EPICURUS IN R(

The role of Greek thought in the final days of the Roman Republic is a topic that has garnered much attention in recent years. This volume of essays, commissioned specially from a distinguished international group of scholars, explores the role and influence of Greek philosophy, specifically Epicureanism, in the late Republic. It focuses primarily (although not exclusively) on the works and views of Cicero, premier politician and Roman philosopher of the day, and Lucretius, foremost among the representatives and supporters of Epicureanism at the time. Throughout the volume, the impact of such disparate reception on the part of these leading authors is explored in a way that illuminates the popularity as well as the controversy attached to the followers of Epicurus in Italy, ranging from ethical and political concerns to the understanding of scientific and celestial phenomena. This title is also available as Open Access on Cambridge Core.

SERGIO YONA is Assistant Professor in the Department of Classics, Archaeology, and Religion at the University of Missouri. He is the author of *Epicurean Ethics in Horace: The Psychology of Satire* (2018).

GREGSON DAVIS is Andrew W. Mellon Professor Emeritus at Duke University. His major publications include: *Polyhymnia: The Rhetoric of Horatian Lyric Discourse* (1984) and *Parthenope: The Interplay of Ideas in Vergilian Bucolic* (2012).

EPICURUS IN ROME

Philosophical Perspectives in the Ciceronian Age

EDITED BY

SERGIO YONA

University of Missouri, Columbia

GREGSON DAVIS

Duke University, North Carolina

CAMBRIDGE
UNIVERSITY PRESS

CAMBRIDGE
UNIVERSITY PRESS

University Printing House, Cambridge CB2 8BS, United Kingdom

One Liberty Plaza, 20th Floor, New York, NY 10006, USA

477 Williamstown Road, Port Melbourne, VIC 3207, Australia

314–321, 3rd Floor, Plot 3, Splendor Forum, Jasola District Centre, New Delhi – 110025, India

103 Penang Road, #05–06/07, Visioncrest Commercial, Singapore 238467

Cambridge University Press is part of the Cambridge University Press & Assessment.

It furthers the University's mission by disseminating knowledge in the pursuit of education, learning, and research at the highest international levels of excellence.

www.cambridge.org
Information on this title: www.cambridge.org/9781009281393
DOI: 10.1017/9781009281416

© Cambridge University Press 2022
Reissued as Open Access, 2022

First published 2022

A catalogue record for this publication is available from the British Library.

Library of Congress Cataloging-in-Publication Data
NAMES: Yona, Sergio, editor. | Davis, Gregson, editor.
TITLE: Epicurus in the Roman Republic: philosophical perspectives in the e Age of Cicero / edited by Sergio Yona, University of Missouri, Columbia, Gregson Davis, Duke University, North Carolina.
DESCRIPTION: Cambridge, United Kingdom; New York, NY, USA: Cambridge University Press, 2021. | Includes bibliographical references and index.
IDENTIFIERS: LCCN 2021038882 (print) | LCCN 2021038883 (ebook) | ISBN 9781108845052 (hardback) | ISBN 9781108949446 (paperback) | ISBN 9781108954402 (epub)
SUBJECTS: LCSH: Epicurus–Influence. | Philosophy, Ancient. | Cicero, Marcus Tullius. | Lucretius Carus, Titus. | BISAC: PHILOSOPHY / History & Surveys / Ancient & Classical
CLASSIFICATION: LCC B573 .E6425 2021 (print) | LCC B573 (ebook) | DDC 187–dc23
LC record available at https://lccn.loc.gov/2021038882
LC ebook record available at https://lccn.loc.gov/2021038883

ISBN 978-1-009-28139-3 Paperback

Contents

Illustrations

Contributors

ELIZABETH ASMIS is Professor of Classics at the University of Chicago. She is the author of *Epicurus' Scientific Method* (1983) and articles on Plato, Philodemus, Lucretius, Seneca, Epictetus, Marcus Aurelius and others. Her current research focuses on Epicureanism and Stoicism, Cicero's political philosophy and ancient aesthetics, and her teaching covers Greek and Roman philosophy, rhetoric and medicine.

MONICA R. GALE is Professor in Classics at Trinity College, Dublin. She is the author of *Myth and Poetry in Lucretius* (1994), *Virgil on the Nature of Things: The Georgics, Lucretius and the Didactic Tradition* (2000) and other books and articles on Lucretius and on Late Republican and Augustan Poetry. She is currently working on a commentary on the complete poems of Catullus for the Cambridge Greek and Latin Classics series.

T. H. M. GELLAR-GOAD is Associate Professor of Classics and Zachary T. Smith Fellow at Wake Forest University. He specializes in Latin poetry, especially the funny stuff: Roman comedy, Roman erotic elegy, Roman satire and – if you believe him – the allegedly philosophical poet Lucretius. He is the author of *Laughing Atoms, Laughing Matter: Lucretius'* De Rerum Natura *and Satire* (2020) and *Plautus: Curculio* (2021).

NATHAN GILBERT is Assistant Professor at Durham University. He completed his PhD in 2015 at the University of Toronto and has published articles and given conference papers on Cicero, his Epicurean contemporaries and intellectual culture in the late Republic. He is currently working on a new edition of the fragments of Metrodorus of Lampsacus.

PAMELA GORDON is Professor of Classics at the University of Kansas. She is the author of *The Invention and Gendering of Epicurus* (2012), the essay "Epistolary Epicureans" in *Epistolary Narratives*, edited by Owen

Hodkinson and Patricia Rosenmeyer (2013) and the introduction to *The Complete Works of Sappho*, translated by Stanley Lombardo (2016). Her research interests beyond Epicureanism include gender studies, Greek vase-painting and Greek and Roman poetry.

DANIEL P. HANCHEY is Associate Professor of Classics at Baylor University. His research interests lie chiefly with the dialogues of Cicero, both their form and content. He has published several articles on these topics and is currently at work on a monograph entitled *Building Friendship:* De Amicitia *and the Architecture of Cicero's Dialogues*, which synthesizes many of these ideas.

MATHIAS HANSES is Assistant Professor of Classics and Ancient Mediterranean Studies at Penn State University. His research interests lie primarily in Roman drama, the history of ideas and Black classicism. He is the author of *The Life of Comedy after the Death of Plautus and Terence* (2020), which examines Roman comedy and its influence from the stage onto the pages of Latin literature from Cicero to Juvenal.

GEERT ROSKAM is Professor of Greek Studies at the Catholic University of Leuven. He is the author of many articles and edited volumes on ancient philosophy and of *On the Path to Virtue: The Stoic Doctrine of Moral Progress and its Reception in (Middle-)Platonism* (2005), *Live Unnoticed: On the Vicissitudes of an Epicurean Doctrine* (2007), *A Commentary on Plutarch's De latenter vivendo* (2007) and Plutarch's *Maxime cum principibus philosopho esse disserendum. An Interpretation with Commentary* (2009).

KATHARINA VOLK is Professor of Classics at Columbia University and has published widely on Roman poetry and philosophy. Her books include *The Poetics of Latin Didactic: Lucretius, Vergil, Ovid, Manilius* (2002), *Manilius and his Intellectual Background* (2009) and *Ovid* (2010); she is the co-editor with Gareth Williams of *Roman Reflections: Studies in Latin Philosophy* (2016). Her latest monograph is *The Roman Republic of Letters: Scholarship, Philosophy, and Politics in the Age of Cicero and Caesar* (2021).

SERGIO YONA is Assistant Professor of Classics at the University of Missouri. He is the author of *Epicurean Ethics in Horace: The Psychology of Satire* (2018). His latest monograph project is entitled *Gods, Religion and Superstition in Early Vergil and Horace* (forthcoming).

Acknowledgements

The late Diskin Clay played a crucial nurturing role in our earliest researches into the reception of Epicurean thought among the major Augustan poets, especially early Vergil, which led to extensive reading of the burgeoning editions of the Philodemus papyri from Herculaneum and to the study of the Diogenes of Oenoanda inscription. The memory of his convivial conversations on all aspects of Epicureanism continues to provide consolation for the loss of his intellectual companionship. Phillip Mitsis and David Konstan, both ex-colleagues at New York University, were no less inspiring in stoking the embers of inquiry into the teachings of the Garden and their prolific afterlife. We are grateful to Duke University for its support of our work by granting a timely leave of absence that greatly facilitated the task of co-editing this volume of essays.

We would also like to acknowledge the support of David Armstrong, whose intellectual generosity and guidance over the past few years have contributed in many ways to the organization of the present volume. The University of Missouri likewise facilitated progress by the granting of a leave of absence for the 2019–2020 academic year.

Additionally, the present state of this collection of studies owes much to the valuable feedback of the anonymous readers, whose suggestions did much to improve the overall quality of the work. Our thanks also to the editorial staff at Cambridge University Press, especially Michael Sharp and Katie Idle, and copy-editor Joshua Hey along with Sindhuja Sethuraman, for overseeing and coordinating everything relating to the publication process.

Finally, we thank every one of our contributors, whose expertise is clearly the focus of this edited volume and whose patient collaboration made the entire endeavour a very enjoyable and memorable one. And, of course, we owe a debt of gratitude to our wonderful families, who, as always, are an indefatigable source of support and encouragement to us in all that we do.

This title is part of the Cambridge University Press *Flip it Open* Open Access Books program and has been "flipped" from a traditional book to an Open Access book through the program.

Flip it Open sells books through regular channels, treating them at the outset in the same way as any other book; they are part of our library collections for Cambridge Core, and sell as hardbacks and ebooks. The one crucial difference is that we make an upfront commitment that when each of these books meets a set revenue threshold we make them available to everyone Open Access via Cambridge Core.

This paperback edition has been released as part of our Open Access commitment and we would like to use this as an opportunity to thank the libraries and other buyers who have helped us flip this and the other titles in the program to Open Access.

To see the full list of libraries that we know have contributed to *Flip it Open*, as well as the other titles in the program please visit http://www.cambridge.org/fio-acknowledgements

CHAPTER I

Introduction

Sergio Yona

The popularity of Epicureanism in Republican Rome among people of all backgrounds, including men, women, farmers, poets, politicians and many others, would seem – at least according to some prominent sources – to be somewhat paradoxical. Indeed, it is difficult to ascertain how an allegedly introverted, apolitical and atheistic philosophical tradition, foreign to Italy and espousing unorthodox doctrines regarding issues fundamentally integral to Roman society, could attract so many followers. Epicurus, for example, provocatively declared that gods are not concerned with human affairs (KD 1; *Men.* 123–124) and that political ambition poses serious challenges to true happiness (DL 10.119: οὐδὲ πολιτεύσεσθαι).[1] Furthermore, he preached pleasure over virtue for its own sake (*Men.* 129) and encouraged private communities (οἱ οἰκεῖοι, who engage in fruitful conversations and forge bonds not experienced by "outsiders" or οἱ ἔξωθεν) as opposed to universal networks of power and influence (cf. *Men.* 135).[2] And even though such views challenge many notions undergirding the commonest platitudes that frequent the works of influential Roman conservatives, their promise of tranquility through

---

[1] The KD 1 statement is as follows: Τὸ μακάριον καὶ ἄφθαρτον οὔτε αὐτὸ πράγματα ἔχει οὔτε ἄλλῳ παρέχει· ὥστε οὔτε ὀργαῖς οὔτε χάρισι συνέχεται: ἐν ἀσθενεῖ γὰρ πᾶν τὸ τοιοῦτον, "That which is blessed and immortal neither has trouble itself nor causes trouble to another being; thus, it experiences neither anger nor favor, for this sort of thing pertains to weakness." Cf. Lucr. 1.44–49 (= 2.646–651). Also important are Epicurus' observations in *Men.* 123–124. See Rist: 1972, 140–163, Mansfeld: 1993, Lorca: 1996, 852–855, Tsouna: 2007, 244–246 and, more recently, Torres: 2018, 455–487 and Erler: 2020, 79–94 for a convenient overview of Epicurean theology. For qualification regarding Epicurean involvement in politics tailored to a Roman audience, see Fish: 2011.

[2] For the importance of communal living and interaction for Epicureans in general, see the edition of Konstan et al: 1998 of Philodemus' treatise *On Frank Criticism*. See Nussbaum: 1994, 117–136 for an overview of what the typical experience of philosophical education within the Epicurean community might have been like. Cf. Clay: 1998, 75–102 for cults and communal gatherings devoted to Epicurus. For general introductions to Philodemus, see the following overviews: Tait: 1941, 1–23, Asmis: 1990, Gigante: 1995, Yona: 2018, 18–27 and Armstrong and McOsker: 2020. Introductions to editions of his treatises also include bibliographical information.

fellowship in the midst of extreme civil strife in the final years of the Republic proved particularly attractive. As Cicero observes in *On Ends*, Epicurus' universal call to philosophy (cf. *Men.* 122) appealed not only to educated Romans, but also to rustics and farmers (2.12): *vos de plagis omnibus colligitis bonos illos quidem viros, sed certe non pereruditos*, "you gather from every quarter of the countryside doubtless respectable but certainly not profoundly learned adherents."[3] The apparent popularity of Epicureanism among commoners, whose testimony is regrettably unavailable to modern scholars, is difficult to understand precisely because the evidence comes exclusively from elite and often biased sources, like Cicero himself.

What emerges is an obviously incomplete account characterized by tension and contradiction on all sides, even among social elites: On the one hand is Cicero's calculated criticism of the Garden as incompatible with *Romanitas* in every way, while on the other is the opposite witness of Atticus and also Lucretius' powerful endorsement of Epicureanism in *On the Nature of Things* as the antidote to contemporary turmoil. Somewhere in the middle are important figures like Julius Caesar and Catullus, whose attitude toward the sect is in each case ambiguous and therefore debatable. The essays in this volume consider all of this and collectively ask broader questions: What exactly does Roman Epicureanism entail, at least from the perspective of prominent citizens, in terms of identity and culture? Furthermore, what possible solutions does it offer contemporary Romans and how do these correspond to the political and social trends of the day? Although answers are not eminently forthcoming, the following chapters strive to elucidate many nuances of the rhetorically charged debate among the likes of Cicero and Lucretius regarding the presence of Epicureanism in the Roman Republic's final days.

This volume offers a fresh take on the complex tension between Epicurus and Rome through examinations that, in contrast to many recent collections, focus on a single philosophical tradition while considering the voices of more than one prominent author within that particular group. Unlike relatively recent volumes such as Miriam Griffin and Jonathan Barnes' *Philosophia Togata* (Oxford 1997) and Myrto Garani and David Konstan's *The Philosophizing Muse* (Cambridge 2014), for example, this study is exclusively centered on Epicureanism as opposed to Greek philosophy in Rome generally speaking.[4] In considering the works of authors

---

[3] See Yona: 2018, 252–253.

[4] Additionally, the horizon of our project is further expanded by Mitsis: 2020, which extends the timespan of reception into the Renaissance and beyond. Finally, there is Volk: forthcoming a.

like Cicero, Caesar, Atticus, Catullus and of course Lucretius, the following examinations also provide a broader scope than volumes like Daryn Lehoux, A. D. Morrison and Alison Sharrock's *Lucretius: Poetry, Philosophy, Science* (Oxford 2013) and Clara Auvray-Assayas and Daniel Delattre's *Cicéron et Philodème: la polémique en philosophie* (Paris 2001), but without reaching beyond antiquity to discussions of later reception such as Brooke Holmes and W. H. Shearin's *Dynamic Reading* (Oxford 2012). Additionally, this collection does not consider the development of Epicurean tradition per se in connection with difficult ethical and theological doctrines, like Jeffrey Fish and Kirk Sanders' *Epicurus and the Epicurean Tradition* (Cambridge 2011); instead, it tackles the thorny issue of how to justify – or not – the lifestyle of Romans, especially powerful and influential ones, who were sympathetic to a philosophical tradition (with everything it entailed) that ran contrary to mainstream culture. What this volume does, then, is attempt to understand the paradoxical appeal of a system allegedly incompatible with Roman politics and culture through the contrasting (and at times seemingly dialectical) accounts of its most prominent opponents as well as proponents.

One of the major challenges to exploring the popularity and nature of Roman Epicureanism in the late Republic is the unreliability of mostly biased sources, especially Cicero. His public attacks on Epicureanism and its apparent incompatibility with Roman culture, particularly in *On Ends*, is framed within a rhetorical context designed to highlight the un-Epicurean attributes of famous Romans of the past.[5] Thus, he exploits tradition and the *mos maiorum* by selectively introducing exempla that fit his narrative and thereby cleverly establishing a false dichotomy: The fluidity of culture – in this case Greek and Roman – is replaced by a hard-and-fast distinction, again designed to establish insurmountable distance between Epicureanism and *Romanitas*. As the chapters of Geert Roskam ("*Sint ista Graecorum*: How to Be an Epicurean in Late Republican Rome – Evidence from Cicero's *On Ends* 1–2") and Daniel P. Hanchey ("Cicero's Rhetoric of Anti-Epicureanism: Anonymity as Critique") in this volume demonstrate, however, contemporary Epicureanism is more nuanced than Cicero would allow one to believe. In fact, rather than being unqualifiedly prohibited, political involvement for Epicureans was, depending on one's situation, permissible and even

---

[5] Cf. Essler: 2011, who examines Cicero's use and abuse of Epicurean theology in representing such doctrines in his work *On the Nature of the Gods*. A similar study, in relation to Cicero's misrepresentation of the Epicurean hedonic calculus, is that of Hanchey: 2013b.

preferable (perhaps reflecting an adaptation to tradition spurred on by the criticism of Roman statesmen like Cicero). The issue, then, is not as one-sided as Cicero suggests, although tension still remains: The idea of calculating pleasure and pain, for example, which is certainly practical, still poses – at least for Cicero – a fundamental threat to the collective progress of Roman society.

In his private communications, too, the statesman mentioned immediately above offers concerted resistance to Epicureanism and even impassioned critique of individual Romans, such as close friends and colleagues, who were possibly members of the Garden or at least seem to have sympathized with its teachings. As Nathan Gilbert argues in his chapter entitled "Was Atticus an Epicurean?," Cicero's correspondence with his friend Atticus, who was most likely an Epicurean, underscores the former's familiarity with and passionate rejection of the philosophical tradition in question. At the same time, his analysis of the hybridization of tradition and philosophy in the person of Atticus makes a crucial point: His limited engagement with politics and successful but controlled financial success, all of which are consistent with Epicurean tenets, prove (to Cicero's chagrin) that it is indeed possible for a prominent Roman to be involved with such a philosophical system – to be a "serious Epicurean" – without completely abandoning local tradition. At the same time, the question of what it meant to be a "serious Epicurean" was not always easy to answer. A case in point is Katharina Volk's chapter on the Epicureanism of Julius Caesar ("Caesar the Epicurean? A Matter of Life and Death"), which hits the reset button, so to speak, on the issue of identity. The evidence from sources in this particular regard is inconclusive. How many Romans were Epicureans and how can one know for sure? This is a slippery question, and one that emphasizes the overwhelming mutability of a moving target such as an individual's affiliation to any given intellectual tradition. A similar challenge arises in connection with the covert Epicureanism of another suspected enthusiast of the Garden who was quite familiar with Caesar, namely, Catullus. Here again the evidence, which is perhaps even more problematic since its origin is an author who famously drew a clear distinction between a poet and his work,[6] is not forthcoming. Monica

---

[6] Cat. 16.5–6: *nam castum esse decet pium poetam | ipsum, versiculos nihil necesse est*, "For the honorable poet must be chaste himself, but it is not at all necessary for his verses to be so." Cf. Lee: 2008, xx: "In literary studies, as in most other departments of life, fashion swings from one grotesque extreme to the other. In the nineteenth century many scholars took poetic statements as too literally related to

Gale, in her chapter entitled "*Otium and Voluptas*: Catullus and Roman Epicureanism," provides a fresh reconsideration of this evidence and argues that, despite the language Catullus employs in his poems (some of which focus on *otium* and *voluptas* – two very Epicurean concepts), the poet's antagonism toward prominent Epicureans like Lucius Calpurnius Piso Caesoninus (cos. 58), Philodemus and Lucretius ultimately precludes any association of him with that philosophical sect.

Turning from problematic sources or unreliable evidence to the work of a Roman Epicurean like Lucretius undoubtedly involves an obvious shift in focus, from how fellow citizens view the sect from the outside to how Roman Epicureans view the world and society around them. Like Cicero, the work of Lucretius is understandably biased in its tone, although his testimony represents countervailing convictions that both problematize the discussion and somewhat neutralize the negative criticism of Epicurus' detractors. In other words, Lucretius' *On the Nature of Things* offers modern scholars a glimpse into the inner workings of the mind of a contemporary Epicurean enthusiast and devoted follower, thus countering Cicero's forceful criticisms about its inability to provide solutions to Romans of his day and age. Actually, in the context of civil strife, violence and death, Lucretius' advice on living a complete life and not fearing the inevitable (death) turns out to be rather relevant. That is to say, for all of the interconnectedness and fluidity that characterizes society's hybridization of Epicurean and Roman traditions, Lucretius draws a stark contrast between the incorrect, popular (Roman) view toward death and the correct (Epicurean) understanding of the unavoidable or, as Lucretius puts it, *mors immortalis* (cf. 3.869).[7] Elizabeth Asmis, in her chapter "'Love it or Leave it': Nature's Ultimatum in Lucretius' *On the Nature of Things* (3.931–962)," masterfully explains the arguments Lucretius introduces in Book 3 on the fear of death.[8] This, however, is more than just an intellectual performance: Natura's therapeutic (if harshly frank) advice is

---

real life; in the twentieth many have believed that poetry has no relation at all to life but exists in a self-referential vacuum or self-contained world of literary allusion." The truth, as usual, is probably somewhere in between. For persona theory, particularly in relation to Horace and Roman satire, see Freudenburg: 2010, 271–272, Anderson: 1982, 9–10 and Freudenburg: 2005, 27–29. For a study of the "Lucretian ego," see Gellar-Goad: 2020, 127–163.

[7] Epicurus regards the fear of death in general as the "most horrible of evils" (*Men.* 125: τὸ φρικωδέστατον ... τῶν κακῶν) because of its complexity and profoundly destructive effects on human beings.

[8] As Fish: 1998, 101 n. 12 notes, the bibliography on Epicureanism and death is "immense." For extremely helpful documentation of the debate, see Nussbaum: 1994, 204–212, Armstrong 2003, 28 n. 28 and D. Armstrong: 2004, 31 n. 36. For a general study of the topic, Wallach: 1976, Warren: 2004, Torres: 2018, 347–362, Long: 2019, 115–151 and Erler: 2020, 42–58.

potentially beneficial not only for Lucretius' immediate audience, but for all Romans suffering from this irrational fear, which introduces a paradox of sorts. The very philosophical tradition that some view as detrimental to the Republic (and Roman society in general) claims to have the solution to problems this same society has created for itself. Indeed, Lucretius associates greed, ambition and crime in general with a profound fear of death,[9] for which Epicurus has the remedy.

But Lucretius' defense and promotion of the conviction that "death should not be feared" goes beyond the popularization of arguments and maxims; indeed, Lucretius challenges Romans to face head on the gruesome reality that death entails: decomposition, decay and more. In this sense, Pamela Gordon's chapter, entitled "Kitsch, Death and the Epicurean," invites readers to consider the uncomfortable truth about the human condition; only then can one accept mortality and begin to focus attention on living. Beginning with a definition of kitsch as that which "excludes everything from its purview which is essentially unacceptable in human existence," Gordon provides a novel reading of Lucretius' diatribe against the fear of death as an attack against the denial of human mortality and its logical consequence: putrefaction. By introducing passages that feature vivid and often grotesque descriptions of decomposition, she shows how Lucretius attempts to combat the refusal to acknowledge the truth of human existence. Finally, she explains how the poet's censure of excessive grief through "clichéd lamentations" at the death of a loved one is consistent with the Epicurean view of frank criticism as therapeutic, which also plays a role in Philodemus' *Epigrams* and is the topic of one of his surviving ethical treatises.

Lucretius' attack on false beliefs, however, does not stop at personifications of nature or disturbingly detailed literary descriptions of death; indeed, he is acutely aware of the dangerous influence of popular

---

[9] Lucr. 3.59–64:

> denique avarities et honorum caeca cupido,
> quae miseros homines cogunt transcendere fines
> iuris et inter dum socios scelerum atque ministros
> noctes atque dies niti praestante labore
> ad summas emergere opes, haec vulnera vitae
> non minimam partem mortis formidine aluntur.

Greed, moreover, and the blind lust for honor, which compels wretched humans to transcend the limits of justice and contend day and night, sharing and scheming crime, to climb with exceeding toil to the summit of riches, all of these sores of life are nourished in no small way by the fear of death.

entertainment on average Romans through various sensory (visual, oral, aural etc.) experiences. This of course includes dramatic performances, which were vastly popular at the time, as well as wall paintings, many of which depicted scenes from traditional mythological stories involving vengeful gods. One of the most prominent of these tales, as Mathias Hanses discusses in his chapter "Page, Stage, Image: Confronting Ennius with Lucretius' *On the Nature of Things,*" is the sacrifice of Iphigenia. It is important to recognize that the majority of Romans were exposed to such visual representations and, according to Lucretius, at risk for developing (or feeding already developed) false beliefs about menacing gods. More specifically, Hanses provides new evidence of Lucretius' engagement with Rome's first national poet. Through a consideration of the language and content of various passages of *On the Nature of Things*, Hanses underscores the Epicurean poet's efforts to challenge his predecessor's influence as a mythological, religious and even philosophical authority. This study, however, examines far more than the intertextual connections between Lucretius and Ennius. Hanses' exploration of the Lucretian sacrifice of Iphigenia passage, which he argues is Ennian in its language, leads to considerations of the popularity of this scene as part of dramatic performances as well as the subject of works of art. Such venues would have made the horrors of *religio* more accessible and perhaps more appealing to the general public, he suggests, thus prompting Lucretius to provide his readers with a "toolkit" for confronting such displays through his didactic epic. To be sure, this criticism of Ennius is a boldly direct challenge to average Romans to reconsider certain aspects of their received tradition in light of Epicurus' teachings. Lucretius' outspoken criticism of Rome's premier poet at the time, however, is not a complete rejection of *Romanitas* for Epicureanism, but rather a further (salubrious, for Lucretius) "hybridizing" of the two.

This emphasis on visual arts and the importance of perception also relates to natural phenomena, such as the well-known question of the actual size of the sun. The final chapter in the volume is more scientific than the rest, but it is consistent with the notion of "thinking like an Epicurean" and viewing the outside world – to the degree that it can be understood at all, given our limitations – as a follower of the Garden living in Rome. In his examination, entitled "Lucretius on the Size of the Sun," T. H. M. Gellar-Goad tackles a rather curious epistemological conundrum. He begins with an overview of criticisms of Epicurus' claim that the sun is the size it appears to be before offering careful analysis of key passages from Epicureans, especially one from Book 5 of *On the Nature of Things* regarding the sun's heat. This passage's content and intricate syntax, Gellar-Goad explains, is designed to emphasize the difficulty of drawing accurate conclusions about celestial phenomena (thus posing an indirect challenge to those who claim to have done so). By means of an explanation of the Epicurean theory of knowledge, which is founded upon the ability to acquire clear sense perceptions, he identifies the many challenges associated with the observation of objects as distant as the sun. The result, he suggests, is that regarding this issue the Epicureans were careful to suspend their judgment in order to avoid drawing false – and potentially harmful – conclusions. For the Epicureans, then, the sun is in fact "perceived" to be the size of a foot, since for them sense perceptions are infallible; the "actual" size of the sun, however, is undoubtedly beyond our limits to determine.

The overall objective of the essays collected in this volume is to present to modern audiences the rhetorical intricacies of the social, political and essentially philosophical conversation (or rather debate) that was a central feature of the final days of the Roman Republic. The manner in which Cicero's mischaracterization of Epicurus' teachings clashes with Lucretius' zealous promotion of the same tradition powerfully underscores Romans' desperate struggle to provide their countrymen with meaningful solutions, especially at such a crucial turning point in their history. At the same time, this tension reflects the collective identity crisis of a people undergoing a violent transition from republic to empire and struggling to mitigate – or even prevent – such a tumultuous and fundamental change. These are the voices of citizens seeking stability and, above all, answers to the question "What does it truly mean to be Roman?" For Cicero, this involves political engagement and striving for traditional virtue for its own sake, all of which are at odds with Epicureanism; for Lucretius, the Master's teachings offer his fellow compatriots knowledge, peace and physical as well as psychological repose, all of which seemed like impossible ideals in the midst of so much civil strife. The answer, again, is likely somewhere in between, and the contrasting (though interconnected) arguments in the following chapters provide a starting point for understanding the complex compromise that the label "Roman Epicureanism" implies.

PART I

Epicurus and Roman Identities

CHAPTER 2

Sint Ista Graecorum: *How to be an Epicurean in Late Republican Rome – Evidence from Cicero's* On Ends *1–2*

Geert Roskam

A Philosophy for Dummies all over the World?

Imagine: One day you discover the ultimate truth – what do you do? Of course, you are delighted and enthusiastically want to share your discovery with the rest of the world. Your predecessors have already published, after arduous research and a painstaking thinking process, all the little bits of truth that they had fished out of a nature that – as Heraclitus already knew – likes to hide (fr. 22 B 123 = Themistius, *Orat.* 5.69b). Then, after this age-long tradition of careful searching, the day comes that light definitively breaks through and the decisive truth is found, a turning point in intellectual history. From that moment on, there is no need for further discussions, as the clear truth is available to everyone.

This is what happened at the end of the fourth century BC, and the "divine mind"[1] who discovered the truth was Epicurus. For later followers such as Lucretius, his discoveries eclipsed all previous achievements. They were even more precious than the gifts of Ceres and Liber, more impressive than Hercules' labors (*DRN* 5.13–54; cf. also 3.1–30). No wonder, then, that Epicurus also wished to communicate his insights to all other people. He addressed his letters to everyone, men and women alike,[2] to both young and old (*Men.* 122), to both upper and lower classes, including slaves.[3] He even showed a fundamental openness to other philosophical traditions, provided that they were compatible with the truth he discovered.[4] And this

---

[1] Lucr. 3.15; cf. also 5.8.
[2] Plutarch, *De lat. viv.* 1129A (πᾶσι καὶ πάσαις); *Adv. Colot.* 1126F (πρὸς πάντας ἐγράφετο καὶ πάσας); Seneca, *Ep.* 14.18; cf. also Epicurus, *Hdt.* 37; *Pyth.* 85; fr. [59] Arr.² For the women living in the Garden, see esp. Gordon: 2004; cf. Erler: 1994, 287–288.
[3] Such as Mys (DL 10.3 and 10), who also received letters from the master (fr. 152–155 U). According to DeWitt: 1954, 95, Mys' position "was comparable to that of Tiro in the household of Cicero."
[4] See *Nat.* 14, col. 1–17 Leone; Erler: 2011, 19–22.

eagerness to divulge the Epicurean truth *urbi et orbi* was taken over by later
followers. It still seems to have lost nothing of its original enthusiasm in the
second century AD, when Diogenes of Oenoanda published his inscription
for the sake of everyone: the young, the old, and those who are somewhere in
between, "not yet old, but not indeed young either,"[5] including not only
Greeks but foreigners, too.[6] And since he explicitly addresses future generations as well (fr. 3.IV.13–V.4), we may even in our own day witness the
appeal of the school.[7] Epicurean philosophy, in short, has a remarkably
strong universalizing tendency.

Although this tendency is well known, we sometimes risk forgetting
how radical it was and how far-reaching its consequences actually were.
After all, we may reasonably presume that Epicurean philosophy meant
something completely different for a female slave at Demetrius' court in
Epicurus' day and for a male aristocrat in the Rome of Vespasian. It is not
evident that all the differences in time, place, external circumstances and
prevalent ideological presuppositions can be bracketed without any problem.
If philosophy, indeed, "does have a geography,"[8] it is worth re-examining
seriously Epicurus' claim of the universalizability of his philosophy.

In *On Ends*, Cicero suggests that the Epicureans recruit their followers
among the uncultivated peasants (2.12). This may be no more than a
polemical smear, in line with Cicero's generally unfavorable view of
Epicureanism,[9] but we may take it as an excellent point of departure for
a thought experiment. Let us, for the time being, leave Cicero's world and
return to that of Epicurus in order to take a few local farmers – say Gorgias
and Daos, the characters of Menander's *Grouch* – from their plough in
order to turn them into Epicureans. Of course, Gorgias and Daos are not
very learned, to say the least, and are entirely ignorant of philosophical
speculation. Is it possible to transform them in a satisfactory way into
genuine Epicureans?

Yes, it is. Epicurus insisted that no erudition is required to understand
his truth and live according to it,[10] and in spite of the impressive learning

---

[5] Fr. 29.III + NF 207.I.13 – NF 207.III.13.

[6] Fr. 3.V.4–8; 30.I.14–II.2; 32.II.9–III.1; 119.III.2–3.

[7] See Bergsma, Poot and Liefbroer: 2008 for an assessment of the applicability of Epicurus'
philosophy to the situation of our own day.

[8] Woolf: 2015, 5.

[9] Cicero usually places Epicurus' philosophy at the lowest level, associating it with beasts and with
vulgar, effeminate, narrow-minded hedonism; see esp. Görler: 1974, 63–83.

[10] See, e.g., DL 10.6 (= fr. 163 U); Athenaeus, 13.588a; Plutarch, *Non posse* 1094D (= fr. 117 U);
Lactantius, *Div. inst.* 3.25.7 (= fr. 227ᵃ U); Cicero, *Fin.* 1.71–72 and 2.12; *Nat. D.* 2.74; cf. Erler:
1992b, 317–319.

of later Epicureans such as Philodemus, we should not tone down the radical nature of Epicurus' original claim. Metrodorus even went so far as to say that we should not be dismayed if we do not know on which side Hector fought, or if we cannot quote the opening lines of the *Iliad* (Plutarch, *Non posse* 1094E = fr. 24 K.). Gorgias and Daos, then, can even do without the absolute minimum in this respect. But what *do* they need? First of all, if they swallow Epicurus' "fourfold remedy" (τετραφάρμακον), they will no longer be afraid of the gods and of death, and they will gain a sound insight into pleasure and pain. On that basis, they can begin to pursue their pleasures in their own way, since Epicurus left much room for individual judgment of concrete circumstances.[11] What they further need, then, is a careful calculus of pleasure and pain, and in that field, sober-minded farmers like Gorgias and Daos, who stick to common sense, may well have some advantage over sophisticated minds.[12] Beyond this, we cannot expect that they will have deep insight into the Epicurean canon, in epistemological theories about preconceptions and perception, in complicated details of Epicurean theology, atomism and the swerve, or in the tenets of other philosophical schools. In that sense, their Epicureanism will be rudimentary,[13] but they will experience all the pleasures of their belly – which, we should not forget, is the principle and root of every good[14] and the region that contains the highest end (Plutarch, *Non posse* 1098D = fr. 40 K.) – they will not be seduced by excessive and unnecessary luxury or by empty desires, and they will be free from superstition and the fear of death. The Epicureanism of Gorgias and Daos will be an Epicureanism sui generis, no doubt, but it will be perfectly in line with their character, condition and the particular circumstances of their lives. In other words, it will be precisely the kind of Epicureanism that is fitting for them. We can conclude, then, that it is indeed possible to turn them into genuine Epicureans.

Similar thought experiments can be set up about female slaves at the royal court in Epicurus' day, about old sculptors, ordinary cobblers or barbarian traders. All their situations are different, but all of them can in their own way adopt Epicurean philosophy. In this essay, I would like

---

[11] See on this Roskam: 2007a, 147–148 and *passim*. Such openness is the logical implication of the choice for pleasure as the final end.

[12] In that respect, Epicurus' statement that "prudence" (φρόνησις) is even more precious than philosophy itself (*Men.* 132) makes perfect sense indeed.

[13] Perhaps not unlike the simplified Epicureanism propagated by authors like Amafinius and Catius (Cicero, *Acad.* 1.5; *Tusc.* 4.6–7; *Fam.* 15.16.1–2 and 15.19.2); Roskam: 2007a, 84–85.

[14] See Athenaeus 7.280a and 12.546f (= fr. 409 U).

to focus on a completely different context, viz. the world of the late Cicero. In a way, the challenge is here even greater, since we are now dealing with a completely different place (Rome), date (the first century BC) and (social, political, ideological) context, yet our basic question remains the same: Is Epicurus' truth still equally relevant in this particular situation or do the new circumstances ask for significant modifications or even undermine the whole doctrine? Our question, in short, is: How can one be an Epicurean in late-Republican Rome?

This, of course, is quite an ambitious question and a full answer would require a book-length study, if only because several alternatives are possible. In all likelihood, Amafinius would come up with a view that differs from those of Philodemus, Lucretius or Cicero. For reasons of space, I confine myself to one author (Cicero) and one work (*On Ends*). This double limitation implies that our conclusions will only yield a partial answer. Nevertheless, we will see that Cicero's discussion of Epicureanism in the first two books of *On Ends* raises several general questions that are particularly relevant for our topic and even allow us to reach more generic conclusions.

The Greek Perspective of *On Ends* 1–2

In the proem to *On Ends* (1.1–12), Cicero defends his decision to write philosophical works in Latin against the widespread aversion to philosophy and against a certain snobbish preference for Greek works. Although this proem is not without relevance for our question, as it thematizes in a direct and programmatic way the confrontation between the Greek and Roman intellectual world in Cicero's day, I nevertheless prefer to skip it and immediately turn to the actual discussion, both because the proem stands on itself and may have been conceived earlier[15] and because it has been well studied recently.[16] We will have some opportunities, though, to refer to it in the course of our analysis.

Before Torquatus starts his defense of Epicurus' doctrine of the final end in Book 1, Cicero first launches a short general attack against Epicurean philosophy, rejecting in a fairly systematic way its natural philosophy (1.17–21), logic (1.22) and ethics (1.23–25). One of the striking aspects of this initial criticism is its predominantly Greek intellectual framework. In the domain of natural philosophy, for instance, Cicero focuses on the

---

[15] It may have been one of the proems gathered in the separate *volumen prohoemiorum* (*Att.* 16.6.4).
[16] See esp. Baraz: 2012, 113–127.

relation between several views of Democritus and Epicurus. What he offers us, in other words, is the kind of brief, technical discussion we also find in Greek theoretical polemics,[17] and what we do not find at all are clear traces of a specifically Roman input. The same holds true for his discussion of logic. As far as ethics is concerned, Cicero compares Epicurus' position with that of Aristippus and the Cyrenaics – again, the same Greek school tradition. Yet here we at last find a Roman element, too: Cicero confronts Torquatus with the impressive achievements of his own ancestors. This is the first encounter with the Roman world in the discussion. I shall come back to it later and examine how "Roman" this argument actually is. For the time being, I confine myself to the observation that Triarius ignores it in his recapitulative summary of Cicero's attack (1.26). There, Aristippus' name is at least mentioned, while the famous Torquati are not.

Torquatus' survey of Epicurus' philosophy shows the same general tendency. Just like Cicero, he usually refers to a Greek intellectual framework. He even explicitly states that he will say nothing new (1.28), which is an interesting disclaimer in our context. Of course, the phrase *nihil novi* need not imply that Torquatus directly takes over everything from Epicurus himself – we shall see in a moment that he also takes into account later developments. Still, it is not without importance that he begins his account by underlining that his approach is perfectly in line with Epicurus, "the author of the system himself" (1.29). The whole emphasis, then, is on continuity.

Moreover, throughout Torquatus' survey, we find many clear references to the Greek tradition. Epicurus' understanding of pleasure as the absence of pain is illustrated with a reference to an Athenian statue of Chrysippus and opposed to the Cyrenaic view (1.39). Several sections contain an accumulation of material that can be related to the Greek tradition and to the position of Epicurus himself,[18] and even Torquatus' examples sometimes sound rather Greek. His reference (in 1.58) to a city rent by faction reminds one of the well-known "Greek" problem of a πόλις ruined by internal στάσις, and as examples of true friendship, Torquatus lists Theseus and Orestes (1.65).

The overall impression, so far, is that the intellectual framework of *On Ends* 1 is to a very significant degree that of the Greek tradition. A similar

---

[17] See, e.g., Plutarch, *Non posse* 1100A and esp. *Adv. Colot.* 1108E–1111E, with the discussion of Kechagia: 2011, 179–212 and Castagnoli: 2013.
[18] Just a few other examples, of which there are many more: 1.38 ~ KD 18; 1.40 ~ KD 2 and 4; 1.45 ~ KD 29; 1.57 ~ KD 5; 1.63 ~ KD 16 and 19; 1.65 ~ KD 27; 1.68 ~ KD 28.

conclusion holds true for the second book as well, although the Roman element there becomes more prominent. But as we shall see later, the Greek pole is not forgotten, to say the least. Cicero often refers to Epicurus and to his "alter ego" Metrodorus (2.7 and 2.92). This observation in itself already undermines the hypothesis[19] that the founding fathers of the school were no longer relevant in Cicero's day and that Cicero only read the works of contemporary Epicureans. It is true that Cicero elsewhere claims that Epicurus' and Metrodorus' works are only read by the Epicureans themselves (*Tusc.* 2.8), but such polemical statements should not be taken at face value. Even more, ancient polemicists as a rule tend to take the orthodox position of the founders of the school as their point of reference rather than dealing with later modifications, and Cicero is not different in this respect. Although he was interested in contemporary developments (see below), he undoubtedly regarded the writings of the ancient masters as the principal criterion for determining the orthodox position.

Just like the first book of *On Ends*, the second contains many references to technical discussions that were held in the Greek philosophical schools. Cicero more than once recalls the position of Hieronymus of Rhodes (2.8; 2.16; 2.32) and of Aristippus (2.18; 2.20). In the context of a doxographical survey of views regarding the final end,[20] he mentions the views of Aristotle, Callipho, Diodorus, Hieronymus and Aristippus (2.19), and again, more elaborately, those of Aristotle and Polemo, Callipho, Diodorus, Aristippus, the Stoics, Hieronymus, Carneades, Pyrrho, Aristo and Erillus (2.34–35; further developed in 2.36–43). Remarkably enough, all of these thinkers belong to the old, Greek tradition. Should we conclude, then, that Cicero could not come up with one Roman thinker who developed a relevant thought about this issue? Perhaps we should, at least in the sense that no Roman thinker at that time had become a paradigmatic figure whose philosophical position was regarded as innovative and worth mentioning alongside the views of the great Greek philosophers. The latter, by contrast, often appear in Book 2: Cicero mentions the seven Sages (2.7), Democritus (2.102), Socrates (2.1–2; 2.90), Plato (2.2; 2.4; 2.45; 2.52; 2.92), Aristotle (2.17; 2.106), the Cyrenaics (2.114), the Stoics (2.13) – including Zeno (2.17), Cleanthes (2.69) and Chrysippus (2.44) – and Carneades (2.59). More than once, their names

---

[19] Put forward by Delattre: 1984.

[20] The whole survey rests on the traditional *Carneadea divisio* and follows the polemical approach of the New Academy; see Lévy: 1984; cf. Brittain: 2016.

also occur concerning points of secondary importance.²¹ Occasionally, Cicero's references to the Greek tradition even risk becoming pedantic. A case in point is his elaborate discussion of the conflict between Socrates and sophists like Gorgias (2.1–2) – as if Torquatus and Triarius, who are both explicitly characterized as learned men (1.13; cf. 1.26), really needed such a lesson.

Moreover, the "Greek framework" of Book 2 is not confined to the philosophical tradition but also includes illustrious statesmen and warlords (2.62, 67, 97 and 112) and famous examples of friendship (2.79). One may add to all this anecdotes such as the one about Themistocles and Simonides (2.104) and several highlights of the Greek literary tradition: a reference to the famous story of Solon and Croesus (2.87, referring to Herodotus 1.29–33), an allusion to Xenophon's description of the Persians' diet (2.92, cf. Xenophon, *Cyr.* 1.2.8), a translation of a verse from Euripides (2.105; *TrGF* 5.1, fr. 133) and a reference to famous Greek authors and artists (2.115).

This long list may be tedious and prosaic, but it is important in that it shows how relevant the Greek tradition is for Cicero in these first two books of *On Ends*. On the basis of this survey, we can already come to some conclusions.

First, the above list illustrates how Roman aristocrats like Torquatus and Cicero actually engage in philosophy. Their whole thinking is moulded by the traditional framework of the Greek philosophical schools. They have no problem with linking their different views to that of the great Greek thinkers of the past. When Torquatus, for instance, expresses his preference for continuous speeches, Cicero immediately – almost naturally, one might say – connects this with the position of Zeno the Stoic.²² As already observed above, moreover, no attempt can be found to relate the opinions of Torquatus and Cicero to that of important Roman thinkers. The overall philosophical framework of Books 1 and 2 of *On Ends* is Greek.

This is the direct consequence of Cicero's thorough familiarity with Greek philosophy. Since he attentively followed at Athens the courses of Zeno and Phaedrus in his youth,²³ we can be sure that he even knew the

---

²¹ E.g. in 2.15 (Heraclitus and Plato), 2.17 (Zeno and Aristotle) and 2.52 (Plato).

²² We may well discover a subtle trace of malice in Cicero's attempt to connect the position of his Epicurean friend with that of the Stoic Zeno. In the context of this friendly dialogue, this suggestion is probably *sine ira*, but not necessarily *sine studio*. Later, Diogenes of Oenoanda would offer a clever Epicurean retort by publishing his Epicurean inscription on a Stoa.

²³ See esp. *Fin.* 1.16 and *Fam.* 13.1.2; cf. *Nat. D.* 1.93 and *Phil.* 5.13. On Phaedrus, see esp. Raubitschek: 1949 and Erler: 1994, 273.

Garden from the inside. Moreover, he in all likelihood deepened his knowledge by reading the works of contemporary Epicureans[24] and by discussing Epicurean philosophy with his learned friends (including Atticus, his former fellow student in the Athenian Garden).[25] This background, then, also helps to explain the great significance of the Greek tradition in the first two books of *On Ends*: Cicero had so thoroughly appropriated this tradition that it simply had become part and parcel of his own philosophical frame of reference.

This conclusion strongly problematizes the clear-cut opposition between "Greek" and "Roman" that can often be found in scholarly literature. Fundamental questions about happiness, the final end, the successful life and so on have a general scope and cannot really be pegged down to one specific world (either Greek or Roman). If indeed Roman thinkers like Cicero prove to reflect about such problems on the basis of the rich Greek tradition that they have entirely appropriated, a rigid dichotomy between "typically Greek" and "typically Roman" makes no sense at all. One might object, though, that such radical opposition can to an important extent be traced back to the works of Cicero himself. This is true, indeed. Especially in the programmatic proems to his dialogues, such an opposition can be found more than once, but it occurs elsewhere, too. In the second book of *On Ends*, for instance, Cicero repeatedly argues that some topics are not permitted to Romans and should be left to the Greeks: *sint ista Graecorum* (2.68; cf. 2.80). Moreover, such opposition between "Greek" and "Roman" is not merely a rhetorical construct of Cicero himself, but seems to rest on broader contemporary debates and convictions.[26] Yet even though all this is true, it is appropriate to maintain an attitude of caution towards oversimplified applications of such labels. As we saw, Cicero and Torquatus have made traditional Greek thinking their own to such an extent that it had become part and parcel of their thinking. Cicero elsewhere claims that he has always combined Greek and Latin elements (*Off.* 1.1), and even more instructive than such explicit statements are passages such as *On Ends* 2.105–106, where he smoothly combines Greek material (Epicurus, Euripides, Aristotle) with Roman

---

[24] Such as Lucretius (see Gatzemeier: 2013, 27–47) and Philodemus (see Delattre: 1984 and Tsouna: 2001; Erler: 2001 is more skeptical about Philodemus' importance for Cicero's discussion of Epicureanism, although he too agrees that Cicero probably read Philodemus' works).

[25] For the Epicureanism of Atticus, see Gilbert (Chapter 4) in this volume.

[26] See Baraz: 2012, 13–42.

(T. Manlius Torquatus, Marius, Scipio Africanus).[27] That Cicero does not deem it necessary to comment on such combinations tellingly shows that to his own mind, and probably to those of his intellectual friends, the clear-cut distinction between "Greek" and "Roman" was far less evident than he himself sometimes suggests.

Second, this conclusion throws further light on the situation of the Epicurean school in Cicero's day. The philosophical community of the Garden in Athens still existed, and we may presume that it even had some doctrinal authority, although it had ceased to be the only institution where the "orthodox" position was defined. Other circles, like that in Campania where Philodemus was active, had meanwhile come into existence[28] and saw no problem in disagreeing with the Athenian Garden. In such a context, the Epicurean school is no longer synonymous with the Athenian Garden.[29] In other words, a man can also be a full member of the Epicurean school when he endorses the Epicurean point of view during a discussion on Cicero's estate at Cumae or when he pursues Epicurean pleasures in Piso's villa in Herculaneum. Epicureanism was not merely institutionally embedded, but had become a school of thinking that was spread over many local communities. From such a perspective, then, the Torquatus of *On Ends* is no less a full member of the Epicurean school than a student of the Athenian Garden, and can no less participate actively in the philosophical debates that are held within the school. This evolution raises two further questions.

First, did it entail innovations in communicative patterns within the school? The different participants in the discussion in *On Ends* show a remarkable friendliness, being lavish in giving compliments to one another. They prove to be open-minded, as a rule try to be fair, and while drawing out their friends (1.26 and 1.72) they confirm their willingness to listen to each other's arguments and even to be persuaded (cf. 1.15; 1.23).[30] How all this relates to traditional communication patterns in

---

[27] In this context, Cicero's repeated use of Greek poets in their Latin translation also deserves mention. See on this also Cicero's own comments in *On Ends* 1.4–5. A survey of the material can be found in Dueck: 2009.

[28] Even in Epicurus' own day, several such communities already existed, such as that of Lampsacus, and Epicurus kept in touch with its members through a lively correspondence.

[29] Cf. Fuhrer: 2012.

[30] A further indication of this fundamental open-mindedness is the open end of the discussion; cf. Schofield: 2008.

the Epicurean Garden (e.g. to the ideal of frank speech and to the notorious polemical laughter) is a topic that calls for further study.[31]

Second, did it entail doctrinal innovations? Both Cicero and Torquatus attach great importance to their own critical judgment (1.6; 1.12; 1.72), and three times Torquatus indeed expresses his personal opinion about a discussion that is carried on in his school. In 1.29–31, he distinguishes between three views on the choice for pleasure as the final end. Epicurus himself regards this choice as self-evident, relying on the senses. Other Epicureans aim at a more subtle position, thinking that sense perception should be supported by further rational arguments. Yet others are less confident and acknowledge that the issue requires a lot of theoretical speculation. This list, then, is not a merely neutral juxtaposition of three contrasting views, but also contains a concise critical evaluation of them. Again, it is evident how thoroughly Torquatus has appropriated this school tradition. Furthermore, and quite remarkably, he himself opts for the third view, which to a certain extent disagrees with Epicurus himself. Torquatus no doubt qualifies as a loyal Epicurean, but he never gives up his critical sense. Somewhat further (1.55), he points to the complicated question of the relationship between mental and corporeal pleasures and pains. Again, he admits that many Epicureans adopt a different position, but insists that these are ignorant. Here, too, Torquatus expresses his own judgment, deciding for himself who are the *imperiti* and whose view is correct. The third section where Torquatus deals with internal disagreements in the Epicurean school concerns friendship (1.66–70). Some Epicureans insist that every friendship rests on utility and personal pleasure, others argue that the pursuit of pleasure constitutes the initial impetus for friendship but that we later begin to love our friends for their own sake, and yet others believe that friendship is based on a kind of contract. The particularities of these different theories need not detain us here.[32] Important for us is that Torquatus here again expresses his personal judgment. In his opinion (1.66: *ut mihi videtur*), the first position is well tenable, whereas the second one is advocated by Epicureans who are a bit more timid yet still fairly acute (1.69).

---

[31] For the importance of frankness in an Epicurean context, much interesting information can be found in Philodemus' *De lib. dic.* As to the issue of polemical laughter, relevant is, for instance, the difference between Torquatus' courtly behavior in *On Ends* and Velleius' aggressive approach in *On the Nature of the Gods*; see on the latter Classen: 2010.

[32] They are often discussed in secondary literature; see, e.g., Mitsis: 1988, 98–128; O'Connor: 1989; O'Keefe: 2001; E. Brown: 2002; Evans: 2004; D. Armstrong: 2011; Frede: 2016.

These three passages may help in refuting a prejudice that existed for a long time in scholarly literature and has only gradually been abandoned, viz. the belief that the Epicurean school was one monolithic tradition, in which no real discussion was possible and where every adherent unquestioningly agreed with what Epicurus said.[33] This view was to a significant extent influenced by un-Epicurean sources such as Seneca (*Ep.* 33.4), Numenius (Eusebius, *PE* 14.5.3 = fr. 24 des Places) or indeed Cicero, who suggests in *On Ends* that Epicurus' position is the "light" of his followers (2.70) and that a great multitude of people will be glad to accept everything Epicurus teaches them as true (2.28). Torquatus, for his part, appears as an enthusiastic admirer of Epicurus.[34] But we now see that this admiration for and loyalty towards his master is not uncritical and that he sometimes even defends positions that run counter to those of Epicurus. Torquatus, in short, is a genuine Epicurean who is not afraid of following his own *iudicium*.

Moreover, it is not just on minor details that he dares to express his own opinion, but on fundamental issues like pleasure and friendship, and he deals with these questions in a fairly technical way that echoes the theoretical debates in the schools. It has been observed that all the participants in the philosophical discussions of Cicero's dialogues are aristocratic Romans and that professional (often Greek) house-philosophers are glaringly absent.[35] This observation is pertinent indeed, but it should be (re) interpreted in light of the conclusions reached above. As a matter of fact, in his capacity as a follower of Epicurus, Torquatus adds no less to the position of his school than would a professional philosopher. Even more, as Cicero presents the situation in *On Ends* 1–2, the difference between the professional philosopher and the aristocratic members of Cicero's erudite circle is slight. Nor is there any significant difference concerning the "Greek" and the "Roman" perspective.[36] We have seen that Torquatus adopts precisely the Greek traditional framework that the professional Greek house-philosophers had and that he considers his own position to be in line with that of his Greek philosophical predecessors. What we find in *On Ends* 1–2, then, is not a dynamic of opposition between "Greek"

---

[33] Seminal studies that did much to undermine this unjustified view include Angeli: 1988, 82–102; Sedley: 1989; Erler: 1992a; 1992b; cf. also Roskam: 2007a, 149–150.

[34] He regards his master Epicurus as "the only person who has discerned the truth" (1.14) and as the "great explorer of the truth, the master-builder of human happiness" (1.32); cf. also 1.63 and 1.71–72. The translations, here and elsewhere, are borrowed from the Loeb edition.

[35] Fuhrer: 2012, 243; Steel: 2013, 229; Gildenhard: 2013, 261–262.

[36] *Contra* Blyth: 2010/11, 73, and Gildenhard: 2013, 261–263.

and "Roman" but a dynamic of completion and culmination of the Greek tradition. That this was indeed how Cicero himself saw it is further corroborated by his provocative claim at the outset of the *Tusculan Disputations* that the Romans generally improve upon what they have received from the Greeks (1.1). Torquatus, Cicero and others, then, do not merely receive and appropriate the Greek tradition, but also improve on it from the inside.

The question then remains: How did they manage to do this? Their approach is much less radical than Cicero suggests. Again, we should not be misled by the rhetoric of Cicero's proems. In dialogues like *On Ends*, we see more clearly how the process of reception and appropriation in Cicero's circle concretely works. The Roman aristocrats follow the traditional paths of the (Greek) school and lay their own accents, often on the basis of views that, again, had already been elaborated by previous (Greek) members of the schools. It is striking indeed that nowhere in the aforementioned passages from *On Ends* are the "improvements" Cicero has in mind or Torquatus' personal opinions influenced by the changed circumstances or by peculiar insights that have been derived from any specifically Roman context. On the contrary, concerning the discussions about both pleasure and friendship, Torquatus refers to the polemical objections of other philosophical schools (1.31 and 1.69). Throughout his survey, then, Torquatus follows the internal logic of traditional school debates without borrowing a single argument from the specifically Roman attitude towards friendship or pleasure.

Finally, all this has important implications for the question of Cicero's sources. On the basis of the results of the German tradition of *Quellenforschung*, the bulk of the first book of *On Ends* was long traced back to a treatise of a later Epicurean author; the second one (and the polemical attack in 1.17–25), so it was argued, was directly influenced by a lost treatise of Antiochus.[37] This hypothesis obviously provides an easy explanation for the omnipresence of the Greek element in the first two books of *On Ends* (as it regards the whole discussion as mere ἀπόγραφα of two Greek works), but it does so at a high cost, by unduly reducing Cicero to his sources. Nowadays, scholars have become much more sensitive to the *voluntas auctoris* of later writers.[38] Cicero was no mere slave of his

---

[37] The hypothesis was elaborated by Hirzel: 1882, 630–668 and accepted in the *RE* article by Philippson: 1939, 1136–1137.
[38] See, e.g., D'Anna: 1965, 32–52 on Cicero.

sources, nor were his dialogues mere "copies" of earlier Greek works.[39] As noted above, Cicero had an excellent knowledge of Epicurean philosophy and was perfectly able to present the core of Epicurus' philosophy while adding his own criticism and his own arrangement (1.6).

One element, however, is often neglected in such discussions of Cicero's sources: the importance of social contacts in the aristocratic circles of Cicero's day. The literary setting of *On Ends* and other dialogues is not merely a matter of fictional *ornatus*. These learned philosophical discussions among friends also reflect practices that prevailed in the high society of the late Republic, as is illustrated in Cicero's correspondence.[40] Erudite members of the aristocracy discuss philosophical topics with one another, and during these conversations they fall back on ready knowledge, on what they have learned in their youth, on books they read in their leisure time and on what they remember from earlier discussions. We should not underestimate the influence that this scholarly interaction in such "intellectual communities"[41] had on Cicero's works. It probably helped to shape Cicero's general philosophical view; moreover, isolated passages from the dialogues sometimes even found their direct origin in previous discussions between Cicero and one of his friends.[42]

What about the Romans in *On Ends* 1–2?

We have seen that the clear-cut opposition between "Greek" and "Roman" is problematic in Cicero's case and that the participants in the discussion of *On Ends* have fully appropriated a traditionally Greek perspective as their own frame of reference. The question remains, however, whether this appropriation is entirely unproblematic. Here and there, Cicero suggests it is. In 1.50, for instance, Torquatus explains the Epicurean view of justice and illustrates it with a reference to the recent past (*ut te consule*). By this short phrase, which implies a clever argument *ad hominem*, he claims that his doctrine is corroborated by what recently happened in Rome. Epicureanism, in other words, can smoothly and without any problem be applied in contemporary Rome as well. There are also situations, however, where such an application is prima facie less evident. In what follows, I deal with four domains where input from the specifically Roman

---

[39] In spite of what he claims himself in *Att.* 15.52.3; see Bringmann: 2012 for a recent interpretation of this passage.

[40] See on this esp. Griffin: 1995.   [41] Steel: 2005, 106–114.

[42] A case in point is *On Ends* 1.25, which can only be understood against the background of Cicero's correspondence with Cassius (*Fam.* 15.17.3 and 15.19.2–3); see Roskam: 2019.

context can be expected, and examine to what extent this input entailed modifications and reinterpretations of the Epicurean point of view.

The first domain is that of language. Cicero presents Epicurean philosophy, including its technical terms, in a new linguistic context, which sometimes requires quite a lot of creativity. Cicero often comments upon his work as a translator.[43] In *On Ends* 1–2, however, he seems to minimize the importance of this issue. In 2.10, he deals with the precise meaning of the Latin term *varietas* in order to show that the problem does not lie with the term but with the content of Epicurus' doctrine. In this case, then, the difference in language does not interfere with the understanding of what Epicurus wanted to say. More important in this context is Cicero's discussion of the term *voluptas*, which he regards as the correct translation of the Greek ἡδονή (2.12–15). He defends his translation with unusual insistence, going so far as to claim that "no instance can be found of a Latin word that more exactly conveys the same meaning as the corresponding Greek word than does the word *voluptas*" (2.13). Not every scholar agrees with Cicero on this,[44] and an analysis of the semantics of the two terms may well reveal subtle differences in connotation, but that may not suffice to undermine the whole of Cicero's argument. We should also bear in mind that Lucretius used the same term *voluptas*, which seems to imply that even contemporary Roman Epicureans considered the term the accurate translation of ἡδονή. If they were entitled to do so, Cicero, so it seems, was entitled to do the same. Anyhow, in this case, too, Cicero strongly underlines that the use of a different language nowhere interferes with a correct interpretation of Epicurean doctrine.

The upshot of all this is that Epicurus' Greek language is no obstacle at all to introducing his philosophy to Rome. Conversely, nowhere in *On Ends* 1–2 can there be found any claim that new insights, derived from the use of Latin terminology, require substantial modifications in Epicurus' philosophical doctrine. A translation can sometimes cause some problems, perhaps, but the content is much more important than the words (2.20).

The second domain concerns virtue. Torquatus deals at length with the virtues of wisdom, temperance, courage and justice (1.42–53). This is an interesting section that has elicited much discussion. Phillip Mitsis has found in this passage influence of a typically Roman perspective, as opposed to the orthodox Epicurean point of view.[45] David Sedley agrees with Mitsis about the presence of much non-Epicurean material in this

---

[43] See, e.g., Powell: 1995c; Reinhardt: 2005; Blyth: 2010/11; Glucker: 2012.
[44] See Powell: 1995b, 299.   [45] Mitsis: 1988, 69–70.

section but finds a different explanation, arguing that Torquatus rather uses a more general framework closely connected to the Platonist ethical tradition and to widespread values.[46] Yet others have shown – correctly, to my mind – that we should not underestimate the amount of orthodox Epicurean material in Torquatus' argument.[47] But this discussion above all shows, once again, that we should avoid using such labels as "Greek" or "Roman" in an absolute way, as if this were self-evident. In fact, both Torquatus and Cicero know and even share basically the same frame of reference, which is that of the traditional philosophical schools, and then deal with it from the perspective of their own philosophical convictions. Cicero's reply to Torquatus in Book 2 is particularly illustrative in this respect. He develops a lengthy argument in order to show that justice cannot be explained in terms of self-interest (2.51–59). Whereas for Epicurus, justice fundamentally rests on fear of detection,[48] Cicero objects that real life proves Epicurus wrong, for shrewd criminals are not stopped by this fear (2.55) and powerful rulers do not even need to be bothered by it (2.57). Here, we can easily detect the influence of Cicero's expertise as a lawyer. He uses his great experience in this field in order to confront Torquatus with a few concrete counter-examples. Especially interesting is the case of Publius Sextilius Rufus. He was left heir to Quintus Fadius Gallus, on condition that he would hand on Fadius' estate to his daughter, but then denied the arrangement and added that he thus observed the (Voconian) law (2.55). In this way, we have here an example of a wicked criminal who does not break the law but is even guilty *by means of* the law (2.55). This example is particularly well-chosen, as it provides a serious challenge to the Epicurean point of view. Apparently, there are criminals who can be certain that their crimes will go unpunished. And thus, so Cicero claims, we need another foundation for justice. If people act justly, their justice rests on the force of nature itself (2.58; cf. also 2.28).

Here, the input of the Roman context seems obvious. Cicero cleverly points to concrete events that happened in Rome and that undermine crucial presuppositions of Epicurus' system. Finally, we have come across clear evidence of the importance of Roman circumstances. Or have we? The conclusion is perhaps not so simple. A closer look shows that the central aspects of Cicero's argument can also be found in the Greek

---

[46] Sedley: 1996, 335–338; similarly Morel: 2016, 82–87.
[47] Tsouna: 2001, 168–169; D. Armstrong: 2011, 107–108; Fish: 2011, 88.
[48] KD 34–35. See on the Epicurean position, e.g., V. Goldschmidt: 1977; Vander Waerdt: 1987; Alberti: 1995; Cosenza: 1996; J. M. Armstrong: 1997; Van den Steen: 2009.

tradition. Epictetus, for instance, also emphasizes that a powerful criminal can sometimes be sure that he will go unpunished (3.7.13–14).[49] Cicero expresses precisely the same conviction, but illustrates this idea by means of examples that are closer to his Roman readers. Thus, he opts for Crassus and Pompey (2.57) rather than for, say, Alexander the Great, but fundamentally the core of his argument does not differ at all from what we read in Epictetus. Again, Epictetus emphasizes the power of nature in his polemics against Epicurus (1.23.1–10) – the context of the argument is different, but its essence is the same. Or one could take the example of Publius Sextilius Rufus, who knew that nobody could prove what the dead Fadius had asked him. This is a concrete elaboration of a theoretical question that Epicurus raised himself, viz. whether the sage would break the law if he would be sure that his crime would not be detected.[50] What Cicero is doing in all these cases, then, is bringing issues and arguments that he received from the Greek tradition closer to his readers by illustrating them with examples borrowed from Roman life. This conclusion is further supported by the last example with which Cicero closes this section, that is, Carneades' argument about the viper: Suppose you know that a viper is hidden somewhere, but you do not warn somebody whose death would be useful for you, then you definitely commit a wicked deed and yet can be absolutely sure that your crime will not be detected (2.59). Fundamentally, this is the same argument, though now more hypothetical and borrowed from the Greek tradition. Whereas Carneades devised a theoretical case, Cicero the lawyer knew of comparable cases that actually happened and deployed them against Epicurus.

We may conclude, then, that in this case too, Cicero's use of material that is directly derived from what happened in contemporary Rome does not entail substantial innovations in or modifications of traditional philosophical arguments. Instead the reference to Roman events and examples helps in mediating the Greek tradition to Cicero's Roman readers, and as such supports and contributes to the applicability and universalizability of Greek philosophy in general and discussions about Epicurean philosophy in particular.

A similar conclusion holds true for the many examples derived from the third domain: the achievements of famous ancestors. Cicero already elaborates this argument in his first attack at the beginning of *On Ends* 1. While we have seen above that the general perspective of this attack is that

---

[49] Cf. also Atticus, Eusebius, *PE* 15.5.5 = fr. 3 Baudry and fr. 532 U.
[50] See Plutarch, *Adv. Colot.* 1127D (= fr. 18 U); G. Seel: 1996; Roskam: 2012.

of the Greek school tradition, we should now give due attention to the one Roman element that it contains. Cicero at length recalls the celebrated heroic fight of Titus Manlius Imperiosus Torquatus and his condemnation of his son, and also mentions a later Titus Manlius Torquatus who banished his own son (1.23–24), pointing out that these men were not pursuing pleasure but were led by a sincere concern for the public interest. Yet this is no mere panegyric on the Roman tradition as opposed to Epicureanism. These examples are not chosen at random, but focus on the achievements of Torquatus' own ancestors. As such, they are a challenging *ad hominem* argument against Torquatus, who picks up the message (1.34).

Nevertheless, there is much more to it than a mere rhetorical *ad hominem* argument. This is evident from Book 2, where analogous arguments frequently occur, and not only about Torquatus' illustrious family. In 2.63–65, for instance, Cicero opposes Lucius Thorius, an inveterate clever hedonist, to the consul Marcus Regulus, who decided to return to Carthage in order to be tortured to death, and claims that the latter was not only more virtuous but even happier than the former. The argument rests on the power of Regulus' exemplary behavior, which seems completely at odds with Epicurean rationality and yet seems preferable. To a certain extent, this is a "false dilemma,"[51] not only because Thorius is not an acceptable paradigm of the Epicurean philosopher, but also because one could think of an alternative.[52] This whole argument is an intelligent rhetorical construct that strategically appeals to the instinctive feelings of the reader.[53] Near the end, Cicero also refers to panegyrics and epitaphs (2.116–117), which do not focus on pleasures but on great accomplishments – again the same argument, but now in the light of death and the afterlife, a context which makes the challenge even more radical and difficult to ignore.

What is especially interesting for our purposes, however, is that Cicero in such passages appears to refute the claims of the Epicureans by means of arguments derived from the great Roman tradition. Cicero, in other words, seems to construct a clear opposition between the Epicurean position and the Roman tradition. The impressive heroic exploits that he recalls time and again are (a) completely at odds with Epicurus' ideals and convictions and (b) typically Roman. However, on closer inspection the case proves,

---

[51] See on this argumentative technique, which also occurs in Cicero's speeches, Seager: 2011.
[52] Roskam: 2007b, 64.   [53] Cf. Brinton: 1988.

once again, more complicated. In fact, both claims require further explanation.

(a) Cicero insists that the Epicureans are not interested in great achieve-
     ments. Nor do they ever mention them in their discourses (2.67). At
     first sight, this looks like a polemical exaggeration. There can be no
     reasonable doubt that erudite Epicureans knew their history.
     Philodemus, for instance, uses history as an argument for his own
     Epicurean position,[54] Atticus was writing history (2.67) and
     Torquatus had no problem in assessing the value of Cicero's histor-
     ical information (1.34). But these Epicureans read history through
     another lens, as appears, for instance, from Torquatus' own evalua-
     tion of the achievements of his distinguished forefathers. All these
     exceptional deeds, so Torquatus argues, are inspired by a concern for
     personal security and thus, ultimately, pleasure (1.34–36). This is a
     direct application of Epicurus' *Principal Doctrines* 6 and 7, which
     provided the Epicureans with an interpretative key for the evaluation
     of the past. In that sense, Cicero's argument that "history is dumb in
     the Epicurean discourses" is indeed problematic. Yet we should not
     dismiss it too early. Interestingly enough, here he speaks in the first
     person singular: He claims that he has "never heard" (*numquam
     audivi*) in Epicurus' school one mention of all these famous states-
     men who are always on the lips of other philosophers (1.67). We
     know that Cicero studied in the Garden; if we believe his testimony,
     polemical though it may be, we may conclude that the Athenian
     Epicureans of Cicero's day were largely ignoring these topics, and
     this, after all, is not implausible, for the issue reflects more the
     interests of other philosophical schools like Platonism and Stoicism.
     If the Epicureans were confronted with an objection derived from the
     illustrious political tradition, they had their answer ready (along the
     lines of *Principal Doctrines* 6 and 7), but within their own school
     their focus was on different things. What mattered for them was
     maximizing their personal pleasure: Why should they bother with the
     heroic deeds of Themistocles? Why would they even take the trouble
     to ridicule such great actions during their meetings? Of course, the
     value of Cicero's testimony also depends on what courses he followed
     in the Garden – if he only took lessons in physics, his testimony
     would be right but quite uncharitable – and on the question of

---

[54] *Rhet.* II, 209, col. 6.28–30 S.; Roskam: 2007a, 107.

whether we can indeed take the claim of *numquam audivi* at face value, but in the not unlikely case that we are indeed entitled to do so, this passage offers us an interesting glimpse into internal school discussions of the Garden in Cicero's day.

(b) Cicero emphatically presents the great achievements of the past as something typically Roman. He contemptuously admits that the Greeks could adduce a few examples of heroic behavior, but insists that many more examples of such heroic self-sacrifice in the service of the public interest can be found in Roman history (2.62). The question, of course, is whether this is more than a piece of overblown rhetoric. The Greeks, one may presume, had no real difficulty in enumerating a list of analogous examples from their own history. In this respect, Plutarch's *Parallel Lives* are the perfect reply to Cicero. This suggests that Cicero's passing remark is ultimately little more than a challenging hyperbole inspired by unwarranted chauvinism.

However, there may be more to it than this. In order to understand fully Cicero's argument from illustrious Roman history, we should consider it in light of the philosophical tradition. For the core of Cicero's argument can indeed be traced back to a rich (Greek) tradition of anti-Epicurean polemics. Plutarch, for instance, is offended at Epicurus' criticism of great heroes such as Themistocles, Aristides and Epaminondas, and he extols their virtues against the trivial results obtained by the Epicureans.[55] Fundamentally, Cicero and Plutarch perfectly agree on this point, but Plutarch of course takes his examples from his own, Greek tradition. In other words, their concrete examples differ, but their basic argument is the same. Against that background, it should not surprise us that both Cicero and Torquatus conclude their discussion of concrete examples with a general phrase: In 1.24 Cicero deals with *optimus quisque* and in 1.37 Torquatus refers to "the glorious exploits and achievements of the heroes of renown." Such general phrases in fact express the gist of the argument, which can easily be made more concrete in different contexts. Cicero, then, is borrowing an argument from the philosophical tradition while giving it a "Roman flavor." This adaptation may have been partly motivated by his popularizing goals[56] – turning the introduction to philosophy into an introduction to the great Roman past – but Cicero's popularizing aim is no sufficient explanation. The focus on the Roman tradition is also a

---

[55] Plutarch, *Non posse* 1097C (= fr. 559 U) and *Adv. Colot.* 1127AB (= fr. 560 U); cf. Roskam: 2007b, 24–25.
[56] Thus Powell: 1995a, 9; cf. Maso: 2008, 15.

necessary condition for the efficiency and persuasiveness of the argument.[57] The more strongly these great examples appeal to the readers,
the more cogent the argument becomes. What Cicero needs, then, is
models that are well known to his readers, that are part and parcel of their
intellectual world; in short, models like Lucretia and Regulus (2.65–66)
rather than Epaminondas or Cimon, or models indeed like T. Manlius
Torquatus Imperiosus (1.23; 2.60; 2.72–73; 2.105), one of the direct
ancestors of his friend Torquatus.

   In that sense, Cicero's focus on the "typically Roman" tradition is no
less the result of his enthusiasm for the *mos maiorum* than of his familiarity
with the philosophical school tradition and the demands of rhetorical
persuasiveness. For Cicero indeed realized very well that for his aristocratic
readers it was hard to reject any such argument. They could ridicule
famous *Graeculi*, perhaps, but it was not so easy to laugh at the distinguished Romans of old. And Torquatus could make use of *Principal
Doctrines* 6 and 7 in order to reinterpret the great deeds of his own
ancestors from an Epicurean point of view, but this argument has its limits
in that it cannot be used in order to save all heroic achievements in the
history of Rome. What about the rest, then? Was Marcus Regulus a simple
fool, like Lucretia and Lucius Verginius? Epicurus was prepared to take the
consequences and make fun of great paradigmatic figures such as
Epaminondas, even if he knew that this would be very offensive to many
people, because he did not pursue the favor of the multitude.[58] It is not
evident, however, that an aristocrat like Torquatus would be as ready to
neglect the demands of *decorum*. This brings us to our last point.

   In the second book of *On Ends*, Cicero blames Torquatus for an
embarrassing inconsistency. Whereas Torquatus claims to do everything
for the sake of pleasure, he cannot possibly maintain this stance while
addressing the senate (2.74–77). On such occasions, he prefers to dwell on
duty, fair-dealing, moral worth and so on; in short, to switch to the
vocabulary of the Stoics and Peripatetics. And not without reason, for to
be honest about his real political motivations when talking to the senators
would almost surely ruin his later political career (2.76). And thus, Cicero
concludes, Torquatus is forced to employ artificial language in order to
conceal what he really thinks, or "change his opinions like his clothes,"

---

[57] *Contra* Striker: 1995, 58 ("he has the annoying habit of . . . interrupting or inflating an argument by
more or less irrelevant stories from Rome's glorious past or deplorable present").

[58] See fr. 187 U; cf. Seneca *Ep.* 29.10 and 25.6 (= fr. 209 U) and Porphyry, *Marc.* 30 294.2–3
N. (= fr. 489 U).

confining his true convictions to a small circle of intimate friends and defending counterfeit opinions in public (2.77). This, to my mind, is one of the strongest arguments in Book 2 of *On Ends*. Cicero knew very well what kind of discourse was usually heard in the Roman senate and saw an obvious contrast with Torquatus' Epicurean ideals. The whole passage is characterized by a strong rhetorical tone,[59] but also makes a valid philosophical point, on the basis of the specifically Roman political context. What could Torquatus say in reply to this challenge?

At first sight, hardly anything at all. Nowhere in *On Ends* 1–2 does Torquatus develop new arguments that take into account the political context at Rome. He could have pointed to the exceptional situation at the end of the Republic, which required political engagement, but apparently did not think of this line of reasoning.[60] Nor is there any trace in Torquatus' exposition of an "over-riding sense of obligation to [. . .] non-philosophical fellow-citizens."[61] Even *Principal Doctrines* 6 and 7 are not used as an argument in favor of political engagement. We have seen that Torquatus used these doctrines as keys for an Epicurean interpretation of history, and that is probably what they were also meant for. Of course, they also offer interesting opportunities: If earlier politicians were right in pursuing their personal security and pleasure through a political career, the same argument may be valid for contemporary politicians, too.[62] Yet it is probably no coincidence that such an argument can nowhere be found in our extant sources. *Principal Doctrines* 6 and 7 focus on the past rather than the present, and prove especially useful as a defense against polemical attacks. They were never meant as a positive argument in favor of a political career, and later Epicureans never understood them as such. Epicurus was open-minded, no doubt, and made room for exceptions, but usually he rather recalled people from politics than stimulating them to all the dangers and pains that a political career necessarily involves.

---

[59] See Inwood: 1990; cf. also Roskam: 2007b, 65–68.

[60] Nor, by the way, did Cassius explain his decision to kill Caesar along these lines; cf. Griffin: 1989, 30–31.

[61] Sedley: 1997, 46–47, suggests that this may explain why so many Epicureans were involved in politics at the end of the Roman Republic. But Torquatus never seems to allude to such a motivation. He admits that "in certain emergencies, owing to the claims of duty or the obligations of business," pleasures may be rejected and pains chosen, but this is too vague to warrant the conclusion that Torquatus is thinking of the kind of "over-riding sense of obligation" that Sedley means. The *tempora* and *necessitates* can perfectly be understood as emergencies *of the Garden* (Roskam: 2007b, 37–41) and the claims of *officia* as duty towards friends.

[62] Cf. Fish: 2011, 75–76.

In *On Ends*, Torquatus brings forward only one argument in reply to Cicero's attack. At the very end of Book 2 he confidently asserts that he can fall back on greater authorities, namely, on Siro and Philodemus (2.119). For the time being, Cicero and Triarius kindly enough accept this argument *ex auctoritate*, although Torquatus has clearly failed to convince them. On that point, the dialogue ends, but we may well go on and wonder whether Philodemus could really help Torquatus on this issue. As far as I can see, he could not.

That is not to say, however, that Philodemus would run into problems himself. In his *Rhetoric* he makes an interesting distinction between the task of the philosopher, who should give his advice to the politician, and that of the politician, who should take into account this philosophical advice while making his political decisions. Such a collaboration between philosopher and politician yields advantages for the whole community (*Rhet.* III, col. 14ᵃ, 30–15ᵃ, 31 Ham.).[63] An interesting illustration of Philodemus' theoretical view may be found in the political career of Piso, who opted for a friendly, reconciliatory political course and avoided excessive ambitions that were a menace to the existing political order.[64] But Philodemus' position rests on a fundamental dichotomy between the field of the philosopher and that of the politician, both of which have their own autonomy.[65] Philodemus, then, adopts the perspective of the professional philosopher who looks at politics as an outsider. He has an interesting reply to Cicero's attack, but this reply cannot simply be taken over by a politician such as Torquatus.

Does this imply, then, that all the Roman Epicureans who engaged in politics indeed had a problem and that Cicero's criticism was correct? Not necessarily. One can take Piso as an example and assume, for the sake of argument (and perhaps correctly), that he indeed regarded himself as an Epicurean: Was such self-understanding credible at all? In my view, Piso's Epicureanism was no less credible than that of the simple farmer Gorgias with whom we began. Of course, there are some obvious differences between the two. Since Piso was an intellectual, we can presume a greater acquaintance with the theoretical details of Epicurean philosophy. He probably had no fundamental problem in accepting the great outlines of Epicurean physics: atomism, the mortality of body and soul, and even the conception of the gods. The Epicurean epistemology and canon were equally unproblematic, as was the basic goal of pleasure and even its

---

[63] Cf. Roskam: 2007a, 122–123; D. Armstrong: 2011, 120–121; Fish: 2011, 95–96.
[64] See on this esp. Griffin: 2001.   [65] Roskam: 2007a, 104–119.

implications, such as the interpretation of pleasure as absence of pain, the simple life concerned with the gratification of limited natural pleasures or the interpretation of virtue as a means for pleasure.[66] If Piso could readily endorse all of these doctrines, his philosophical outlook is not to be seen as "Epicureanism light" but as genuine Epicureanism adapted to his own situation.

Furthermore, the most important adaptation was probably his political career. Here we come across a problem, a problem that should not be overemphasized, perhaps, but is still real, and Cicero was right in detecting it. The question is, however, whether this suffices to undermine fully the credibility of Piso's claim to be an Epicurean. Much depends on how careful Piso's calculus of pleasure and pain was. If he could, in the long run, derive more pleasure than pain from his political career, this career could be perfectly justifiable from an Epicurean point of view. And as a matter of fact, it has been repeatedly argued that the choice of an unnoticed life would have been much more difficult for an aristocratic man like Piso, who was born into a family that already counted many consular members.[67] If he had preferred private pleasures to the public *cursus honorum*, he would have fallen short of expectations. This is an important observation indeed, and in all likelihood it at least partly influenced Piso's course of action. Yet it is only one side of the coin. If we for a moment stick to the Epicurean point of view, we may insist that political commitment also entailed much trouble – even Cicero agreed on that (*Rep.* 1.4–6; *Orat.* 3.63) – and that most of Epicurus' arguments against participation in politics remain valid in Piso's case. We may presume, for instance, that Cicero's vitriolic speech *Against Piso* did not really contribute to Piso's Epicurean pleasures.

Thus, Piso faced the challenge of having to judge whether the choice for politics was, *rebus sic stantibus*, the one that would maximize his personal pleasures. All in all, Epicurus might well have recalled Piso (cf. Cicero, *Rep.* 1.3) as he recalled Idomeneus (Seneca, *Ep.* 22.5–6 = fr. 133 U), adding, though, that he should wait for the right opportunity[68] and that the decision ultimately lies with Piso himself. The choice is not self-evident, and scholars may disagree on what Piso should have chosen if he consistently followed the Epicurean criterion of pleasure (cf. KD 25); but even if

---

[66] Cf. the position of Cassius in *Fam.* 15.19.2–3, with Griffin: 1989 and Roskam: 2019.
[67] See, e.g., Morford: 2002, 107; Fish: 2011, 96; D. Armstrong: 2011, 118–119; cf. Benferhat: 2005a, 69, on Albucius.
[68] Roskam: 2007a, 48–49.

his calculus is wrong, he need not be embarrassed by Cicero's argument, for Piso can simply regard himself as a politician who listens to the advice of an Epicurean philosopher while retaining his own autonomy as a politician. From Philodemus' perspective, Piso occupies the place of the politician, not that of the professional philosopher, and in this capacity he should not meet the same demands of strict philosophical consistency.[69]

It is clear, then, that neither Philodemus nor Piso should be troubled by Cicero's argument. Torquatus, however, does have a problem. We have seen that he wants to be taken seriously as a full member of the Epicurean school. In that respect he assumes, as it were, the role of the professional philosopher. At the same time, he is about to assume the praetorship (2.74) and thus also plays the part of the politician. He thus combines the positions of Philodemus and Piso, and there the problem arises: Torquatus wants to have his cake and eat it, too, and Cicero is absolutely right in making this point. At the end of the second book of *On Ends*, he puts Torquatus on the spot. He should *either* opt for pleasure *or* become a benefactor of the entire human race (2.118). In other words, he has to choose between the role of the professional Epicurean philosopher who is pursuing his individual pleasures and that of the statesman whose concern is with the public interest. A combination of both roles is out of the question. And strikingly enough, Metrodorus agrees. He points out to his brother Timarchus that there is no need to save Greece, but to eat and drink in a way that will do the flesh no hurt and gratify it.[70] Metrodorus and Cicero thus agree on the basic opposition between the alternatives and on the need to choose between them (though not, of course, on what would be the correct choice). Torquatus for his part muddles up things by combining what is incompatible. In this respect, Cicero's criticism is entirely correct.

At this point, however, it is necessary to underline an obvious fact that is all too often forgotten: The Torquatus of *On Ends* is a *literary fiction*.[71] It is

---

[69] Torquatus' remark near the beginning of *On Ends* is telling in this respect: He supposes that Cicero rejects Epicurus mainly for stylistic reasons, since he can scarcely believe that he regards Epicurus' doctrines as untrue (1.14). We could never suppose that a public-spirited and ambitious politician like Cicero would be able to agree with Epicurus' philosophy – such an inconsistency is simply too strong. Torquatus apparently sees things differently. Of course, his challenge is primarily a means to draw Cicero out, yet it suggests that he has no major difficulties in connecting Epicureanism with active politicians.

[70] *Adv. Colot.* 1125D (= fr. 41 K); cf. also *Non posse* 1098CD and 1100D; Westman: 1955, 211–212; Roskam: 2007a, 72–73.

[71] Cf. Morel: 2016, 80. See also Hanchey (Chapter 3) in this volume for more on Cicero's anti-Epicurean rhetoric.

far from certain whether the historical Torquatus took the same course. Probably he indeed regarded himself as an Epicurean,[72] but in this he may have followed the course we attributed above to Piso. If so, he probably answered Cicero's argument from inconsistency with a shrug. The Torquatus of *On Ends* is different: For him, the demand of philosophical consistency between words and deeds is much more urgent. The historical Torquatus can regard the choice between pleasure and a political career as a "false dilemma," but Torquatus the literary character is less entitled to do so. This implies that Cicero's argument is only valid in the specific argumentative context he has carefully constructed himself. In other words, Cicero's argument is especially revealing for his own attitude towards philosophy (not for the general outlook of people like Piso or the historical Torquatus). Ultimately, he cannot prove that a Roman aristocrat (even a consul) can never be an Epicurean, but he at least makes the point that a professional Epicurean philosopher cannot easily become a consul without betraying his own philosophical convictions. Cicero's criticism of the character he has created in his dialogue is convincing, but his literary Torquatus is in the end a chimaera.

Conclusion

In this chapter we have examined whether Epicurean philosophy could be applied in the late Roman Republic, or whether the new context also entailed new problems that required modifications and innovations.

We have seen that Torquatus saw no problems in presenting his Epicurean convictions as relevant for his own life and that he did not feel the need for far-reaching compromises or adaptations. Instead, the Romans rather appropriated the Greek intellectual perspective. As we have seen, the general theoretical framework of the discussions in *On Ends* 1–2 is that of the Greek school tradition. Whenever Torquatus mentions new developments in Epicurean doctrine, these prove to be the products of the school tradition rather than modifications inspired by specifically Roman circumstances. And whenever Cicero refers to the Roman tradition in his critical reply, his references prove to rest on argumentative patterns that can already be found in the Greek tradition. What we have only rarely found in *On Ends* 1–2 is the development of new insights that are based on the peculiar context of Rome as opposed to that of Athens. The most interesting argument in this respect is probably that against the political

---

[72] See Castner: 1988, 40–42; Benferhat: 2005a, 266–270.

engagement of the Roman Epicureans. This, as we have seen, is a clever and convincing argument that seems to be directly derived from the concrete Roman political situation, although it does not entirely reflect historical reality but is based on a theoretical construct of Cicero.

All this has implications for the current hypothesis that Epicurean philosophy is fundamentally opposed to the typically Roman tradition, and that Stoic and Peripatetic philosophy yield much better opportunities to assimilate the traditional *mos maiorum*.[73] The principal problem with this view is that it rests, at least to a certain extent, on ideological pre-suppositions and constructs that unduly privilege specific interpretations of the Roman tradition, developed by men such as Cicero. But what is "typically Roman" or "typically Greek"? Such clear-cut oppositions and oversimplifying labels repeatedly occur in the rhetorical proems of Cicero's dialogues (and elsewhere, too), but they do no justice to the complexity of this matter. Cicero himself agrees – in no less rhetorical vein – that the Epicureans "occupied all Italy" (*Tusc.* 4.7). Even if this is rhetorical hyperbole, the statement may at least not be totally unfounded. But if Epicureanism were incompatible with "typically Roman" culture, then its success would be hard to explain. Moreover, we should then have to conclude that men like Torquatus and Cassius were not true Romans,[74] that Lucretius was not a true Roman, that even Atticus was not a true Roman. In spite of all his rhetoric, Cicero could never go that far.

---

[73] See, e.g., Erler: 1992b, 308; Baraz: 2012, 3; Woolf: 2015, 6 and 144; cf. also Hanchey: 2013b.

[74] A conclusion Cicero himself would strongly disagree with. He praises Torquatus' qualities in *Brut.* 265 and *Att.* 8.11b.1, and underlines Cassius' virtue and *dignitas* (*Fam.* 15.16.3). Of course, such friendly statements are influenced by the context, but this is no less true for the rhetoric of the proems.

CHAPTER 3

Cicero's Rhetoric of Anti-Epicureanism: Anonymity as Critique

Daniel P. Hanchey

It is perhaps unfair to the Epicureans that one of the richest – or, at least, one of the best-preserved – sources for Epicurean thought is also one of its most vocal critics. But fair or not, over the course of the last decade of his life, Cicero made the Epicureans a regular feature of the philosophical and ethical dialogues that constituted much of his public voice at the time. Cicero's critiques of Epicureanism are further augmented by the fact that for him – orator, statesman, philosopher – the Epicureans are consistent antagonists across several spheres of his own activity and thought. For example, not only does Cicero take issue as a philosopher with the Epicurean *finis* of pleasure, but, as a statesman, he also disagrees with the Epicurean aversion to (or at least reticence regarding) political involvement.[1] And as an orator, Cicero claimed no benefit could be derived from the Epicureans, who, he seems to have believed, rejected παιδεία and had little need for a skill so entwined with public deliberation.[2]

In truth, for Cicero these spheres of thought were not distinct. The Scipio of *On the Republic* claims at the end of Book 6 that the highest virtue involves service to the state (*Rep.* 6.29). Crassus makes clear throughout *On the Orator* that genuine oratory is likewise ingrained in public service (e.g., 3.76). And in Cicero's first book of *Tusculan Disputations* the lead interlocutor presents an argument for an immortal soul that closely recalls the activity of the orator.[3] Each of the three

---

[1] Fish: 2011 and others have gone a long way to debunking the idea that Epicureans, especially Roman Epicureans, rejected political involvement unilaterally. This chapter, though, will as a general rule describe Epicureanism from a Ciceronian perspective. For Cicero's critique of the Epicurean aversion to politics, see the chapters of Roskam (2) and Gilbert (4) in this volume.

[2] Cicero at *Orat.* 3.63 discounts the value of Epicurean thought for the orator. On the Epicureans and παιδεία, see Chandler: 2017, 1–17.

[3] This argument especially occupies the central part of the first *Tusculan*, from 1.50 to 1.67. A fuller consideration of the way Cicero makes this connection can be found at Hanchey: 2013a.

spheres to which Cicero most fully devotes himself – oratory, politics, philosophy – informs and depends on the others. The union of these three spheres is part of what Robert Hariman calls "Cicero's republican style."[4] Cicero spent much of his life and career trying to articulate, validate and perform this "style," this unified approach to public living and private morality.

It just so happened that the Epicureans were at odds with him in each facet of his program. For the Epicureans, these spheres of activity were not a program per se; the overlap between them did not play for them the privileged role it did for Cicero. Cicero was developing a socio-political system, whereas the Epicureans were developing a philosophical one. As a result, not only did Cicero feel the need to criticize the individual tenets of Epicureanism, but he did so from a very specific paradigm and according to a specific set of rules. Cicero and the Epicureans were not playing on the same field, so to speak; this, however, never stopped Cicero from criticizing Epicureans as if they were supposed to be on his field and playing his game.

Finally, to compound the whole picture of Cicero's anti-Epicureanism, even as he strove to establish and fortify his brand of republicanism, he faced the ever-growing inevitability of its defeat at the hands of Julius Caesar. Caesar posed a threat to Cicero's real Republic and his theoretical one, with the result that Cicero's criticism of the Epicureans was further fueled by existential angst over his whole project. If indeed Caesar had Epicurean sympathies, encouraged by his father-in-law or otherwise, it can only have added to Cicero's antipathy.[5]

Taken together, these factors produce a tangled web of criticism that stretches throughout Cicero's theoretical works. But perhaps because of

---

[4] Hariman: 1995, 95–140. Cappello: 2019 explores the effects of this "style" within Cicero's *Academics*, where he identifies Cicero's skeptical philosophical method with a community-oriented approach to philosophy. A Republic implicitly provides the right mood and backdrop for philosophical inquiry. Gurd: 2007 does something similar in considering how many of Cicero's letters depict his deep interest in collaboration as part of his compositional practice. Again, the back-and-forth of republican community finds its parallel in Cicero's practice of writing.

[5] For competing views on the extent of Caesar's Epicureanism, see Bourne: 1977, who argues for its influence in much of Caesar's behavior, and Mulgan: 1979, who is less convinced. Belliotti: 2009 marshals the evidence and reasonably concludes that it is a stretch to identify Caesar as an "Epicurean *as such*" given the limited evidence (109, emphasis in original). But he also admits that many of his ideas, particularly on religion and death, mirrored those of the Epicureans and may have borne their influence (107–109). And now Valachova: 2018 reaches a similar conclusion to that of Belliotti. See also Volk's chapter (5) in this volume for the possibility of Caesar's Epicureanism.

Cicero's opposition to Epicureanism on such a fundamental level, he can extend his criticism of the sect into any topic or area that he feels threatens his general republican perspective.[6] In this chapter I will focus not so much on the explicit doctrinal criticisms that Cicero levels at the Epicureans in, for example, *On Ends* 2 or *On the Nature of the Gods*,[7] but on one facet of his rhetorical criticism throughout his theoretical writings, viz., his tendency to avoid explicitly naming the Epicureans, a technique whose consistent reappearance indicates its significance for his overall project, style and literary technique.[8]

Circumlocution

When in the course of the discussions dramatized in Cicero's dialogues an interlocutor wishes to invoke the Epicureans, he will occasionally do so by invoking the founder himself by name.[9] At other times Cicero uses the adjectival form *Epicureus*, either in reference to specific adherents of the school or to Epicureans as a collective. He uses it in both of these ways most often in discussions where Epicurean thought specifically is under thorough review, especially in *On Ends* and *On the Nature of the*

---

[6] The bibliography on Cicero's anti-Epicureanism is copious. See Griffin: 1989, Nicgorski: 2002, Stokes: 1995, Striker: 1996 and especially Lévy: 1992, who emphasizes Epicureanism's threat to the *mos maiorum*. Zetzel: 1998 considers *On the Republic* and Lucretius; Maslowski: 1974 concentrates on the speeches. Cicero's specific distaste for the pleasure calculus appears in *Against Piso* (*passim*), *For Sestius* (23, 138–39) and *For Caelius* (39–42). Inwood: 1990 focuses on Cicero's criticisms in *On Ends* 2, which are his most concentrated and pointed rebukes. He concludes that Cicero's arguments aim primarily "to air the issues raised by Epicurean hedonism … and to kill its influence at Rome … by showing that it was not in fact compatible with the traditional *Roman* attachment to prima facie moral virtue" (163, emphasis in original). Cf. Annas and Betegh: 2016. Benferhat: 2001 explores Cicero's anti-Epicureanism in the *Tusculan Disputations*.

[7] On Cicero's representation and critique of the Epicureans in *On Ends*, three chapters dedicated to the subject in the volume edited by Julia Annas and Gabor Betegh (2016) are well worth reading. Warren (ch. 2), Morel (ch. 3) and Frede (ch. 4) explore Cicero's cases against Epicurean understandings of pleasure, virtue and friendship, respectively.

[8] Charles Brittain: 2016 provides an example of what I mean by Cicero's literary technique. He cannily observes that the conversations depicted in *On Ends* appear in reverse chronological order (according to dramatic date). Thus, according to the conceit of the dialogue, the Cicero of Book 2 has already heard, and rejected, the arguments advanced in Books 5 and 3, respectively. As Brittain shows, this timeline calls into question interpretations of the dialogue that suggest Cicero is slowly advancing closer to the truth through his discussions. The literariness of the dialogues plays an invaluable role in shaping his arguments.

[9] E.g., *Fat.* 18 or *Div.* 1.61, but there are numerous examples of this kind of reference, not only to Epicureanism, but to many different schools of thought. Democritus (e.g., *Acad.* 1.7) and Metrodorus (e.g., *Fin.* 1.25) also occasionally appear paired with Epicurus as representatives of elements of Epicurean thought (as well as Philodemus and Zeno in *On Ends*).

Gods, and *passim* throughout *On Fate*, the *Tusculan Disputations* and the *Academics*.[10]

But at other times, both in these works and others where Epicurean doctrines, though not the focus, still come under some consideration, the interlocutor regularly invokes the Epicureans obliquely, using a periphrasis that identifies them as "those who refer all things to pleasure" or the like.[11] Cicero uses a formulation of this sort at least twenty times in his theoretical works. At least a dozen of these formulations occur across five works where the Epicureans go unnamed in the passage or the larger context.[12] So, for example, in *On Friendship* Laelius offers the following judgment (32):

> Ab his qui pecudum ritu **ad voluptatem omnia referunt** longe dissentiunt, nec mirum; nihil enim altum, nihil magnificum ac divinum suspicere possunt qui suas omnes cogitationes abiecerunt in rem tam humilem tamque contemptam.

> Those people who, in the manner of beasts, refer all things to the standard of pleasure, differ greatly from these men I've just named [i.e. friends who esteem love over profit]. And it's not surprising. For those who have cast all their thoughts upon a thing so base and so contemptible cannot observe anything exalted, estimable and divine.

There are several possible explanations for Cicero's circumlocution in passages like this, and Jonathan Powell details two of the most plausible in his commentary on *On Friendship*. Laelius' discourse on friendship, as he indicates, is that of a self-declared amateur. Of course, all Ciceronian interlocutors are amateurs in a certain sense, for he intentionally populates his dialogues with Roman aristocrats in lieu of philosophers in the Greek tradition.[13] Some of these speakers are still experts in their subject matter, as with Crassus in *On the Orator* or Scipio in *On the Republic*. Others are not experts but still speak and conduct themselves as if they have expertise, even if that expertise is historically implausible (e.g., Balbus in *On the Nature of the Gods* or Lucullus in the *Prior Academics*). But Laelius

---

[10] He mentions the "Epicureans" as such eleven times in *On Ends*, thirteen in *On the Nature of the Gods*. Forms of *Epicureus* occur two or three times each in *Acad.*, *Div.*, *Fat.* and *Tusc*, but rarely ever outside of these works.

[11] E.g., *Amic.* 32, quoted below, *Orat.* 1.226, *Fin.* 2.58, *Sen.* 43, *Off.* 3.118. This and other formulations are considered in more depth below.

[12] *Orat.* 1.226, 3.62, 3.63; *Sen.* 43; *Leg.* 1.39, 1.41, 1.42, 1.49; *Amic.* 32, 86; *Off.* 1.5, 3.12.

[13] Cicero's letters offer unique insight into his mindset in choosing his interlocutors. See, e.g., *QFr.* 3.5, *Fam.* 9.8, *Att.* 13.12 and 4.16. Such letters suggest he is concerned not only with the social status of figures from the past, but that contemporary political pressure and his own friendships affect whom he chooses as speakers.

forswears such expertise explicitly first at *On Friendship* 17, where he rejects the Greek rhetoricians and the *schola*, then again at *On Friendship* 24, where he avoids the company of those *qui ista disputant*.[14]

Powell suggests first that Laelius' aversion to identifying the Epicureans by name extends in part from his resistance to being identified as a philosopher of the Greek sort, whose knowledge of philosophy is too specific and subtle.[15] To buttress this case, Powell also notes that Laelius avoids naming any philosophical school at all in the dialogue.[16] As a second possible explanation for the anonymity of the Epicureans, Powell proposes that Cicero himself wishes to avoid giving offense to Atticus, the dedicatee of the dialogue and the companion who was himself an Epicurean and whose friendship had in some way inspired the work.[17]

This second argument is plausible but seems insufficient to explain Cicero's pattern of describing the Epicureans while leaving them unnamed, since by 44 BC Atticus was certainly well-acquainted with Cicero's attacks on Epicureanism.[18] The first argument, however (about Laelius avoiding Greekness), bears consideration. On the one hand, Cicero's Laelius undoubtedly wished to avoid appearing Greek, but it is also worth noting that Laelius' main objection is to Greek-style display centered on the rhetorical method, the fielding of any sort of question and the formulation of a clever argument in response. Crassus objects to the same kind of scenario in a mirror-passage in *On the Orator* 1 (98–110), and Cicero, in the process of reassuring Torquatus about his intentions, is critical of this rhetorical method in his opening words in *On Ends* 2.

Posing objections to Greek disputation or to the inviting of questions does not necessarily entail avoiding mention of Epicureanism. Cicero seems generally and consistently opposed to both things, but his criticisms of the two modes tend to be different. In the opening paragraphs of *On Ends* 2, Torquatus and Cicero have to work toward a compromise regarding modes of philosophical discourse. Cicero, without Torquatus' objection, wants to avoid the *schola* (2.1–4), but Torquatus ultimately grows impatient with the dialectical approach Cicero offers in its place (2.17–18).

---

[14] The *schola* form and the verb *disputare* are repeatedly rejected by Ciceronian interlocutors. For a discussion of these terms and how they are used in Cicero, see Gildenhard: 2007, 7–21 and Gorman: 2005, 65–67.

[15] Powell: 1990, 16.   [16] *Ibid.*

[17] *Ibid.*, 20. Gilbert's chapter (4) in this volume explores Atticus' Epicureanism in more detail.

[18] Cicero in fact associated with and respected many Epicureans, including Atticus, Cassius and Torquatus. Powell's argument that Cicero wanted to avoid causing offense to these is entirely plausible. In a sense, the emphasis on certain Epicurean traits allows Cicero to distance the people he is talking about from the Epicureans he admired.

In the end, Cicero returns to a rhetorical mode after having made his aversion to the *schola* clear. This compromise is one of several literary tools for suggesting that, far from being the kind of Greek philosophers that traffic in displays of cleverness, the Epicureans in fact lack subtlety and erudition (cf. 2.12–13: *bonos ... sed certe non pereruditos*). They are not, like Greek sophists, misleading the audience; they are, as the compromise of *On Ends* 2 suggests, misleading themselves by failing to understand fully what they are saying.[19]

Likewise, in *On the Orator* Crassus fully wants to avoid associations with the likes of the sophist Gorgias, but he promotes philosophical inquiry. Rejecting the Greekness of the *schola* does not mean rejecting philosophy or even the knowledge of philosophy. In fact, in Book 3 he mentions a number of philosophers and philosophical schools by name several times, including the Stoics,[20] but he does not name the Epicureans. Instead he resorts to the periphrastic formula, calling the Epicureans at *On the Orator* 3.63 *hi qui nunc voluptate omnia metiuntur* ("these who now measure all things on the scale of pleasure"). Then, a paragraph later, he speaks at 3.63 of *ea philosophia, quae suscepit patrocinium voluptatis* ("that philosophy that has taken up the patronage of pleasure"). This circumlocution seems to be a different sort of rhetorical move than the critique levelled at Greek scholastic philosophy at *On the Orator* 1.105, where Crassus explicitly associates such philosophy with a Peripatetic named Staseas.

So, while Powell's suggestions tell part of the story, Cicero must have a further reason for avoiding mention of the Epicureans by name. And the reason may not in fact be all that hard to determine: Cicero identified the Epicureans as he did to place the focus on, and to avoid any confusion over, what he considered to be true Epicureanism and why he considered it a true problem.

Epicurean Fundamentals

Like the other philosophical schools, Epicureanism had to negotiate a tension in its fidelity to the principles of its founder versus its role within evolving or shifting cultural contexts.[21] This burden was particularly

---

[19] Cicero's arguments in *Fin.* 2 are designed to point out internal inconsistencies in Epicurean doctrines about pleasure. Cf. Morel: 2016.

[20] See esp. *Orat.* 3.59–68. Cf. Scaevola's initial skepticism about the union of philosophy and oratory at *Orat.* 1.41–44, where he lists a number of schools.

[21] Certainly this is true for Epicureanism at Rome. Chandler: 2017, 8–9 considers this tension in the context of παιδεία. And Philodemus, who borrows vocabulary from the Stoics, says outright in *On*

pronounced for the Epicureans, who had great reverence for Epicurus himself. Cicero mentions this reverence in the *Tusculan Disputations* (1.48):

> soleo saepe mirari non nullorum insolentiam philosophorum, qui naturae cognitionem admirantur eiusque inventori et principi gratias exsultantes agunt eumque venerantur ut deum.

> It is my usual tendency to marvel at the unusualness of many philosophers who themselves marvel at the study of nature, and leap to give thanks to its inventor and originator, and worship him like a god.

Philip Hardie suggests that in his reference to *non nulli philosophi* Cicero has in mind Lucretius in particular, but regardless of the specific identification, Cicero's *philosophi* are undoubtedly the Epicureans and the *inventor* is Epicurus himself.[22]

Here, too, Cicero avoids specific mention of Epicurus' name, and in doing so he highlights a contrast. On the one hand, many Epicureans go so far as to worship Epicurus; on the other hand, in doing so they reveal the height of their foolishness. In *Tusculan Disputations* 1 they worship Epicurus for freeing them from the fear of the mythological terrors of the underworld. But since that fear is unfounded and silly to begin with, the Epicureans effectively worship Epicurus for an unfounded and silly reason. When he avoids naming them Cicero accomplishes two rhetorical effects. First, he slights them, treating them as if they are not worth naming. And secondly, he suggests that their fundamental principles, as advanced by Epicurus, are so manifestly wrong that simply by identifying what he understands those principles to be he is making a rhetorical argument against them. Giving them a name would give them credit. Withholding the name discredits them, and identifying them by one of their beliefs brings that belief under scrutiny.

Cicero is also insisting that any Romanized versions of Epicureanism are not fully genuine. Epicureanism in Rome had advanced and evolved to meet new and different cultural and moral contingencies, but Cicero uses his periphrases to orient his reader to what he considers Epicurus' core ideas. In the response to Torquatus in *On Ends* 2, Cicero the interlocutor introduces a scenario where a man dying intestate asks his friend to ensure his estate passes to his daughter. Cicero assumes Torquatus, as the friend in

---

Property Management that Epicureans have no problem receiving what is good and true from other schools into their own tradition.

[22] Hardie: 2007, 113; Cf. Pucci: 1966, 93–95. Roskam's chapter (2) in this volume analyzes the Epicureanism of Torquatus.

such a situation, would oblige the dying man. But he would do so in spite of, not because of, his Epicureanism (2.58):

> sed ego ex te quaero, quoniam idem tu certe fecisses, nonne intellegas eo maiorem vim esse naturae, quod ipsi vos, qui omnia ad vestrum commodum et, ut ipsi dicitis, ad voluptatem referatis, tamen ea faciatis, e quibus appareat non voluptatem vos, sed officium sequi. . .?

> But I ask you, since you would no doubt have done the same thing, don't you realize that the force of nature is so great that you, you who refer all things to your convenience and pleasure, as you put it, even you would do these things that make it clear that you are pursuing not pleasure, but duty. . .?

Here again Cicero uses the circumlocution (*vos, qui omnia ad vestrum commodum et . . . ad voluptatem referatis*) to point out what he considers one of the fundamental principles of Epicureanism and to express his belief that this core quality of Epicureanism, understood in the most straightforward way, is manifestly foolish even to Torquatus. Despite the best efforts of figures like Torquatus to Romanize Epicureanism, Cicero consistently tries to make clear that, to him, Epicureanism is ultimately defined by certain baseline qualities. At the most fundamental level, by avoiding the name of the Epicureans so often and by replacing the name with circumlocutions, Cicero concentrates on highlighting and marginalizing these basic Epicurean qualities.

And for Cicero, there are three basic qualities to which he returns, corresponding roughly with elements of Epicurean physics, logic and ethics: the mortality of the soul, an animal-like failure to employ *ratio* and *oratio* and a penchant for quantifying ethical decisions.

Soul Mortality

Following Democritus, the Epicureans famously held the soul to be a physical, mortal substance that dissolved with the rest of the body at death.[23] When Cicero needles Lucretius and the *non nulli philosophi* (in *Tusc.* 1.48, quoted above), it is because he (or his interlocutor) strongly doubts that Epicurean arguments about death come close to the mark. In two other places, *On Friendship* 13 and *On Old Age* 85, Cicero's interlocutors scoff mildly at philosophers who deny soul immortality.

The Epicureans, of course, were not the only philosophers to claim that the soul was mortal. Cicero admits as much at *Tusculan Disputations* 1.77,

---

[23] Cf. Lucr. 3.830–869.

where he mentions Dicaearchus as an example of one disbelieving in the immortal soul. But Cicero's characteristically condescending tone in both *On Friendship* 13 and *On Old Age* 85 suggests that the Epicureans are the primary group he has in mind. At *On Old Age* 85, he refers to them as *minuti philosophi*; then in *On Friendship* 13, in the voice of Laelius, he describes philosophers who have "recently" (*nuper*) come on the scene – a sort of rhetorical deauthorization of their ideas. In all three passages (*Tusc.* 1.48, *Sen.* 85 and *Amic.* 13) Cicero avoids naming the Epicureans while mocking their ideas. The references are rhetorically dismissive of soul mortality. But though he scoffs, generally this core belief of the Epicureans is the one least emphasized by Cicero, perhaps because, even to Cicero, there is no prima facie evidence that a belief in a mortal soul is absurd, or perhaps because the belief was shared by non-Epicureans.

Likeness to Animals

The second core characteristic he presents relates in a way to logic: Cicero regularly connects the Epicureans to beasts or animals. In *On Duties* 1.11, Cicero offers a Stoic-influenced understanding of how humans and animals differ.[24] He argues that both animals and humans have instincts for self-preservation and procreation, but animals lack the human capacities for *ratio* and *oratio*, i.e., for reason, which allows humans to think logically and to process the relationship between past, present and future, and for speech, which allows humans to form communities.

These two complementary ideas form the bedrock of Cicero's work and thought. The dialogue form he so often uses embodies both reason and speech, and the fact that Cicero outlines the joint significance of *ratio* and *oratio* for humans first in the opening paragraphs of his first theoretical work (*Inv.* 1–2) and then returns to it in his final work (*Off.* 1.11) serves as another testimony to the fundamental role the paired ideas play in the theoretical works as a whole.[25]

And yet, these two capacities for reason and speech are precisely the two capacities that animals lack. As a result, when Cicero compares Epicureans to animals, he is doing more than offering a simple slight. He is instead pointing to a fundamental flaw in their philosophy, one that discredits anything else they might say. They can neither synthesize ideas nor operate effectively in communities.

---

[24] Cf. *Inv.* 1–2, *Fin.* 2.45 and *Leg.* 1.30.
[25] These ideas are more fully explored in Hanchey: 2014.

Cicero associates Epicureans with animals regularly. Twice in *On Friendship* (20, 32) Laelius makes brief, summary critiques of the Epicureans, saying first that seeking out pleasure in place of all other things is "the goal of beasts" (*beluarum extremum*; 20) and later that Epicureans refer all things to pleasure "in the manner of cattle" (*pecudum ritu*; 32). In *Academics* 1.6 and *On Ends* 2.109, where Epicureans are explicitly named, Cicero reaffirms that pleasure is the chief end for beasts and that Epicureans share this quality with them. And in *On the Nature of the Gods* 1.122, Cicero implies that Epicureans value and treat their friends as if they were *pecudes*. All of these comparisons are meant to reinforce the parallel critiques that Epicureans are irrational (fail to employ *ratio*), are self-interested (fail to pursue community through *oratio*) and are pleasure-seekers.[26]

Emphasis on Measuring and Quantification

But by far the most common circumlocution, and hence the one that most closely and completely identifies the Epicureans for Cicero, is a two-part formula exemplified succinctly at *On the Orator* 3.62: *hi qui nunc voluptate omnia metiuntur*.[27] With this pattern Cicero takes aim at what he considers the Epicureans' most fundamental flaw: their ethics. The first and most obvious part of the formula is the reference to pleasure, and Cicero considered the Epicureans hedonists fundamentally. But equally significant for the formula is the verb *metiuntur*. The Epicureans make two mistakes: They use pleasure as the standard and they make decisions through a process of measuring.[28]

Cicero returns to this formula over and over again, with slight variations. The Epicureans regularly weigh or measure things in accordance with pleasure (or pleasure and pain) in order to make decisions.[29] Very often Cicero says specifically that the Epicureans (unnamed, except in

---

[26] Cicero is in part able to make the comparison between animals and Epicureans because of Epicurus' own words. In DL 10.137, Epicurus points to the natural impulse of pigs and babies towards pleasure. The comparison to animals and babies is not meant to inspire Epicureans to imitate them, but to justify the innate quality of the desire for pleasure. Cf. Lucretius 5.932–959. See also Warren: 2002, ch. 5, on the Epicurean origin of the pig comparison, and, of course, cf. Horace *Ep.* 1.4.16.

[27] Leeman, Pinkster and Wisse: 1996, *ad loc.*, note that Cicero used a similar formula in the contemporary speech *Against Piso*, which serves as a reminder both of the breadth of Cicero's characterization of the Epicureans and of the invective potential of the formula. The *nunc* here also recalls the dismissive *nuper* at *Amic.* 13.

[28] Parts of the discussion that follows were first articulated in Hanchey: 2013b.

[29] See *Orat.* 3.62, *Leg.* 1.39, *Fin.* 2.56, *Fin.* 5.93, *Sen.* 45 and *Off.* 3.12.

On Ends) "refer things to pleasure" (e.g., *omnia, quae faceremus, ad voluptatem esse referenda; Sen.* 43).[30] The valence of the verb *referre* retains the sense of measuring, the idea that pleasure is a standard or calculus by which to make a judgment. In some cases the Epicureans "refer" or "measure," but do so to or by standards apart from or in addition to pleasure. So, in *On Laws* 1.41 the Epicureans measure on a calculus of "convenience" (*commodus; metietur suis commodis omnia*), as they do at *On Duties* 1.5 and 3.12, while at *On Ends* 2.58 they refer all things *ad vestrum commodum*. At various times they measure by or refer to "benefit" (*emolumentum*), "utility" (*utilitas*), "reward" (*praemium*), "profit" (*merces*) and the "stomach" (*venter*).[31]

As variations in the formula clarify, the pleasure/measure pairing has a broader application. Pleasure functions as the most common stand-in for selfishness, while measuring encompasses a decision-making process that values nothing but self-interest as inherently worthy per se.[32] That is to say, measuring denies or limits the capacity of nature to endow certain concepts with inherent value. Value is instead assessed through a process of weighing or measuring.

Both selfishness and measuring ultimately have the same fault: They undercut the function of the Republic. The threat posed to the Republic by selfishness is clear.[33] The threat of measuring is perhaps not as clear, but what is clear is that Cicero, with the rarest of exceptions, uses the rhetoric of measuring in social and ethical decision-making contexts negatively.

The examples related to Epicureans constitute the vast majority of Cicero's appeals to measuring, but even when the Epicureans are not the specific target, measuring carries an unfavorable connotation. In *On the Orator* 1.7 and 2.335, Cicero mentions people who measure on a scale of utility, but in both cases they seem to be using the wrong process of decision-making because they arrive at the wrong conclusions.[34]

---

[30] See also *Orat.* 1.226, *Fin.* 2.58, *Sen.* 43 and *Amic.* 32.

[31] For *emolumentum*: *Fin.* 2.85 and *Off.* 3.12; for *utilitas*: *Leg.* 1.42 and *Off.* 3.118; for *praemium*: *Leg.* 1.49; for *merces*: *Fin.* 2.85; for *venter*: *Nat. D.* 1.113.

[32] Cf. Morel: 2016, 78: "By subordinating morality to pleasure, Epicurean ethics starts out from an unacceptable principle and therefore leads, regardless of its doctrinal content, to disastrous consequences."

[33] *Off.* 1.22 (*non nobis solum nati sumus*) perhaps most famously and succinctly summarizes Cicero's general position.

[34] *Orat.* 1.7: *Quis enim est qui, si clarorum hominum scientiam rerum gestarum vel utilitate vel magnitudine metiri velit, non anteponat oratori imperatorem?* ("Who in the world would not place a general before an orator, if his concern was to measure the knowledge of illustrious men by the usefulness or greatness of their accomplishments?"); 2.335: *quarum fructum utilitate metimur*, in a critique of utilitarianism.

The Epicureans are simply a subset of these individuals. Cicero describes the virtuous as measuring the highest good with *honestas* in *On Ends*, but the passage is focalized by Epicurus, who would, by Cicero's assessment, understand the conflict between virtue and pleasure in terms of measuring.[35] In *On Friendship* 21, it is actually the Stoics who measure, when they overvalue the *magnificentia verborum*, by speaking about preferred indifferents and tightly restricting the meaning of words like *bonus* and *sapiens*. A pair of examples come in the *Tusculans*, at 1.90 and 5.94: In both cases the interlocutor is responding to people who use the senses or the body as a standard of decision-making, and he then offers alternative, worthier standards (the health of the Republic in the first instance, traditional Roman social divisions in the other). These examples, though more haphazard than Cicero's association of measuring with the Epicureans, only reinforce the insufficiency of measuring as a tool for making social and ethical decisions.[36] The instrumental process of measuring requires the decision-maker to quantify ethical goods and to judge them in relation to other goods. Cicero occasionally uses such language when his interlocutor introduces it, or when another figure focalizes the words, but he avoids it when describing his preferred ethical decision-making processes.

Why, then, is Cicero so opposed to measuring? A passage from the first book of *On Laws* summarizes many of the different ways Cicero considers the use of measuring a threat to the Republic, beginning at 1.39. The interlocutor Cicero is making the case for natural law and the inherent value of virtue, an argument upon which the ideal laws of his ideal Republic will rest. He says:

> Sibi autem indulgentes et corpori deservientes atque omnia quae sequantur in vita quaeque fugiant voluptatibus et doloribus ponderantes, etiam si vera dicant (nihil enim opus est hoc loco litibus), in hortulis suis iubeamus dicere, atque etiam ab omni societate rei publicae, cuius partem nec norunt ullam neque umquam nosse voluerunt, paulisper facessant rogemus.

> And regarding those who indulge themselves and are slaves to their bodies, and measure on a scale of pleasure and pain all the things they should do or

---

[35] *Fin.* 2.48: *hanc se tuus Epicurus omnino ignorare dicit quam aut qualem esse velint qui honestate summum bonum metiantur* ("Yet your Epicurus tells us that he is utterly at a loss to know what nature or qualities are assigned to this morality by those who make it the measure of the chief good").

[36] The only other example I find comes at *Brutus* 257, where Cicero argues against using utility or profit as a means for weighing someone's worth (*quare non quantum quisque prosit, sed quanti quisque sit ponderandum est*). Cf. the examples from *Orat.* This passage in *Brut.* is charged with implicit criticism of Julius Caesar and commodity exchange. See Hanchey: 2015.

flee from in life; even if these should speak the truth—there is no need here to go into detail about it—let us beseech them to do their talking in their little gardens, and let us ask them to retire a little from the society of the Republic, about which they neither know anything nor want to know anything.

The cluster of elements from Cicero's formula makes the identification of the Epicureans secure, as does the reference to *hortuli*.[37] Here Cicero excludes the Epicureans from a discussion of the Republic by placing emphasis on their wont to "weigh on a scale of pleasure and pain" (*voluptatibus et doloribus ponderantes*). This characteristic is fundamentally what disqualifies them from commenting on the running of the Republic.

Just a few paragraphs later, despite his stated intention to avoid arguing against the Epicureans, Cicero repeats the same set of premises (*Leg.* 1.42). The discussion has moved on to the priority of universal law over the written laws of individual states. Cicero insists that without universal law, written laws have no ultimate, absolute authority to which to appeal, and may therefore be rejected in some instances. Specifically, Cicero speaks of the sort of individual (*idem*) who claims that everything is to be measured by "self-interest" (*utilitate*) and who will even break laws if he stands to profit. The same criticisms of selfishness resurface here, coupled with a reference to measuring (*metienda sunt*), all in the context of a rejection of nature. Here the threat of the Epicureans is even greater: Not only should they not participate in setting laws for the Republic, but their methodology poses a direct threat to the existing laws and their foundations.

In *On Laws* 1.49, Cicero again makes the association between Epicureans and utilitarian measuring: *Qui virtutem praemio metiuntur, nullam virtutem nisi malitiam putant* ("Those who measure virtue based on reward think there is no virtue but vice"). By prioritizing *praemium* the Epicureans devalue a whole set of virtues: *beneficentia, gratia, amicitia* and ultimately *societas, aequalitas* and *iustitia* (1.49–50). Such a self-interested calculus is most troubling to Cicero because it threatens the Republic, its laws and the very bonds of society.

In this way, measuring is closely connected to the parallel category of quantification and commerce. Like measuring, commerce is interested in relative value, and Cicero, on multiple occasions, connects the Epicureans

---

[37] Dyck: 2004, 172 *ad loc.*, offers two interpretations of Cicero's hesitation to name the Epicureans in this specific passage. He first names the rhetorical strategy of *tacito nomine*, i.e., the slighting of the opponent by leaving them unnamed. He also postulates, like Powell: 1990 in his *On Friendship* commentary, that Cicero is showing sensitivity to the feelings of Atticus, who is of course both present for the discussion and an Epicurean.

with the commercialization or commoditization of friendship. Three of the most striking examples come from dialogues that engage Epicureanism explicitly (*On Ends* and *On the Nature of the Gods*). In *On Ends* 2, Cicero twice rejects Torquatus' idea of Epicurean friendship by associating it with ideas of commerce. First, at 2.83, Cicero discusses the claim voiced by Torquatus (at *Fin.* 1.70) that the Epicureans enter into "pacts" (*foedera*) of friendship. He concludes:

> An vero, si fructibus et emolumentis et utilitatibus amicitias colemus, si nulla caritas erit, quae faciat amicitiam ipsam sua sponte, vi sua, ex se et propter se expetendam, dubium est, quin fundos et insulas amicis anteponamus?

> But if we cultivate friendships for their benefits and gains and utility, if there is no love, which produces friendship of its own accord, by its own force, sought from and for its own sake, can one doubt that we would prefer acquiring land and real estate to acquiring friends?

Foedus itself is not an explicitly commercial term. Torquatus had used it himself (1.70) to describe what he perceived as the elevated character of Epicurean friendship. Cicero here claims that, if the Epicureans can transcend their doctrine of self-seeking through contract, they might also attain to other non-Epicurean virtues through contracts.[38] In fact, though, Cicero mocks the Epicurean understanding of a *foedus*. Their contract is not designed to assure fairness to all parties, but to ensure the opportunity for individual profit. Cicero suggests that if friendship is a matter of this kind of contract, then friends are merely another commodity (and perhaps a less profitable one), in the vein of real estate purchases, like *fundi* or *insulae*.

In his use of *fructus*, *utilitas* and *emolumentum*, Cicero directly echoes his description of the Epicureans in *On Laws* 1.42 and 49, where measuring is designed to produce just such outcomes, and the parallel vocabulary suggests that measuring and contracting are parallel processes. The self-interested disposition typical of the Epicurean finds its complementary action in treating communal virtues as commodities through a process of measuring. In *On Ends* 2.83, the argument in favor of virtue is contrasted

---

[38] The earliest citations in the *TLL* all use *foedus* with legal force. Asmis: 2008 considers the meaning of *foedus* in an Epicurean context in Lucretius. She looks specifically at the phrase *foedus naturae* (or *foedera naturai*) and the relationship between treaties and the physical world. Cicero may be building off *foedus* as an Epicurean watchword, but, with his emphasis on commodities here, he has clearly appealed to something different than the limits of the natural universe discussed by Lucretius.

not with an argument against pleasure, but with one against commercialized friendship. That is to say, Cicero's fundamental criticism of the Epicureans, though often connected to pleasure, can equally be expressed through a critique of ethical measuring.

Cicero again identifies Epicurean friendship as a form of commercial transaction at the end of *On Ends* 2 (117). Here he contrasts what he considers true friendship and its emphasis on the mutual appreciation of virtue with the utilitarian friendship of the Epicureans. Cicero explicitly connects Epicurean friendship with *commodus* and *faeneratio*.[39] In *On the Nature of the Gods* 1.122, the connection is even more direct. To conclude his criticism of Epicureanism in that book, Cotta states emphatically that the friend who seeks "his own benefit" (*ad nostrum fructum*) is participating not in "friendship" (*amicitia*) at all, but in "commerce" (*mercatura*). Friends become the equivalent of *prata et arva et pecudum greges* ("land and fields and herds of cattle").[40] Here the measuring critique is paired with the animal critique, highlighting another reason the animal connection works for Cicero and synthesizing his positions. Measuring, quantifying and commoditizing friends all disembed value from nature and place the individual's prerogative over that of the community.

The passage that best synthesizes Cicero's periphrastic criticism of the Epicureans is *On Friendship* 26–32, which brings us back to the opening observation of this chapter. The last of Cicero's dialogues, this work puts a period of sorts on several of the themes that emerge in his theoretical works of the 50s and 40s. And, as a text dedicated specifically to social attitudes and practices, *On Friendship* is uniquely positioned to criticize Epicureanism, if it is understood that Cicero's basic criticism of the Epicureans is their failure to observe the natural social bonds that undergird the Republic.

Laelius insists repeatedly throughout the dialogue that friendship should not be predicated on exchange. His position implicitly obviates the need for measuring or utilitarianism. In the structure of the work, as is typical of the genre, the text begins with Fannius and Scaevola asking Laelius for his thoughts on friendship. Laelius immediately offers a brief summary of

---

[39] Forms of *commodus* appear three times in reference to the Epicureans in 2.117, along with the reference to usury. It is true that *commodus*, its connection to commodity notwithstanding, need not carry a strictly commercial meaning (cf. *Nat. D.* 1.122), but its connection to other self-interested calculi makes its meaning clear (cf. not only *Leg.* 1.41 and *Fin.* 2.58, but also *Off.* 1.5 and 3.12). When paired with *faeneratio* in *On Ends* 2.117, the commercialized sense of *commodus* becomes readily apparent.

[40] Cf. the *fundi* and *insulae* of *On Ends* 2.83 above.

these thoughts and claims to have had his say. But his sons-in-law insist that he speak more, and so beginning at 26 he enters upon a fuller discussion. He immediately lays out two types of friendship: The first is characterized by exchange (especially *dandis recipiendis meritis*), while the second is attached to *amicitia*'s root, *amor*. Fannius and Scaevola, who applied a sort of overly aggressive social pressure (*vim*) to oblige Laelius to keep speaking, seem to have been adhering to the former, disapproved version, while Laelius naturally prefers the latter.[41] The Epicureans play no role in the discussion, but almost as if it cannot be helped, the talk of exchange relationships and the implied quantification and commercialization of friendship lead Laelius to invoke them (31–32):

> Ut enim benefici liberalesque sumus, non ut exigamus gratiam (neque enim beneficium faeneramur sed natura propensi ad liberalitatem sumus), sic amicitiam non spe mercedis adducti sed quod omnis eius fructus in ipso amore inest, expetendam putamus. Ab his qui pecudum ritu ad voluptatem omnia referunt longe dissentiunt.

> For just as we do not do good and show generosity so that we may extract *gratia* (for we do not lend good deeds at interest, but are by nature prone to generosity), so too we think friendship should be sought not because of a hope for the profit it will bring, but because its every benefit is contained in the very idea of love. These ideas differ sharply from the ideas of those who, in the manner of cattle, base all their decisions on pleasure.

The Epicurean watchwords *merces, fructus, voluptas* and *referre* appear in full force here, and the broader themes appear as well: the commercialization of friends, measuring and animals. Then, of course, all these ideas are set against concepts like *beneficium, gratia, liberalitas, natura* and, inevitably, *amicitia*. The Epicureans are Cicero's stock foil for correct social behavior, and since right social behavior lies at the root of Cicero's republican philosophy the Epicureans are Cicero's most basic, most fundamental object of criticism.

Cicero spent the last decade or more of his life arguing for the value of a rational and virtuous society in the face of the looming, then realized, autocracy of Julius Caesar. He did so in the belief that the Republic represented something abstractly good. Thus, Scipio can claim in the final paragraph of his *somnium* that "the greatest cares are concerned with the health of the nation" (*sunt autem optimae curae de salute patriae*; *Rep.* 6.29). It is such *curae* that speed the soul's ascent to the heavens at bodily death.

---

[41] When his sons-in-law reject his demurral, Laelius exclaims: *vim hoc quidem est adferre* (26).

The opposite of serving the Republic – that is, the thing that slows souls down – is capitulation to the pleasures of the body. Cicero's great good, the Republic, found its greatest political enemy in Julius Caesar, who hastened its demise. Cicero's Republic, however, found its greatest theoretical enemy in the Epicureans, whose recourse to measuring and quantification led them to reject the inherent good of the virtues that hold a society together. This tendency of the Epicureans to resort to measuring on a self-interested scale was such a crucial element of Cicero's critique that he could and did use it to identify the Epicureans even without naming them explicitly.

Conclusions

Cicero's periphrastic references to the Epicureans reveal that Epicureanism functions as much more than a philosophical school for him: It serves as a symbol of many of the ideas he finds most distasteful, and in the end this symbolic function most clearly and fully explains why Cicero often avoids naming them. In part he wants to discredit them, and in part he wants to foreground their core beliefs. Both of these goals, moreover, work in service to his larger goal: He does not want his criticism to be limited to a philosophical school alone but to a mindset, which, in Cicero's understanding, the Epicureans most fully embody. It is an unnatural mindset because it promotes the comparison of relative values instead of adhering to absolute values instilled by nature. Furthermore, it is fundamentally antisocial because it uses profit, utility, pleasure, convenience and reward as its standards. In both these ways it is also an animal mindset that sets aside the human capacities for *ratio* (the true understanding of nature), *oratio* (the vehicle for social engagement) and the divine soul that houses both of them. And in all these ways it is a mindset indifferent to the foundations and institutions of the Republic.

Cicero the philosopher claims in the preface of *On Divination* 2 (among other places) that, in the face of an externally enforced *otium*, he has turned to the writing of theory as a means of serving the state. He goes on to claim that he has done so by educating the youth in the study of philosophy. But it is equally clear that he has set as his goal not educating them in Greek philosophy but in Roman philosophy. It is also clear that Roman philosophy, for Cicero at least, emanates from the institution of the Republic. At *On Divination* 2.7, he says: *In libris enim sententiam dicebamus, contionabamur, philosophiam nobis pro rei publicae procuratione substitutam putabamus* ("For it was in my books that I was offering up my opinion, in my books that I was holding forth in speeches to the assembly. I considered that philosophy had for me taken up the role of the care of the Republic"). It is no accident, then, that so many of Cicero's works containing criticisms of Epicureanism take the form of dialogues that dramatize and exemplify the working of Roman social bonds.[42]

The Epicureans are a philosophical target, to be sure, in the traditional sense: Cicero takes aim at their philosophy at length in *On Ends* and *On the Nature of the Gods* especially. But they are also a philosophical target in the context of the republicanized philosophy of Cicero because they represent an anti-republican ideology (the celebration of self-interest) and methodology (the quantification and measuring of all things, often by utilitarian criteria). They play the role of villain in both capacities in Cicero's dialogues, and, with his rhetorical circumlocutions, Cicero repeatedly represents them as posing a grave threat to republican values.

---

[42] See Hall: 1996.

CHAPTER 4

Was Atticus an Epicurean?

Nathan Gilbert

Book 5 of *On Ends* opens with a vivid scene of Cicero and his friends during their student days in Athens in 79.[1] Memory plays an important role in the dialogue:[2] During a leisurely stroll each interlocutor is drawn to monuments and memories relevant to their own philosophical or literary interests. Cicero, the Academic skeptic, is drawn to the Academy and imagines the great Carneades lecturing and refuting arguments; his brother Quintus, an amateur tragic poet, claims he can almost see and hear Oedipus speaking lines from Sophocles' plays. Their mutual friend T. Pomponius Atticus, however, thinks of Epicurus and his Garden, while offering a mild complaint about Cicero's teasing (*On Ends* 5.3):

> As for me, you are accustomed to harass me as being devoted to Epicurus (*at ego, quem vos ut deditum Epicuro insectari soletis*), and I do indeed spend a good amount of time with Phaedrus, whom you know I cherish singularly (*unice diligo*), in Epicurus' Garden, which we just now passed by ... even if I wanted to, I am not permitted to forget Epicurus, whose likeness my friends have not only in paintings, but even on their cups and rings.

Marcus[3] adds "our Pomponius seems to be joking" (*iocari videtur*). Why is Atticus joking? And what about those rings? More generally, how seriously should we read Atticus' Epicurean interests?

---

[1] All dates are BC. I follow Shackleton Bailey's translations of the letters, slightly modified; other translations are my own. My thanks to Katharina Volk for comments (cf. her Chapter 5 in this volume on the Epicureanism of Caesar, as well as Chapter 6 of Monica Gale on a similar topic involving Catullus).

[2] Emphasized by a reference to the *ars memorativa* (*Fin.* 5.1.2; cf. 2.32, where its inventor Simonides is named); memory/remembering also resonate with the book's assessment of Antiochus' historical appeals to the Old Academy. The treatise more generally uses memory to critique Caesar, under whose dictatorship *On Ends* was written: The two other dialogues of the work pointedly depict Cicero debating amiably with two stalwart republicans who had recently died resisting Caesar (Torquatus and Cato).

[3] Hereafter, for the sake of clarity "Marcus" refers to the character of Cicero in a dialogue; "Cicero" to the author and statesman, who may or may not concur with the opinions of "Marcus."

There is no reason to believe that this conversation happened, but the rings did exist. A few have even survived,[4] while Pliny the Elder mentions that some Epicureans went so far as to have portraits of the Master in their bedrooms (*NH* 35.2.5). And Epicurean philosophers and adherents did speak as though allegiance to the master meant something life-changing. Take, for example, Philodemus of Gadara's injunction (*On Frank Criticism* fr. 45.8–11 Olivieri; cf. Konstan et al.: 1998) that the basic and most important principle is that "we will obey Epicurus, according to whom we have chosen to live" (πειθαρχήσομεν Ἐπικούρῳ, καθ' ὃν ζῆν ᾑρήμεθα); Caesar's assassin Cassius' citation of Epicurus in Greek to justify his conduct (*Fam.* 15.19, citing Epicurus, KD 5); the celebration of Epicurus' birthdays;[5] or the suggestive funerary inscription of a Syrian freedman "from the joy-filled Epicurean chorus" (*ex Epicureio gaudivigente choro*).[6] A Greek philosopher in Naples, a Roman senator, a Syrian freedman – and Atticus, a knight: The diversity of these republican Epicureans is striking.[7]

This essay considers what such a commitment might have meant to an educated Roman. What did it mean for a Roman to wear a ring of Epicurus, celebrate his birthday, present himself or herself as an Epicurean on a tombstone or "obey Epicurus"? More generally, did a commitment to the school affect the way a Roman approached politics? Or should we instead, as sometimes suggested, dismiss philosophy as an intellectual pastime segregated from real life or as the cynical manipulation of Hellenic cultural capital for political or networking purposes?[8]

This chapter claims that Atticus offers a fruitful case study of Epicureanism in the late Republic and can thereby contribute to broader questions of philosophical allegiance in the ancient world.[9] There has, of

---

[4] Images in Richter: 1965, figs. 1221–1222 with p. 199; cf. Frischer: 1982, 87 n. 1 and Zanker: 1995, 206.

[5] See Philodemus' dinner invitation to L. Calpurnius Piso (epigram 27 in Sider: 1997); for Epicurus' birthday, see *ibid.*, 152–153. Relevant here is Lucretius' exultation of Epicurus as a god (5.8).

[6] *ILS* 7781 = *CIL* X.2971, funerary epigram of C. Stallius Hauranus, Naples, first century (see Rigsby: 2008).

[7] I do not suggest that Epicurus' diverse following was a particularly *Roman* phenomenon, only that his popularity in Rome is worth investigating. There is evidence for the school's popularity well beyond Athens: Syria was a hotspot, boasting Philodemus, Hauranus and others. Further references in Crönert: 1907.

[8] I cite specific charges below. These interpretations accord with general appraisals of republican uses of Greek culture: e.g. Gruen: 1992 or White: 2010, 104–115, esp. 114–115. For another analysis of disputed Epicurean allegiance, see Volk's contribution in this volume (Chapter 5).

[9] A secondary goal of this paper is to draw attention to Cicero's ongoing "teasing" of Atticus for his Epicurean beliefs, a charming and underappreciated subtext that spans decades of Cicero's writings.

course, been valuable discussion of philosophical allegiance in recent years. Some scholars have approached the question from a philosophical perspective and have examined normative statements of Greek philosophers on what philosophy should mean to an adherent;[10] others focus on the relationship between philosophical ideals and political praxis.[11] There has also been a more focused discussion that has long struggled to come to terms with the surprising fact that the late Republic saw several senators engage in politics while simultaneously claiming allegiance to a hedonistic school that has traditionally been read as hostile to political activity.[12]

A reconsideration of Atticus' Epicureanism will fruitfully extend these debates precisely because he is a not a perfect fit for any of these categories. He was not a professional philosopher; in any case, it is dangerous to assume that the thunderings of Lucretius or Philodemus on the Epicurean wise man map reliably onto the complexities of life. As for philosophical politics, Atticus' political activity was at best indirect and informal, and scholars trying to understand the socially engaged Epicureanism of a Cassius or a Piso are tackling a very different issue than Atticus' leisured equestrian lifestyle. Indeed, this latter strand of scholarship, which has discussed Atticus mostly fully, tends to dismiss his Epicurean interests as those of an intellectual dilettante, an unconsidered eclectic,[13] or it labels him, without much elaboration, as an exemplar of "Roman Epicureanism." There are good reasons, then, to reexamine the rich but elusive evidence for Atticus' Epicureanism.

Our evidence is indeed tantalizing: Atticus is present and absent. Present because we have a great deal of testimony about him from his contemporaries.[14] Cornelius Nepos, for example, was his friend and biographer, and Atticus appears in Ciceronian dialogues. Pride of place, however, goes to the sixteen books of the *Letters to Atticus*. On a sometimes daily basis, these letters hint at Atticus' intellectual interests and political advice; in a few passages, Cicero quotes Atticus' *ipsissima verba*. On the other hand, Atticus is absent, for characterization in an ancient biography

---

[10] Sedley: 1989 and Hadot: 1995.

[11] Griffin: 1986 and 1989 (cf. 1995), Brunt: 1975 and 1989, Trapp: 2007, 226–257.

[12] Castner: 1988 and Benferhat: 2005a. The problem stems from notorious Epicurean slogans ("avoid politics" or "live unknown," frr. 8 and 551 U, respectively: for analysis of such slogans, see Hanchey's chapter (3) in this volume 40–42). This "problem" is more apparent than real: see Roskam: 2007a.

[13] Eclecticism is not necessarily a bad thing, but scholars have tended to use the label to dismiss the seriousness of Atticus' Epicureanism. Donini: 1996 (cf. Hatzimichali: 2011, 9–24) provides a valuable history of scholarly use of the term "eclectic."

[14] On Atticus' life and activities see Perlwitz: 1992, Welch: 1995 and Benferhat: 2005a, 98–169.

or dialogue is never beyond suspicion; nor does our collection of letters preserve any from Atticus himself. Even if it did, their use as evidence would still demand scrutiny, since ancient letters are not neutral packages of fact untainted by political and rhetorical objectives.[15] Indeed, I will underline how previous readings of Atticus' Epicureanism have run into problems precisely because the letters do not permit straightforward readings.

Because space is limited, this study will focus on key passages in Cicero's letters and dialogues in order to gauge in what sense he considered Atticus to be an Epicurean. This focus has two consequences: First, it will not provide a biographical reading of Atticus' life in light of Epicurean doctrine in order to judge the seriousness of his commitment; it seems appropriate to analyze Atticus' life in Epicurean terms only *after* his allegiance has been secured by less subjective criteria.[16] Instead, I contend that an assessment of Cicero's well-documented, cross-generic estimation of Atticus' Epicurean beliefs provides a firmer foundation for analysis, and I argue further that Cicero was not likely to be mistaken about these convictions. The second consequence of this focus is that my engagement with Nepos' *Life of Atticus* will largely be limited to chronology or basic information about its subject's life. This is primarily because Nepos is vague on philosophical matters, including Epicureanism,[17] but also because there is so much more varied Ciceronian evidence.

Was Atticus an Epicurean?

Atticus' Epicurean credentials have often been questioned or outright denigrated. For over a century the overwhelming consensus has been that Atticus' philosophical convictions were superficial, insincere or amounted

---

[15] Work on Cicero's letters has multiplied in recent years: White: 2010 offers a good starting point; on philosophical matters, see Griffin: 1995, McConnell: 2014 and Gilbert: 2015.

[16] I offer a few suggestions in this direction in my conclusion. See further Volk: 2021, 104–108 and in this volume (Chapter 5).

[17] Nepos, who himself disliked philosophers (fr. 5 Winstedt) says (17) that Atticus "so firmly held the precepts (*praecepta*) of the chief philosophers that he used them for leading his life, not for ostentatious display (*ad vitam agendam, non ad ostentationem*)." Compare the similar vagueness about L. Saufeius, who was definitely an Epicurean (12): "[Saufeius] lived in Athens for many years, drawn by a zeal for philosophy (*studio ductus philosophiae*)." Nepos also omits Atticus' cozying up to Caesarians during the Civil War (Welch: 1995, 470) and his financial dealings – matters which might be viewed as sordid. The *Life* therefore offers an idealized biography, and work on Atticus' Epicureanism that bases itself on Nepos' testimony yields non-committal conclusions (e.g. Lindsay: 1998; Shearin: 2012 explores Nepos' vagueness). For the *Life*, see Horsfall: 1989, Millar: 1988, Titchener: 2003 and Stem: 2012. Cappello: 2016 offers an interesting Lacanian analysis of Cicero's relationship with Atticus in Cicero's letters.

to a muddled blend of various schools. Gaston Boissier's (1897, 131) judgment is still indicative of the conclusions of more recent treatments, as well as of the confidence with which later verdicts are expressed:

> [Atticus] studied all of the schools for the pleasure that this study gave to his inquisitive mind, but he was determined not to be a slave to their systems. He had found a principle in Epicurean[ism] . . . that suited him, and seized it in order to justify his political conduct. As to Epicurus himself and his doctrine, he cared very little about them, and was ready to abandon them on the first pretext.

Some ninety years later, Rawson (1985, 101) offers a similar verdict with equal confidence: "It is clear that [Atticus] was not a serious Epicurean . . . His adhesion to the School was probably little more than a warrant for the cult of private life, simplicity and friendship . . . ." For others, Atticus emerges as an intellectual dilettante whose knowledge of Epicurus, much less commitment, was superficial and irrelevant. So Shackleton Bailey (1965–70, i. 8 n. 5): "[Atticus] may be supposed to have professed [Epicureanism] partly to be in the fashion and partly because as a devotee of things Hellenic he had to have a philosophy . . . ." Brunt (1989, 197) includes Atticus among Romans who were "light half-believers of their casual creeds," while C. J. Castner (1988, 60) concludes that philosophy amounted to "a cultural mode of expression rather than a philosophical conviction or a guide to action." Olaf Perlwitz (1992, 90–97) has developed these ideas and concludes that, even if we concede that Atticus was an Epicurean, his allegiance would nevertheless be *überflüssig*, "superfluous": Roman traditions are sufficient to explain his actions, leaving no need to consider philosophy at all. Recent treatments have become suspicious of such blanket condemnations, although doubts continue to linger. Yasmina Benferhat believes Atticus was in fact an Epicurean, but that he (in a characteristically "Roman" way) avoided dogmatic allegiance;[18] Miriam Griffin also harbors doubt.[19]

This review of scholarship underlines powerfully that dismissive readings of Atticus' Epicureanism have become commonplace. These conclusions are advanced with confidence and find their way into commentaries and foot-notes without discussion. Even when not described as a pseudo-intellectual,

---

[18] Benferhat: 2005a, 107: "En tout cas, il nous faut admettre que les Romains cultivés de cette époque manifestaient un certain éclectisme, ou plutôt, dans le cas d'Atticus, un refus manifeste d'esprit de chapelle" ("In any case, we must admit that cultivated Romans of this time showed a certain eclecticism, or rather, in the case of Atticus, a clear refusal of factionalism"). This is an elaboration of the conclusions of Leslie: 1950.

[19] Griffin: 1989, 17 n. 28: "I do not think we have grounds for saying that Atticus was not a serious Epicurean, only that he was less serious in manner than many members of the sect."

the orthodoxy of his Epicurean convictions is questioned. The occasional study that does treat Atticus' Epicureanism seriously typically views this allegiance as straightforward and self-evident – not as a difficult concept requiring interrogation.[20]

This study will challenge this dismissive consensus by examining a selection of "problem texts" that supposedly indicate superficial allegiance. I argue that these passages are allusive and complex, that they do not justify the negative conclusions drawn from them and that other readings are available that question neither Atticus' Epicureanism nor his intelligence. Taking as a keystone for my interpretation the comment in *On Ends* cited above, namely, that Cicero liked to harass his friend, I suggest that the playful and charming depictions of Atticus have been read all too literally, with the result that his Epicurean beliefs and Cicero's ironic engagement with them have been obscured.

Problem Passages and Cicero's "Conversion Tactics"

We begin with a letter written in 50, which breezes through a variety of topics: from the health of Atticus and Tiro to Cicero's travel plans and hopes for a triumph. After mentioning their mutual nephew Quintus, Cicero pivots from family to philosophy (*Att.* 7.2):

> filiola tua te delectari laetor et probari tibi φυσικὴν esse τὴν <στοργὴν τὴν> πρὸς τὰ τέκνα. etenim si haec non est, nulla potest homini esse ad hominem naturae adiunctio; qua sublata vitae societas tollitur. "bene eveniat!" inquit Carneades spurce sed tamen prudentius quam Lucius noster et Patron qui, cum omnia ad se referant, <nec> quicquam alterius causa fieri putent et cum ea re bonum virum oportere esse dicant ne malum habeat non quo<d> id natura rectum sit, non intellegunt se de callido homine loqui, non de bono viro.

> I am happy that your little daughter brings you delight and that you accept that there is a natural bond of affection towards our children. For if this does not exist, there can be no natural association of man to man; and if this is removed, then all society is abolished. "Let's hope for the best!" says Carneades—foully—but nevertheless more prudently than our friends Lucius [Saufeius] and Patro, who do not understand that they are speaking of a clever man, not a good man, since they refer all things to themselves, do

---

[20] E.g. Welch: 1995, 451. Several recent scholars are working to rescue Roman Epicureans from dismissive readings (e.g. D. Armstrong: 2011), but Atticus has not yet received his due (Cappello: 2016, 479, 487 is inclined to take Atticus' Epicureanism seriously but does not offer a defense against skeptics).

not think that anything should be done for the sake of another, and say that it is fitting to be a good man only in order to avoid trouble—not because it is right by nature.

Atticus apparently commented that he adored his daughter, and Cicero used this remark to embark on a philosophical sermon on the necessity of a natural social impulse for a functional society – he alludes here to a Stoic/Peripatetic doctrine, "social οἰκείωσις," which grounds ethical obligations to other people in our natural sociability.[21] Linked with this claim is an attack on self-interested Epicurean hedonism, which notoriously denied to humanity any natural sociability.[22] The references to *noster Lucius* and Patro solidify the anti-Epicurean theme. Patro was the head of the Epicurean Garden after Phaedrus, an old friend and teacher of both Cicero and Atticus (cf. *Fin* 5.3); other letters allow us to identify "Lucius" as Lucius Saufeius, a mutual equestrian friend who had studied with Phaedrus and mingled with Epicureans in Athens for several decades.[23]

Several commentators have seen here evidence for a superficial commitment or ignorance of Epicurean philosophy. Since the school rejected any natural affection for our offspring – or for that matter anyone else – Atticus should not have conceded this point. That he does so is, in the words of Shackleton Bailey, "one of the indications that the philosophy of Epicurus was not his lodestar."[24] This is a very literal reading. There is no reason to think that Atticus, in confessing his love for his daughter, was refuting Epicurean doctrine. It is far more likely that Cicero seized on an innocent comment as an opportunity to deliver a clever philosophical provocation. There are other examples of this practice from his correspondence with philosophically literate friends. When L. Papirius Paetus, a Neapolitan Epicurean, used the word "*mentula*," a coarse word for penis, Cicero latched onto it and delivered a philosophical sermon on frankness of speech.[25] In another letter, Cicero tells Cassius that the latter seemed to be present with Cicero as he was writing to him: This mundane pleasantry sets the stage for a sharp critique of Epicurean εἴδωλα (thin films of atoms

---

[21] See Donini and Inwood: 1999, 677–682; in greater detail, Bees: 2004.

[22] This denial is pilloried by critics like, e.g., Epictetus in his *Discourses* (2.20.6 – the verbal parallels are very close to *Att.* 7.2) and Plutarch in *On Affection for Offspring* (495A).

[23] That "Lucius" refers to Lucius Saufeius is certain: The previous letter mentions Cicero giving a letter to Saufeius to deliver to Atticus while the two men were in Athens. For this identification and Saufeius more generally, see Gilbert: 2019, 27–31.

[24] Shackleton Bailey: 1965–70: iii. 286; cf. Benferhat: 2005a, 106 n. 74.

[25] *Fam.* 9.22 (see McConnell: 2014, 161–194).

emitted from objects) and their causal role in thought and imagination.[26]
Cicero does something similar in *Att.* 7.2 by twisting for humorous
purposes what was probably an offhand comment. There is no justification
for the conclusion that Atticus asserted the existence of natural sociability,
nor that he was an eclectic or uninformed Epicurean. This passage tells us
more about Cicero, his philosophical likes and dislikes, and his epistolary
technique, than it does about Atticus.

That said, this letter can help us in another way, since the correspondence reveals that Cicero assumes significant philosophical knowledge
from his friend. That is to say, most letters do not namedrop Carneades,
switch to Greek, or find parallels in Plutarch or Epictetus. Cicero tailored
the content of his letters to the knowledge and interests of individual
readers. This passage, therefore, challenges any view that Atticus had a
limited understanding of philosophical matters. He is expected to get a
high-level joke, and we have no reason to doubt that he did. Finally, if we
take seriously the claim at *On Ends* 5.3 that Cicero liked to harass his
friend, this letter reads as a playful attempt to pounce on Atticus' loose
language in order to trap him into confessing that his school is indefensible
and that Cicero is, in fact, correct.

Next is a roughly contemporaneous passage from the unpublished *On
Laws* (probably written in the late 50s), which may seem to support a
reading that Atticus was willing to betray the principles of Epicurus at the
drop of a hat. In Book 1, Quintus and Atticus suggest that Marcus
compose a book of *Laws*, as Plato did after his *Republic*. Marcus agrees,
but he will not talk about mundanities of civil law. Instead, he explains the
origin of law by providing a Stoic-inspired theory of natural justice; but
first he asks Atticus to concede (*dasne igitur hoc nobis*) the existence of
divine providence. Atticus agrees (*Leg.* 1.21–22):

ATTICUS: Do sane, si postulas; etenim propter hunc concentum avium
        strepitumque fluminum non vereor condiscipulorum ne quis exaudiat.
MARCUS: Atqui cavendum est; solent enim ... admodum irasci, nec uero
        ferent, si audierint, te primum caput viri optimi prodidisse, in quo scripsit
        nihil curare deum nec sui nec alieni.
ATTICUS: Perge, quaeso. nam id quod tibi concessi quorsus pertineat exspecto.

ATTICUS: I certainly grant this point, if you demand it; for due to the singing
        of the birds and the din of the streams, I am not afraid that one of my
        fellow schoolmates will overhear.

---

[26] *Fam.* 15.16 (see Gilbert: 2015, 189–215).

MARCUS: But be careful: for they tend to get quite angry ... and they will
not take it lightly if they hear that you've betrayed the first section of the
book in which that excellent man has written, "God troubles himself not
at all, concerning neither his own affairs nor of others."

ATTICUS: Continue, please, for I am eager to see what my concession will
lead to.

The terminology of *condiscipuli*, "schoolmates," supports Atticus' connection with the Garden. That said, the concession looks like a blunder, for a
dedicated adherent should have denied providence: Epicurean gods take
no part in human affairs.

Once again, this text does not allow a straightforward reading. Consider
that Quintus, another interlocutor, is expected to accept this assumption
about the gods (*nam Quinti novi sententiam*), and Cicero has his brother
defend Stoicism's account of divine action in Book 1 of his *On Divination*.
It would in fact not be surprising for a Roman to express such a conviction,
unless, of course, that Roman were an Epicurean, who would deny divine
interference in mortal matters – as Marcus has foreseen with his Latin
translation of *Principle Doctrines* 1. This objection would mean that the
discussion of natural law had to start with a battle over the nature of the
gods – in other words, the whole project of *On Laws* would become utterly
sidetracked before it even began. Therefore, Cicero needs to signal to his
readers (something he does quite explicitly)[27] that he is making a key
assumption and will bracket the Epicurean objection. He does so by
enacting this bracketing in the structure of the narrative: Marcus asks his
friend to suspend his Epicurean complaint for the sake of argument, and
Atticus politely agrees. Like *On Ends* 5 a decade later, this dialogue
reenacts debates reminiscent of their student days in Athens.

The broader structure of Book 1 of *On Laws* supports this reading.
Marcus makes a similar move when he anticipates the dangers of Academic
skepticism for his topic: "Let us implore the Academy of Arcesilaus and
Carneades to be silent, since it contributes nothing but confusion to all
these problems" (*Leg.*, 1.39). Cicero throughout his works declares that he
is an Academic skeptic, a school that questioned the possibility of certain
knowledge and was therefore adept at attacking providence (years later
Cicero would use these arguments in *On Divination* 2 and *On the Nature
of the Gods* 3). Commentators used to claim, in part on the basis of this
passage, that Cicero lapsed in the 50s from skepticism to Stoicism or the

---

[27] He qualifies his request with "if you do not assent to this, we must begin our case from this point."

school of Antiochus of Ascalon.[28] Woldemar Görler demolished this
reading in an important article by collecting evidence for the practice of
the ancient philosophical and rhetorical schools and showing that the use
of hypotheses/concessions here is fully in line with this practice.[29] Görler's
analysis clarifies Atticus' concession: He is playing the game of philosophical debate and concedes a point so he can hear the discussion that he
requested – or rather, that Cicero the author wanted to write about.

The structural parallel of these two concessions is telling. In order to
offer a treatment of natural law, Cicero needs to sideline certain Epicurean
and Academic objections and does so by making Marcus and Atticus
concede points to which their respective schools would object. The concessions mirror each other, and, unless we go back to doubting Cicero's
Academic allegiance (something nobody really does anymore), this passage
supports the claim that Cicero considered Atticus to be a serious
Epicurean.[30] Nor does this passage provide evidence for superficial or
confused eclecticism. Finally, we once again see Cicero gleefully putting
very un-Epicurean ideas into the mouth of his friend; there are touches of
irony and playfulness when "Atticus" hopes the din of the streams will
prevent his *condiscipuli* from hearing "his" concession.

The next problem text arises in a celebrated letter to C. Memmius,
which is given a prominent position at the beginning of *Letters to Friends*
13 as an example of how to ask a favor politely. Other letters provide
context:[31] Memmius, the exiled politician and dedicatee of Lucretius,
either owned or had control of Epicurus' house. He had apparently
planned something drastic, but what exactly he proposed to do to the
house – demolish it, renovate it or something else – is unclear. What is
clear is that these plans horrified Patro, now head of the Athenian Garden.
Patro pressed Atticus and Cicero to write to Memmius, leading to 13.1.

The letter begins by noting that Patro had entreated Cicero earlier in
Rome. He ignored the request because he did not wish to interfere with
Memmius. When Patro repeated his plea and after Memmius had dropped
his building plans, Cicero felt comfortable interceding. He summarizes

---

[28] E.g. Glucker: 1988.   [29] Görler: 1995.
[30] Cicero characterized his interlocutors carefully: The first edition of the *Academics* was abandoned
     because Lucullus' technical discussions were "παρὰ τὸ πρέπον" (Att. 13.16.1: see Griffin: 1997);
     cf. his justification for the departure of Scaevola in *On the Orator* (Att. 4.16.3) and the careful
     characterizations of Antonius and Crassus, right down to their prose rhythm (von Albrecht: 2003,
     92–94). Dialogues set in the distant past like *On the Republic* of course allowed Cicero more play.
[31] Att. 5.11.6 and 5.19.3. See Griffin: 1989, 16–18, and 1995, 333 n. 36, as well as Benferhat: 2005a,
     74–78.

Patro's request, citing the latter's *officium*, reverence for the *auctoritatem Epicuri*, the memory of Phaedrus and the importance of preserving the "tracks of great men" (*vestigia summorum virorum*). But thereafter Cicero distances himself from Patro: He disagrees with Epicureanism, his support stemmed from fondness for Phaedrus and he concedes that Patro acted boorishly. Atticus clinches Cicero's request: Stressing his friend's close ties to Epicureans, above all to Phaedrus, Cicero underlines Atticus' insistence on the matter. A later letter suggests Atticus was grateful for this intercession – there Atticus is, as in *On Laws*, called a *condiscipulus* of the Garden.[32]

We see, therefore, Atticus working to help two successive Greek heads of the Athenian Garden in a dispute with the dedicatee of Lucretius over the house of Epicurus. Atticus' efforts here and his connections with such a range of Roman and Greek Epicureans over two decades suggests a strong affinity for Epicureanism. This letter has, nevertheless, prompted dismissive readings. The sticking point is the distancing of Atticus from Patro and other Epicureans (*Fam.* 13.1.5):

> is—non quo sit ex istis; est enim omni liberali doctrina politissimus, sed valde diligit Patronem, valde Phaedrum amavit—sic a me hoc contendit, homo minime ambitiosus, minime in rogando molestus, ut nihil umquam magis.

> Now [Atticus]—not because he is one of *those* people, for he's very polished in every branch of refined culture—has great regard for Patro and had great love for Phaedrus—this Atticus, a man not at all self-seeking or troublesome in his requests, pressed me on this point as never before.

Cicero alludes to Epicurus' notorious advice to "set sail from all *paideia*" as well as to his charges elsewhere that Epicureans were bad stylists or myopically fixed on their school's literature.[33] On this reading, Atticus' culture and distance from Patro reveal insincere convictions.[34]

A comparison of the language in this letter and Cicero's characterizations of Epicureans elsewhere dissolves this problem. In *On Ends* 1.13, the Epicurean spokesman Torquatus is described as "a man skilled in every branch of learning" (*homine omni doctrina erudito*), and one may compare the "*omni liberali doctrina politissimus*" of *Fam.* 13.1. In *On the Nature of the Gods*, the Epicurean Velleius is complimented as "more ornate in his

---

[32] *Att.* 5.19.3: "Concerning Patro and your fellow students (*tuis condiscipulis*), I am happy to hear you are pleased with the trouble I took."

[33] Epicurus, fr. 163 U; for charges of sectarianism and poor style, see Cicero, *Tusc.* 1.6, 2.7.

[34] E.g. Shackleton Bailey: 1980, 163; cf. Castner: 1988, 59.

language than [Epicureans] tend to be" (*ornatius quam solent vestri*, 1.58); Zeno of Sidon, Phaedrus' predecessor as scholarch, is praised for his wide learning and style (1.59; cf. *Tusc.* 3.38). Even more strikingly, Philodemus is complimented in *Against Piso*.[35] While Piso is savaged for his crude, debauched Epicureanism, the Greek is characterized in much the same way as Atticus, Torquatus and Velleius: "I am speaking of a man who is exceedingly polished not just in philosophy, but also in other studies as well (*ceteris studiis . . . perpolitus*), something which they say that the rest of the Epicureans commonly neglect" (*Pis.* 70). In each case Cicero politely compliments his friends and distances them from negative stereotypes about crude Epicurean sectarians. If we want to deny that Atticus was an Epicurean on the basis of this letter, then we must do the same for these other Romans and even prominent Greek philosophers like Zeno and Philodemus. That seems a bit extreme. Cicero treats Atticus as he does his other Epicurean friends: He courteously exempts them from his contemptuous attacks on the learning and polish of other devotees of the Garden. This passage provides no grounds to dismiss Atticus' Epicurean credentials; on the contrary, it offers evidence of substantial involvement in the affairs of his life-long Epicurean friends, teachers and even the house of Epicurus.[36]

There is one last problem text, from a letter to Atticus written in late May of 44. Caesar had been dead for two months; Marcus Antonius was pressing his influence. In an effort at jocularity, Cicero writes, "and so it is foolish now to console ourselves with the Ides of March . . . Let us then go back, as you often say, to the *Tusculan Disputations*. Let us keep Saufeius in the dark about you; I will never give you away!" (*itaque stulta iam Iduum Martiarum est consolatio . . . redeamus igitur, quod saepe usurpas, ad Tusculanas disputationes. Saufeium de te celemus; ego numquam indicabo; Att.* 15.4.2; cf. 15.2.4). We meet again L. Saufeius, schoolmate of both correspondents and friend of two Epicurean scholarchs. As before, Saufeius serves as a shorthand for Epicureanism (Castner: 1988, 66). The implication is that this indefatigable Epicurean diehard would not approve of Atticus' appreciation for the *Tusculan Disputations*. The supposed problem

---

[35] On Piso and Philodemus, see Nisbet: 1961, 183–188 and Sider: 1997, 5–11.

[36] The distancing from Patro is also rhetorically motivated: By appealing directly and repeatedly to Cicero, a *Greek* went over the head of the influential – if exiled – Roman Memmius (see *Att.* 5.11.6 for Memmius' annoyance with Patro). This carefully composed letter refocuses the issue as Cicero's desire to oblige Atticus. The effect is to transform the request into a favor between gentlemanly Romans, which pays proper respect to Memmius – unlike the obstinate, presumptuous plea of a *loquax graeculus*. That Atticus is distanced from Patro is therefore not surprising.

is the dialogue's content, an extended discussion of emotions and cognitive therapy indebted to Stoic ideas, in which Epicurus suffers heated criticism, especially in Book 3. Atticus, then, must have been some sort of eclectic interested in Stoicism or, according to Castner (1988, 60–61), have broken away from a youthful enthusiasm for the Garden.

It is impossible to determine exactly why Atticus enjoyed the *Tusculan Disputations*, but there are several plausible explanations. For example, Atticus could have simply appreciated the work as literature. That is to say, given his literary interests, he could have valued Cicero's claims that Latin was no worse than Greek and might have enjoyed the abundant literary and philosophical translations. If so, we have seen that wide reading and style is no strike against a serious commitment to Epicureanism. Second, Cicero drew on a wide range of consolatory traditions – e.g. the treatment of death in Book 1, which included material to which an Epicurean might not object. Alternatively, Atticus might have simply have been complimenting his friend's newest treatise. If so, Cicero has yet again seized on a passing comment to claim that he had *at last* convinced Atticus of the error of his Epicurean ways (and out of courtesy he would not tattle on Atticus to Saufeius). On this reading, Cicero has enacted an imaginary philosophical victory when the chances of a political victory looked increasingly uncertain. These interpretations are speculative but no less plausible than dismissive readings, and this line of argument holds for other problem texts, which should no longer require discussion. To take just one example, Atticus had a bust of Aristotle in a villa and was a fan of the Peripatetic Dicaearchus – evidence, we are told, of an impure, eclectic Epicureanism.[37] It should be clear by now that neither literary taste nor Aristotle's bust justifies the abuse Atticus has taken.

To sum up, Cicero repeatedly links Atticus with Epicureanism in his letters and dialogues. Scholarship favors literal readings of allusive and playful passages. In contrast, I have argued these passages do not offer evidence for a muddled eclecticism or a superficial commitment to, much less ignorance of, the Garden. Furthermore, I have offered readings which make better contextual sense of these complex passages. It turns out that,

---

[37] *Att.* 4.10.1 (Aristotle); 2.16.3 and 13.32.2 (Dicaearchus) – for Benferhat: 2005a, 107–108 such passages are examples of non-dogmatic Epicureanism. The most troubling passage is 2.16.3, where Cicero says that Atticus' "friend" Dicaearchus argued for the πολιτικός βίος, while Cicero's Theophrastus urged contemplation. This contrast is hard to take seriously: Cicero consistently extolls an active political life and questions the value of indulgence in scientific inquiry (e.g. *Off.* 1.19, 1.54–58; cf. *De or.* 2.156 and *Acad. Pr.* 6) – perhaps Cicero ironically swaps their personal predilections in this letter. For Cicero and Dicaearchus, see McConnell: 2014, 115–160.

as often, Cicero is really talking more about himself, but he does so in a way that does not make sense if he did not think Atticus was an Epicurean. Cicero could be wrong, but in light of the consistency of Atticus' treatment across genres and decades, their shared philosophical education in Athens and Cicero's intimate relationship with him, we have good reason to take Cicero's testimony as correct, whereas doubt would be overly skeptical. Finally, I have suggested that Cicero delights, privately and in published works, in "harassing" his friend, depicting him to say very un-Epicurean things and presenting him as finally giving into Cicero's arguments.

Does It Matter?

Cicero thought Atticus was an Epicurean, and, barring evidence to the contrary, we should believe him. But what does it mean to be a "serious" Epicurean? I now tackle one aspect of this slippery question by analyzing the role Epicureanism played in Atticus' political advice to Cicero, in order to see how philosophy interacted with politics. I begin with two letters in which Atticus seems to have made explicit mention of the Epicurean dictum "stay out of politics" (μὴ πολιτεύεσθαι). Both letters were written in 44, shortly after the death of Caesar, and the correspondents were deeply worried about the increasing power of the consul Antonius. At the time of the first letter (early May), Antonius was making a power play: He had been assigned Macedonia as his province but was preparing to force through legislation to swap this for the two Gauls, along with an extended term and several legions. This was of course eerily similar to Caesar's recent actions in Gaul, so Atticus and Cicero were deliberating their courses of action.

In the first letter Cicero replies to three letters of Atticus and addresses various issues his friend had raised. Sandwiched between discussion of their nephew Quintus and efforts to win the support of the consuls designate Hirtius and Pansa, Cicero indignantly writes, "you make mention of Epicurus and *dare* to tell me to 'stay out of politics'? Isn't Brutus' look enough to frighten you away from *that* kind of talk?" (*Epicuri mentionem facis et audes dicere* μὴ πολιτεύεσθαι? *non te Bruti nostri vulti-culus ab ista oratione deterret?*, *Att.* 14.20). Atticus provided advice that explicitly appealed to Epicurus, but skeptics have argued that μὴ πολιτεύεσθαι is a "cultural mode of expression" (Castner: 1988, 60), a trendy line quoted for effect; or alternatively, that philosophy is superfluous, since Atticus would have advised the same thing anyway. Before adjudicating this question, let us turn to the second letter, which has not received the attention it deserves.

Att. 16.7 is dated August 19, by which point Antonius had forced through the provincial swap, Brutus and Cassius were losing ground and hope for a peaceful solution seemed unlikely. Cicero decided in June to take a trip to Athens, ostensibly to check on his son's studies. Elsewhere, however, Cicero speaks of a massacre and says that he is departing not to escape but in the hope of "a better death" (*mortis melioris; Att.* 15.20.2). Over the next two months, Cicero hesitated and delayed, and one recalls his troubled mind in 49.[38] After he finally departed, however, Piso spoke out in the senate against Antonius. Cicero's absence was sorely criticized, his presence required. He returned to Rome and began his final political struggle, which resulted in his *Philippics*, proscription and dismemberment. His return demanded that he justify his departure and sudden change of mind; Atticus anticipated these criticisms and urged Cicero to reconsider. Luckily for us, Cicero was sufficiently annoyed to quote Atticus' words (indicated by *scripsisti his verbis ... deinceps igitur haec*, etc.), highlighted in bold (*Att.* 16.7.3–4):

> illud admirari satis non potui quod scripsisti his verbis: "**bene igitur tu qui εὐθανασίαν, bene, relinque patriam.**" an ego relinquebam aut tibi tum relinquere videbar? tu id non modo non prohibebas verum etiam adprobabas. graviora quae restant: "**velim σχόλιον aliquod elimes ad me oportuisse te istuc facere.**" itane, mi Attice? defensione eget meum factum, praesertim apud te qui id mirabiliter adprobasti? ego vero istum ἀπολογισμὸν συντάξομαι, sed ad eorum aliquem quibus invitis et dissuadentibus profectus sum. etsi quid iam opus est σχολίῳ? si perseverassem, opus fuisset. "**at hoc ipsum non constanter.**" nemo doctus umquam (multa autem de hoc genere scripta sunt) mutationem consili inconstantiam dixit esse. deinceps igitur haec, "**nam si a Phaedro nostro esses, expedita excusatio esset; nunc quid respondemus?**" ergo id erat meum factum quod Catoni probare non possim?

What really did amaze me [in your letter] is what you wrote in these words: "**All right then: you talk of an 'easy death'—all right, forsake your country!**" I was forsaking my country, or you thought I was doing so? You not only made no effort to stop me, but you even approved! There is worse to come: "**I'd like you to polish up a little tract to show that such was your duty, and address it to me.**" *Really*, my dear Atticus? Does my action require defense, to *you* of all people, who enthusiastically approved it? Yes, I will compose this *apologia* of yours, but I'm going to address it to one of

---

[38] See Brunt: 1986.

those men who were against my departure and were dissuading me. But what need is there for a tract now? If I had stuck to my plans, there would have been. "**But this is inconsistent.**" In all the many writings on this theme, no philosopher has *ever* equated a change of plan with a lack of consistency. And then there's this: "**If you were of my friend Phaedrus' school, it would be easy to find an excuse. As it is, what answer do we make?**" So you think that I couldn't justify my action to Cato?

Atticus was rather punchy: His mockery of Cicero's reference to εὐθανασία (the *mortis melioris* of 15.20.2?) is striking, and his demand for an *apologia* clearly rankled Cicero. The palpable anger makes it difficult to reconstruct Atticus' exact position, and our correspondence suggests that he had in fact approved of the trip to Athens. The key, I think, is Atticus' charge of inconsistency: Cicero should never have left, or, since he had, he should have stuck to his guns. Additionally, Atticus had been reading for years in Cicero's dialogues repeated denunciations of the *inconstantia* of Epicurus and his Roman followers (e.g. *On Ends* 2) and may have thrown this criticism in Cicero's face. Cicero's counter-arguments certainly suggest that he took the criticism as philosophical ("no philosopher has *ever* equated a change of plan with a lack of consistency"), and Atticus' final words support this reading: "If you were of my friend Phaedrus' school, it would be easy to find an excuse." I take *excusatio* in its more specific sense of "exemption from public duty" (*OLD* s.v. *excusatio* 2), along the lines of Atticus' earlier advice to μὴ πολιτεύεσθαι. Cicero would not have had a problem if, like Atticus, he sat this fight out on Epicurean grounds. But Cicero is not an Epicurean; his departure and sudden return therefore opened him up to charges of inconsistency. Atticus is rubbing the situation in Cicero's face. In part, perhaps, to get back at all those years of Epicurus-bashing, but almost certainly to press home the danger of leaping into the struggle against Antonius, who, unlike Cicero, had an army.

Atticus' invocation of Phaedrus shows, furthermore, that philosophy offered more than clever one-liners. Atticus does not quote a Greek proverb; he makes a specific allusion to philosophical allegiance and its political consequences, expressed in terms of his personal relationship with Phaedrus. Both correspondents are taking philosophy seriously at a time of crisis. This exchange, then, shows that philosophy helped justify and frame political activity; it also reveals the difficulties Atticus faced when advising Cicero. The Equestrian Atticus urged Epicurean otium, advice which Cicero was simply not inclined to take. These two letters reveal the tension that resulted from fundamental differences in perspective – and anger: Cicero *very rarely* writes to Atticus so sharply. Epicureanism is not a joke anymore.

We can now consider the charge of Perlwitz and others that Atticus' Epicureanism was "superfluous" or a mere pretext: Equestrian life would have advised sitting out the fight, so Epicureanism does not matter.[39] It is true that Atticus might have acted the same without philosophy. This dichotomy between tradition and philosophy is, however, misleading. As soon as a Roman uses philosophy to support prior preferences or shape political deliberation, this belief or motivation is no longer the same: It is hybridized by tapping into some five centuries of philosophical debate. We should not expect philosophy to make Atticus act completely differently but we should rather search for him (or others) using arguments and philosophical principles to structure possible courses of action, and to act with firmness and conviction based on these principles.[40] If we can find evidence of this, and I have argued we can, then we have good grounds for claiming that philosophy should be considered a factor relevant to historical analysis.

By way of conclusion I offer a few suggestions as to what a biographical reading that takes Atticus' Epicureanism seriously might look like. First, Atticus – unlike contemporaries like Cassius, Piso or Torquatus – emerges as a textbook example of an Epicurean intellectual avoiding political office while cultivating friendship. His wide-ranging financial dealings should not surprise, either: Philodemus' contemporary treatise, *On Property Management*, shows that a committed Epicurean could engage in commerce if he understood money had no intrinsic value – there are no signs that Atticus hankered after ostentatious luxury.[41] Indeed, Atticus' financial support to his friends and his survival of wars and proscriptions are perfectly in line with Epicurean doctrine.[42]

---

[39] Perlwitz: 1992, 97: "Die Zurückhaltung des Atticus gegenüber den angestammten Formen politischer Betätigung wird dabei zu großen Teilen aus den politischen Verhältnissen dieser Zeit selbst zu erklären sein und den Rückgriff auf geistesgeschichtliche Erklärungsmuster überflüssig machen" ("Atticus' reservation towards traditional forms of political activity can for the most part be explained by the political conditions of his time, and it also makes superfluous any recourse to an intellectual-historical explanation"). Cf. Maurach: 1989, 52 (on Cato).

[40] Cf. Brunt: 1975, 31; Griffin: 1989, 36–37.

[41] See Tsouna: 2012 (cf. Asmis: 2004) for Epicurean economics (money has instrumental utility in providing security and helping friends) and Nepos' biography for Atticus' moderation. Philodemus argues that money has instrumental utility in providing security and helping friends.

[42] Perlwitz: 1992 and Welch: 1995 argue that Atticus' behind-the-scenes manoeuvring represents an alternative form of politics. This may be right, but this is a more modern category of political activity: When Epicurus warns against politics or Roman sources discuss the *cursus honorum*, they are not talking about back-scenes manoeuvring.

CHAPTER 5

Caesar the Epicurean? A Matter of Life and Death

Katharina Volk[*]

Was Julius Caesar an Epicurean? It seems unlikely. No ancient source identifies him as an adherent of the Garden, nor are we told that he studied with Greek philosophers of any persuasion, as so many of his peers did both at Rome and abroad. In addition, the man who ambitiously maneuvered himself into the power-sharing arrangement known as the First Triumvirate, spent years battling the Gauls, started and won a civil war and then ruled Rome as a quasi-monarch until being assassinated would appear to be an improbable follower of a school that counseled political quietism and the cultivation of simple pleasures. On the contrary, Caesar might be seen as a perfect example of the wretched individual who, in the words of Lucretius, "strives day and night with the utmost toil to reach a position of prominence and assume power" (*noctes atque dies niti praestante labore | ad summas emergere opes rerumque potiri*, 2.12–13). It is on men like these that the enlightened Epicurean looks down with quiet self-satisfaction from the serene temples of the wise.

That Caesar's ambition could be viewed by his contemporaries as the very antithesis of Epicurean ideals is apparent from a passage in Cicero's invective *Against Piso* of 55 BC. Among many other criticisms, Cicero reproaches Piso for his perverted Epicureanism, which has led this Roman aristocrat to his highly un-Roman refusal to seek a triumph for his military exploits in Macedonia. L. Calpurnius Piso Caesoninus, the patron of Philodemus and indeed well-known for his Epicurean leanings,[1] was also the father of Caesar's wife, a fact that enables Cicero to suggest sarcastically that Piso give an Epicurean lecture to his son-in-law, telling him that public thanksgivings and triumphs are just so many meaningless baubles,

---

[*] My heartfelt thanks go to the editors for inviting me to contribute to this volume, to Nathan Gilbert and Jim Zetzel for commenting on a draft and to Raphael Woolf for allowing me to cite unpublished work.
[1] On Piso's Epicureanism, see esp. Griffin: 2001 and Benferhat: 2005a, 173–232, as well as Roskam in this volume (Chapter 2).

"almost the playthings of children" (*delectamenta paene puerorum*, 60).[2] As Cicero goes on to point out, Caesar would be anything but receptive to this kind of argument: "Believe me, that man is carried on by glory; he is aflame, he burns with the desire for a grand and deserved triumph. He has not learned those same things as you" (*fertur ille vir, mihi crede, gloria; flagrat, ardet cupiditate iusti et magni triumphi. non didicit eadem ista quae tu*, 59).

Despite these obstacles, however, scholars have over the past few decades repeatedly ascribed some form of Epicureanism to Caesar.[3] While the evidence, such as it is, is well known and has been discussed from many different angles, it will be worthwhile to consider the question once more. There has been a recent surge of interest – of which this volume is an excellent example – in Roman philosophy in general and Roman Epicureanism in particular, with special attention paid to the intersections of philosophy and politics in the turbulent period of the late Republic.[4] Given that Caesar was the era's foremost political figure, as well as a formidable intellectual,[5] we would like to know what, if anything, he thought about philosophy and especially about the school most popular among his contemporaries, that of Epicurus.

That Caesar was informed about Epicureanism is without doubt. Even if he had undergone no specifically philosophical training himself,[6] basic knowledge concerning the major philosophical schools was, by the first century BC, part and parcel of the Roman aristocracy's cultural competence, and Caesar can hardly have failed to pick up the principles of Rome's most fashionable philosophical creed. Furthermore, as has often been pointed out, many of Caesar's friends and followers were Epicureans. These include not only his father-in-law Piso, but also his trusted lieutenant C. Vibius Pansa Caetronianus and the jurist C. Trebatius Testa. In the

---

[2] Cf. the whole passage, 59–61, with Rambaud: 1969, 412–413, and Garbarino: 2010, 211–212.

[3] Strongly in favor of an Epicurean Caesar: O. Seel: 1967, 77–83; Rambaud: 1969 and 1984; Paratore: 1973, 184–191; Bourne: 1977; and Fussl: 1980. More tentative: Castner: 1988; Benferhat: 2005a; Pizzani: 1993; and Garbarino: 2010. See also Hanchey in this volume (Chapter 3). I have not been able to find out who first suggested an Epicurean affiliation for Caesar.

[4] Roman philosophy: e.g., Williams and Volk: 2016; Epicureanism: e.g., Benferhat: 2005a, Fish: 2011 and Gilbert: 2015. In my own monograph on the intellectual history of the late Republic (Volk: 2021), philosophy and its political implications and applications figure large as well.

[5] For Caesar's intellectual pursuits in general, see Fantham: 2009. On his most significant scholarly publication, the grammatical work *On Analogy*, see Garcea: 2012. For possible Epicurean influences on Caesar's linguistic thought, see Willi: 2010, 239–241, and Garcea: 2012, 114–124.

[6] This is not assured: The biographies of both Suetonius and Plutarch lack or have lost an opening discussion of Caesar's boyhood and schooling. However, they also mention no association with philosophers later in life, as we so often find with Caesar's contemporaries.

case of such other Caesarians as L. Cornelius Balbus, A. Hirtius and C. Matius, we cannot be sure about their philosophical allegiance, but Epicurean leanings have often been suggested.[7] While older views that Epicureanism provided a political ideology for the Caesarian party have long been debunked,[8] and it is well established that Epicureans stood on both sides of the Civil War, the concentration of putative Epicureans in Caesar's circle is still worth noting.

What is especially interesting is the evidence for Epicurean activity in the Caesarian camp during the campaigns in Gaul, Germany and Britain. Trebatius, who had joined Caesar's staff on the recommendation of Cicero, converted to Epicureanism in 53 BC, apparently under the influence of Pansa. His mentor back in Rome reacted in mock horror: "My friend Pansa tells me you have become an Epicurean. That's a great camp you got there!" (*indicavit mihi Pansa meus Epicureum te esse factum. o castra praeclara!*, *Fam.* 7.12.1). Just a year earlier, the leisure hours of the campaigning Caesarian officers may have been taken up with studying Lucretius' brand-new poem. As Christopher Krebs has shown, following F. R. Dale, Caesar himself must have read *On the Nature of Things* in 54, to judge from striking verbal echoes in Books 5, 6 and 7 of his *Gallic War*.[9] It is possible that Caesar, and perhaps other philosophically interested members of his staff, were introduced to Lucretius by Quintus Cicero, who knew the poem by February 54 (Cic. *QFr.* 2.10.3) and joined Caesar's campaign shortly thereafter. Dale (1958, 182) fondly imagines that Caesar "read Lucretius with Quintus in Britain, on a summer evening in his tent."

Familiarity with Epicureans and knowledge of Epicurean writing, however, do not an Epicurean make (after all, the decidedly non-Epicurean Cicero had many Epicurean friends and read Lucretius' poem). What did Caesar actually believe? In the absence of ancient claims that he espoused Epicurean views, all the evidence is circumstantial, which means that the man's philosophical opinions, if any, need to be inferred from his behavior and oral and written utterances. I will not here review all the characteristics of Caesar that have been adduced to demonstrate his Epicureanism. Scholars have pointed to his rationalism and cool aiming at *utilitas*, his religious skepticism, his flair for friendship, his policy of *clementia* or even

---

[7] On Epicureanism in Caesear's entourage, see Fussl: 1980 and Valachova: 2018. On the individuals mentioned and their Epicurean credentials, see Castner: 1988, Benferhat: 2005a and Gilbert: 2015.

[8] See esp. Momigliano: 1941, 150–157, and Benferhat: 2005a.

[9] See Krebs: 2013 with Dale: 1958.

his entire political trajectory and program as indications of Caesar's allegiance to the Garden.[10] Obviously, such arguments are highly speculative. If we assume for the sake of argument that Caesar in fact possessed all the traits ascribed to him (which is not a given), they are far too unspecific to prove his philosophical views. If we knew for certain that Caesar espoused Epicureanism, then we might be justified in wondering to what extent his displayed character, behavior and decisions might have been informed by his creed.[11] In the absence of a more obviously smoking gun, a mere cool and rational religious skeptic and good friend with an aversion to the needless bloodshed of his peers cannot as such be convicted of Epicureanism.

There is, however, one additional and promising set of evidence that scholars have often pointed to and that concerns Caesar's attitude to death. According to Epicurus, of course, fear of death is – together with fear of the gods – the main obstacle to attaining a happy life, and a person cannot achieve ἀταραξία without having internalized the truth that "death is nothing to us" (ὁ θάνατος οὐδὲν πρὸς ἡμᾶς, KD 2).[12] Whatever his other philosophical beliefs may or may not have been, Caesar on a number of occasions displayed a contempt for death that might be seen as at least Epicurean-inflected. Passing over his well-attested physical courage and death-defying acts during his military campaigns, I will concentrate in what follows on a few attested utterances, which combine to allow perhaps some insight into Caesar's views on life and death.

The first is an argument Caesar reportedly made in his speech on December 5, 63 BC, when the senate debated the fate of the convicted Catilinarians. After the consul-designate Silanus had proposed the death penalty and the subsequent speakers had seconded his motion, Caesar suggested instead lifelong imprisonment without the possibility of parole. While the greater part of his speech as reconstructed by Sallust in his *War against Catiline* is concerned with cautioning the senators against

---

[10] Rationalism: Rambaud: 1969, Bourne: 1977, Fussl: 1980, Minyard: 1985, 17–20 and Pizzani: 1993; religious skepticism: Rambaud: 1969, Pizzani: 1993 and Benferhat: 2005a; *clementia*: Rambaud: 1969 and Bourne: 1977; friendship: Rambaud: 1969, Bourne: 1977 and Benferhat: 2005a. Farthest reaching are speculations that Caesar's striving for power and establishing sole rule was motivated by an Epicurean wish to bring about a state of peace and quiet for the benefit of all mankind (see Rambaud: 1969, 419, Paratore: 1973, 190 and Fussl: 1980, 80).

[11] E.g., since we know that Piso had Epicurean interests and associations, it makes sense to ask – as scholars have done (see n. 1) – whether his moderate and conciliatory politics owe anything to his philosophy. If we knew nothing about his philosophical pursuits, by contrast, we would not be justified in inferring his Epicureanism from his political behavior.

[12] On the Epicurean arguments against the fear of death, see Warren: 2004 and Asmis in this volume (Chapter 7).

approving a measure of questionable legality, Caesar also offers a striking argument against the death penalty itself (Sall. *BC* 51.20):

> de poena possum equidem dicere, id quod res habet, in luctu atque miseriis mortem aerumnarum requiem, non cruciatum esse; eam cuncta mortalium mala dissolvere; ultra neque curae neque gaudio locum esse.

> About the punishment I can speak according to the facts: in sorrow and misery death is a relief from grief, not a torture. It dissolves all human ills, and beyond it, there is place for neither care nor joy.

While Sallust is not quoting Caesar verbatim, he presumably availed himself of the senatorial archives in reconstructing the speeches,[13] and the historicity of the remarks on death is confirmed not only by the fact that Sallust's Cato, in responding to Caesar, refers back to them, but crucially also by Cicero's own summary of the discussion in the fourth speech *Against Catiline*. As for Cato, he begins his attack on Caesar's proposal as follows (Sall. *BC* 52.13):

> bene et conposite C. Caesar paulo ante in hoc ordine de vita et morte disseruit, credo falsa existumans ea quae de inferis memorantur, divorso itinere malos a bonis loca taetra, inculta, foeda atque formidulosa habere.

> C. Caesar a little while ago gave this order a well-phrased and well-structured lecture on life and death, apparently deeming false what is said about the underworld, namely, that divorced from the good, the wicked inhabit horrid, desolate, foul and fearful places.

Cicero, finally, paraphrases Caesar's views on death as follows (*Cat.* 4.7–8):

> alter intellegit mortem ab dis inmortalibus non esse supplicii causa constitutam, sed aut necessitatem naturae aut laborum ac miseriarum quietem esse. itaque eam sapientes numquam inviti, fortes saepe etiam lubenter oppetiverunt . . . vitam solam relinquit nefariis hominibus; quam si eripuisset, multas uno dolore animi atque corporis miserias et omnis scelerum poenas ademisset. itaque ut aliqua in vita formido inprobis esset posita, apud inferos eius modi quaedam illi antiqui supplicia impiis constituta esse voluerunt, quod videlicet intellegebant his remotis non esse mortem ipsam pertimescendam.

> The other speaker understands that death was not created by the immortal gods for the sake of punishment, but is either a necessity of nature or freedom from toil and misery. Thus wise men have never undergone it unwillingly, and brave men have often even willingly sought it . . . He leaves

---

[13] We know that the consul Cicero had the debate taken down in shorthand: Plut. *Cat. min.* 23.3.

only life to the criminals. If he had taken that away, he would have removed with one single pain many miseries of mind and body as well as all punishments for their crimes. Therefore, in order that there be some fear left in life for wicked men, those men of old maintained that there were some punishments of this sort set for the impious in the underworld—since of course they understood that without them, not even death would have to be feared.

Even though Caesar's and Cato's words are filtered through Sallust, and it is unclear to what extent Cicero is distorting or embellishing Caesar's argument, there still emerges a reasonably clear image of what Caesar must have said. Apparently, he claimed that the death penalty was not a suitable punishment because death constitutes the absolute endpoint for human experience beyond which a person will be affected by neither good nor ill – and certainly not the punishments of the traditional underworld. As a result, death is not to be feared (*non esse mortem ipsam pertimescendam*, Cic. *Cat.* 4.8).

While the idea that "death is not an evil" is a philosophical common-place, there is certainly an Epicurean flavor to Caesar's argument.[14] Scholars have pointed to the language of dissolution ([*mortem*] *cuncta mortalium mala dissolvere*)[15] and to the debunking of the myths about the underworld.[16] We might also wonder whether Caesar's statement that, beyond death, there is place for neither *cura* nor *gaudium* alludes to the two poles of Epicurean experience, (mental) pain or disturbance and (mental) pleasure. None of this amounts to a sustained exposition of Epicurean doctrine – which would at any rate be out of place in a political speech – but the passage shows that Caesar was well versed in at least some aspects of Epicurean thought. Why he chose to include those in his plea for moderation vis-à-vis the Catilinarians must remain open. Of course, Caesar may simply have been voicing his own, deeply held convictions. Perhaps, however, he was also trying to appeal to his fellow senators with philosophical aspirations: The entire speech is an attempt to induce the

---

[14] In favor of a strong Epicurean interpretation: O. Seel: 1967, Paratore: 1973, Bourne: 1977, Fussl: 1980, Pizzani: 1993, Benferhat: 2005a and Garbarino: 2010; tentative: Castner: 1988; skeptical: Mulgan: 1979 and Wardle: 2009.

[15] See Benferhat: 2005a, 298–299, who points to KD 2, where what is dead is referred to as τὸ . . . διαλυθέν (translated as *dissolutum* in Cic. *Fin.* 2.100), and Garbarino: 2010, 217, who compares the use of *dissolvere* by Lucretius. Of course, the word choice may be Sallust's rather than Caesar's own.

[16] See Garbarino: 2010, 216–217. What was peculiar about the Epicureans was not that they did not believe in punishments in the underworld (if we trust Cicero, no reasonable person took those seriously), but that they continued to make them a topic. Cf. Cic. *Tusc.* 1.10–11; Lucr. 3.978–1023.

audience to approach the question of the conspirators' punishment rationally rather than emotionally, and the observation that "death is nothing to us" may have served both as an argument to calm those carried away by the calls for the malefactors' blood and as an intellectual fig leaf for those who (like Caesar himself) might have had political or private sympathies with the convicted men.

In addition to this soundbite from an early stage in Caesar's career, we also have a number of utterances from the end of his life, when he held sway in Rome as dictator after having emerged victorious from the Civil War. A number of sources report that Caesar was wont to express a feeling that he had lived enough, with the implication that he was unafraid of death. The most prominent incident is one discussed by Cicero in his speech *For Marcellus*, given in the senate in 46 BC. In this rhetorical balancing act, the speaker, on the one hand, bestows extravagant praise on Caesar for his decision to pardon and recall his exiled foe M. Marcellus. On the other, he argues that it is the dictator's duty to restore the republican form of government, insinuating that Caesar will fall short of his potential and miss out on true glory if he allows matters to persist in the present, undesirable status quo.

As part of his argument Cicero cited a phrase that Caesar himself had just used in his own speech, in which the dictator, apparently to rally senatorial sympathy and support, not only complained about Marcellus' past enmity and mentioned current threats against his own life, but also made the resigned claim that he had "lived long enough for both nature and glory" (*satis diu vel naturae vixi vel gloriae*, 25). Since, in Cicero's opinion, Caesar had not lived enough until he had done his duty by the *res publica*, he took it upon himself politely to combat the dictator's assertion, constructing a philosophical counter-argument in which he clearly interprets his opponent's view as Epicurean.[17] As Cicero recognizes, the idea of a point of "enoughness" beyond which life provides no further attractions is peculiar to the teachings of the Garden. The Epicureans held that perfect pleasure cannot be increased by the duration of time and that one may as well quit while the going is good and one has had *satis* of good things. Thus in her diatribe at the end of Book 3 of Lucretius' *On the Nature of Things*, personified Nature tells the man unwilling to die that "there is nothing that I could additionally contrive and invent to please you: Everything is always the same" (*nam tibi praeterea quod machiner*

---

[17] See Rambaud: 1984, Dobesch: 1985, 188–190, Benferhat: 2005a, 300–301, Garbarino: 2010, 212–213 and Volk: 2021, 139–146, and forthcoming b.

inveniamque, | *quod placeat, nil est: eadem sunt omnia semper,* 3.944–945)
and that he ought to leave while "sated and full of things" (*satur ac plenus . . . rerum,* 960). Of course, a true Epicurean has no desire for glory, but Cicero himself points out that this part of Caesar's utterance is heterodox and not part of his Epicurean *sapientia*: "You will not deny that *even though* you are wise, you are most desirous of fame" (*cuius* [sc. *gloriae*] *te esse avidissimum, quamvis sis sapiens, non negabis?,* 25).[18]

From Cicero's perspective, of course, Caesar's view is completely wrong. He may have lived enough for nature and for glory, "but not enough for the fatherland, which is the most important thing" (*at, quod maximum est, patriae certe parum,* 25): If Caesar quits now, he will lose his chance of leaving behind a lasting legacy. Pleasure, even the memory of past pleasure, by which the Epicureans set so much store, will end with death; only true glory lives on. Therefore, there is only one course possible for Caesar, provided that he is truly *sapiens* and not just imbued with Epicurean pseudo-wisdom (27):

> haec igitur tibi reliqua pars est; hic restat actus, in hoc elaborandum est ut rem publicam constituas, eaque tu in primis summa tranquillitate et otio perfruare: tum te, si voles, cum et patriae quod debes solveris, et naturam ipsam expleveris satietate vivendi, satis diu vixisse dicito.

> This part is left for you, this deed remains, to this you must devote your effort: Put the Republic in order, and you first and foremost will be able to profit from it in the greatest tranquility and peace. At that point, once you have paid your debt to the fatherland, and—sated with life—have satisfied nature, you may say that you have lived enough.

While it is theoretically possible that Cicero added an Epicurean slant to Caesar's *satietas vivendi*, it seems to me more likely that he interpreted correctly something that was already present in Caesar's attitude. That the dictator was in the habit, in the last months of his life, of expressing a sense that he had lived his life to the full, and a concomitant lack of fear of death is attested by a number of historical sources.[19] Suetonius reports at length the various explanations given by contemporaries of Caesar's jaded attitude in the face of possible death through attempts on his life (*Iul.* 86): Was his

---

[18] Compare Cicero's depiction of Caesar's un-Epicurean hunger for fame in *Against Piso*, cited above. For the role of personified Nature in Lucretius' *On the Nature of Things*, see Asmis in this volume (Chapter 7).

[19] Cicero, too, mentions that the sentiment was one that Caesar voiced "all too often" (*nimis crebro, Marc.* 25); interestingly, at that point he reports the tag as *satis te tibi vixisse* ("that you have lived enough for *yourself*").

health failing and he therefore "wished to live no longer" (*neque voluisse se diutius vivere*)? Did he prefer "to face danger once and for all rather than always fear it" (*subire semel quam cavere semper*)?[20] Or was Caesar genuinely convinced that he had lived "enough"? According to some of his friends, he was accustomed to state his view as follows:

> non tam sua quam rei publicae interesse, uti salvus esset: se iam pridem potentiae gloriaeque abunde adeptum; rem publicam, si quid sibi eveniret, neque quietam fore et aliquanto deteriore condicione civilia bella subituram.

> [He used to say that] his safety was not so much in his own interest as in that of the commonwealth. For he had long achieved more than enough of power and glory. But if something should happen to him, the commonwealth would not be at peace and would slide back into civil war in a rather worse condition.

This arrogant assertion almost sounds like a response to Cicero's exhortations in *For Marcellus*: Rather than accept his duty to continue working for the common good, Caesar puts the ball firmly back in the court of the *res publica*. If his fellow Romans want peace and quiet, they need to protect Caesar's life. As for Caesar himself, he has long fulfilled his own desires and could not care less.

Suetonius concludes with an anecdote found also in Plutarch and Appian.[21] The night before he was assassinated, Caesar attended a dinner party where the conversation turned to a discussion about what kind of death was the most desirable. The dictator (seemingly predicting his own imminent demise) declared his own preference for one that was sudden and unexpected (*repentinum inopinatumque*).

Considered in combination, Caesar's reported utterances about life and death can – with all due caution – be considered evidence for an attitude in keeping with Epicurean thought. Death is not to be feared: It is a dissolution and absolute end, beyond which there is nothing that concerns us. Conversely, life is not something that can be profitably prolonged forever: Once one has lived enough, one might as well die with equanimity. This attitude is indicative of what Raphael Woolf has described as the Epicurean "small-scale" view of human existence.[22] Since all necessary

---

[20] This same sentiment is reported also by Vell. 2.57.1, Plut. *Caes.* 57.7 and App. *BC* 2.109.

[21] Suet. *Iul.* 87, Plut. *Caes.* 63.7 and App. *BC* 2.115.

[22] Woolf made this point in a paper ("Philosophy and Death in Cicero's Letters to Atticus") that he delivered in April 2016 at the symposium "Philosophy in Cicero's Letters" at Columbia University. He has kindly permitted me to refer to this hitherto unpublished work. See further Warren: 2004,

desires can be easily fulfilled and the *summum bonum* of katastematic pleasure thus easily achieved, Epicurean life is, as it were, not a big deal and, as a result, neither is death. The person who has reached *satietas vivendi* has no reason not to die. As Woolf puts it, "it is only the philosophy that regards life as essentially small-scale that can regard death as essentially a matter of indifference."

Caesar's own life, of course, was anything but small-scale, and when he declared that he had lived enough or achieved the object of his desires, he was clearly not referring to his having met the minimalist conditions of Epicurean hedonism. It is, however, conceivable that it was a small-scale view of life and death that enabled Caesar to aim as high as he did. Someone who considers neither life nor death a big deal can take risks that others will shrink from because he is justified in being unafraid of whatever the outcome will be. The man who told his mother before his election to Pontifex Maximus that he would return as the winner or not at all, and who likened his beginning a civil war to entering a game of chance (*alea iacta est*), may well have been able to keep his cool in these high-risk situations because he was certain that death is nothing to us.

By this point in my discussion, individual readers may be more or less convinced by my claim that Caesar's views on life and death owe something to Epicurean doctrine. I admit that the argument is speculative, and I am willing to push it as far as I have, and no further. If, however, merely for the sake of argument, we accept for the moment the idea that Caesar had adopted the Epicurean maxim "death is nothing to us" for his own purposes, the question still remains: Was he an Epicurean? At the risk of invoking the infamous Curate's Egg, I would be inclined to answer, "in part." Perhaps, though, it is time in turn to question the question and to ask ourselves what it would actually take for an ancient Greek or Roman to "qualify" as an Epicurean (or, for that matter, an adherent of any other philosophical school). Note that I am not now, as at the beginning of the chapter, concerned with the matter of evidence. The question is not how we, with our limited sources, can identify a potential adherent of the school but, rather, what conditions must be fulfilled for us to consider someone an Epicurean.

In the history of philosophy, such labels as "Academic," "Stoic" or "Epicurean" are most often used to designate authors of philosophical

199–212 on the problem that their arguments against the fear of death leave the Epicureans "with precious few resources to explain why continued life is worth pursuing" (210). For the Epicureanism of Atticus, see Gilbert in this volume (Chapter 4).

works that espouse and expound the doctrine of the sect in question. Very often, such individuals were affiliated with the school as an institution or otherwise active as teachers professing a specific philosophical affiliation. Philosophical teachers who did not publish may likewise be labeled according to their school allegiance, as may philosophical writers who had no official connection to a school and did not engage in teaching. By this convention, for example, Chrysippus and Posidonius are both Stoics, as are Cicero's teacher and houseguest Diodotus (who did not, as far as we know, write anything) and even Seneca (who had nothing to do with the Stoic school as an institution and was not a professional teacher). We are in the habit of calling all such persons "philosophers," even if some of them would not have applied this designation to themselves,[23] and modern scholars occasionally feel that particular ancient thinkers and writers do not fit their own understanding of what philosophy is.

Terms like "Epicurean" or "Stoic," however, clearly also have a wider application, and that is what is at issue here. It surely makes sense to use such designations for people who are not philosophers by any description but who for themselves embrace the teachings of a particular school as a convincing mode of theoretical explanation and/or guide to practical behavior. It is in this sense that we call Piso an Epicurean and the younger Cato a Stoic, and it is in this sense that we are investigating whether Julius Caesar might have been an Epicurean. The question remains: What justifies us to claim a particular individual as the adherent of a particular school, if that individual not only had no institutional affiliation but did not even teach or write philosophy? What does it take to make Piso or Caesar or, for that matter, any modern follower of Epicurus, an Epicurean?

The answer, I posit, is very simple. A person is an Epicurean (or Stoic or Academic or Peripatetic) if he or she identifies as such. If a person proclaims, *te sequor, o Graiae gentis decus*, or calls himself *Epicuri de grege porcum*, that person should be considered an Epicurean.[24] Of course, as we have already seen, in the case of many ancient figures, we lack such explicit self-identification and must carefully review whatever additional sources there may be. Thus, for example, we possess no direct testimony to the

---

[23] Hine: 2016 shows that philosophically engaged Romans of the late Republic and early Empire did not refer to themselves as *philosophi* but reserved this term for Greek professionals; as Trapp: 2017 demonstrates, this changed in later periods.

[24] Lucr. 3.3; Hor. *Epist.* 1.4.16. Of course, the declarations of poetic personae cannot be treated as straightforward statements of their authors; by quoting these famous tags, I am making no claims about the historical Lucretius and Horace. For the Epicureanism of Catullus, see Gale in this volume (Chapter 6).

younger Cato's ever referring to himself as a Stoic; however, the fact that his contemporary Cicero repeatedly calls him a *Stoicus* and considers his behavior and utterances from a Stoic perspective makes us reasonably confident that Cato himself identified as a Stoic – and thus, by my definition, was a Stoic.

The posited self-identification criterion may sound banal, but it has an important corollary for our understanding of philosophical allegiance. If, in order to qualify as, say, an Epicurean, it is sufficient merely to consider oneself an Epicurean, then Epicurean orthodoxy and orthopraxy are not necessary conditions. In other words, an Epicurean by this definition may hold opinions incompatible with Epicurean doctrine or may act in ways not conforming to Epicurean ethical teaching. As a matter of fact, unless the person in question happens to be a sage, it is highly unlikely that her thoughts and actions will be in keeping with Epicureanism at all times. As long as she identifies as an Epicurean, however, we should consider her an Epicurean. Of course, she may, as it were, be a bad Epicurean – but that is a different question.[25]

The study of philosophical affiliation in ancient Rome in general and of Roman Epicureanism in particular has long suffered from anxiety over whether individual Romans were really "serious" about philosophy or qualify as, say, "real" Epicureans. Working with an expectation of doctrinal consistency (related to the charity principle conventionally applied to the interpretation of philosophical texts), scholars have struggled with a perceived lack of intellectual coherence and/or ethical commitment on the part of some of the individuals they study, and have attempted to come to terms with this problem in one of three ways. First, there has been a long tradition of flat-out denying philosophical credibility or sophistication even to Romans with proven philosophical interests and expertise. This tendency is found even among scholars who specifically study such individuals and have contributed much to our knowledge of the history of Roman thought. Thus, for example, within the scholarship of Roman Epicureanism, Catherine J. Castner's *Prosopography of Roman Epicureans* (1988) is notorious for its scornful dismissal of the superficiality and "cavalier attitude" (xvii) toward Epicurean doctrine of the very men whom the author identifies as (possible) Epicureans.

---

[25] Similarly, we are accustomed to accept the self-identification of people as, e.g., Christians, Buddhists or Marxists, notwithstanding their occasional or even frequent failure to fully embrace or live up to the tenets of the creed in question (not even to mention disagreements as to what these tenets are and imply).

Such a view has been widely felt to be unfair and unhelpful, and in recent years, important work has been dedicated to the intellectual rehabilitation of Roman philosophy and of individual Roman thinkers, including Epicureans. This second, apologetic approach has succeeded in demonstrating the high level of doctrinal knowledge and the sophistication of argument of many Romans with philosophical interests and allegiances. Focusing not only on the published works of men like Cicero but on the everyday epistolary exchanges of a wide range of individuals, such scholars as Miriam Griffin, Sean McConnell and Nathan Gilbert have put paid to the notion that Roman philosophy was just the fashionable pastime of an upper class in search of cultural capital.[26] At the same time, readings of this type, often fueled by a desire to prove the orthodoxy of the text or figure in question, run the risk of becoming over-charitable and glossing over tensions and inconsistencies. To stick with the school at issue in this chapter: Even the most learned and committed Roman Epicureans do not always conform to what we understand Epicureanism to entail.

This is where the third approach comes in. A number of scholars – first and foremost Michael Erler and Jeffrey Fish[27] – have argued that Roman Epicureans adopted a form of "unorthodox" Epicureanism (cf. the title of Erler: 1992b), one that was deemed more appropriate to their society and their lifestyle as members of the Roman elite. Sometimes the practitioners in question are seen as developing this particular brand of "Roman Epicureanism" on their own, simply adjusting Epicurean teachings to a new context. Often, however, scholars assert the influence of contemporary Greek Epicureans, in particular Philodemus, the friend and protégé of Piso. A case in point is the potentially embarrassing fact that so many Roman Epicureans by no means adhered to their master's injunction to "live unnoticed" and instead followed the typical political careers of the Roman aristocracy.[28] If it can be shown that there was instead a bona fide Epicurean point of view that condoned political engagement, then numerous "bad" Epicureans will have been saved as perfectly orthodox. The problem is that, given the fragmentary nature of Philodemus' surviving

[26] See Griffin: 1995 and 2001, McConnell: 2014 and Gilbert: 2015 in this volume (Chapter 4).
[27] See Erler: 1992, Fish: 2011 and compare now Yona: 2018.
[28] As Roskam: 2007a has shown, the Epicurean injunction to avoid political engagement was never absolute and allowed for various exceptions and escape clauses. Even so, Epicurus appears to have held that for most people in most circumstances, a life spent in politics will not be conducive to ἀταραξία – which means that the political activity of a large number of Roman Epicureans should still be considered, if not a problem, at least a phenomenon that calls for discussion. Roskam in this volume (Chapter 2) explores further what it meant to be an Epicurean in Cicero's Rome.

work (and the near-total lack of information about the teaching of other Greek Epicureans active in Italy), claims of this nature are often inconclusive[29]; even so, the situatedness of Roman Epicureanism in a social and intellectual context quite different from that of Epicurus' original Garden is a point very much worth taking. Despite the school's well-known veneration of its founder, Epicureanism was not an unchanging monolith but developed over time, with first-century Rome and Italy providing a particularly intriguing chapter.

All three approaches discussed capture important aspects of the Epicurean scene at Rome. There are many examples of highly sophisticated orthodoxy and orthopraxy, of which Epicurus himself would have been proud. There are signs of developing new orthodoxies and Epicurean practices, whether homegrown or influenced by the thought of contemporary Greek teachers. And there certainly are cases of individuals who, despite their declared allegiance, did not, or not always or in all ways, conform to Epicurean doctrine and ethics. At the same time, all three approaches, adopting a somewhat narrow focus, risk losing sight of some aspects of Roman Epicureanism, simply because they do not fit their definitions.

I suggest that by freeing ourselves of the consistency requirement – our desire to have Epicureans think and behave in an Epicurean way, with any departure from orthodoxy considered an intellectual and ethical failure – we will be able to gain a wider and deeper appreciation of the phenomenon of Roman Epicureanism (and, indeed, Roman philosophy and the history of philosophy in general). When an upper-class Roman adopts the teachings of Epicurus for himself, it is obviously interesting to determine how sophisticated his philosophical theory and practice turn out to be, and how he goes about living according to the precepts of the Garden. It is equally interesting to see where he either consciously refuses or tacitly fails to adopt Epicurean teaching, or – to take a broader view – which aspects of Epicurean doctrine appeal to Roman society and which ones do not. Once we stop worrying whether particular individuals were "real" or even "good" Epicureans, we can gain a picture of Roman Epicureanism in all its originality, diversity and self-contradiction.

I would like to take this plea for an inclusive and holistic approach to the historical study of philosophy one step further, and this brings me back

---

[29] Since the editing of the fragments continues apace, the study of Philodemus is a rapidly developing field where new readings and interpretations are constantly being (re)formulated. As a result, there have been both exciting new insights into Philodemus' thought and fair amounts of controversy.

to Caesar. Was he an Epicurean or not? Even by my minimalist criterion, the answer – at least as based on the evidence we have – must surely be no. No ancient source comes even close to indicating that Caesar identified as an Epicurean, and we might therefore consider the case closed. I have been arguing, however, that Caesar held certain ideas about life and death that were informed by Epicurean doctrine: Being knowledgeable about Epicureanism, he apparently adopted and adapted some teachings for his own life without taking on board others, let alone declaring allegiance to the school as a whole. In doing so, Caesar was hardly alone. No doubt many educated Romans let themselves be influenced in one way or another by individual tenets of the various philosophical systems they encountered, just as human beings through the ages have picked and chosen from the philosophies, religions, political ideologies and other creeds available in their societies. The history of philosophy, properly understood, needs to consider not only philosophers and their declared followers, but also philosophy's manifold manifestations in human culture as a whole. Moving out from the core of doctrine, it needs to take account of practice and of expressions in a wide variety of media and contexts. Questions of orthodoxy and orthopraxy will of necessity play an important role in this enterprise, but will not, on their own, succeed in unlocking the historical significance of philosophy in either a specific society or its development over time.

As the papers in this volume show, Epicureanism was extremely influential in ancient Rome during the last century BC and beyond, and this influence is on evidence not only in such philosophical writers as Lucretius and Cicero or such self-identified Epicureans as Cassius and Piso. It pervades Roman society as a whole, leaving its traces in poetry, oratory, inscriptions, art work and the thoughts and utterances of many people. One of them was Julius Caesar. Caesar was not an Epicurean, but he very much deserves a place in the history of Epicureanism.

CHAPTER 6

Otium *and* Voluptas:
Catullus and Roman Epicureanism

Monica R. Gale[*]

Catullan *amicitia* vs. Epicurean φιλία

Porci et Socration, duae sinistrae
Pisonis, scabies famesque mundi,
vos Veraniolo meo et Fabullo
verpus praeposuit Priapus ille?
vos convivia lauta sumptuose
de die facitis, mei sodales
quaerunt in trivio vocationes?

(Catullus 47)[1]

Piggy and cut-price Socrates,[2] Piso's left-hand men, plagues on the world with your insatiable appetites, does that rampant Priapus prefer *you* to my dear Veranius and Fabullus? Do *you* indulge in smart dinners all day long, at vast expense, while my friends beg for invitations at the crossroads?

---

[*] Earlier versions of this chapter were delivered as seminar papers in the Universities of Maynooth and Pittsburgh in February and March 2018, and at the Symposium Cumanum in June of the same year. I am very grateful to audiences on all three occasions for stimulating comments and discussion. Warm thanks are due also to the editors of the present volume, both for the invitation to contribute and for their care and attention to detail in preparing the chapter for publication.

[1] Catullus is quoted from the text of Mynors: 1958; for Lucretius, I have used Bailey: 1922. Quotations from Philodemus' epigrams follow the text and numeration of Sider: 1997. All translations are my own, unless otherwise indicated.

[2] As my translation suggests, I find it more plausible that *Socration* is a derisive pseudonym coined by Catullus – along similar lines to *Mentula*, "Prick," with reference to Caesar's associate Mamurra, in poems 94, 105, 114 and 115 – than a nickname adopted by Philodemus himself (so Sider 1997: 34–37). Sider is surely right to link the pseudonym with the cycle of epigrams addressed by Philodemus to Xanthippe/Xantho, whose name implicitly connects her with Socrates' wife and thus lends the poems in which she appears a potentially philosophical coloring; given the Epicureans' generally negative attitude towards Socrates, however, a more attractive hypothesis, to my mind, is that the delicate self-irony thus implicit in the identification remains tacit until "actualized" by Catullus. In the context of poem 47, the diminutive form suggests disparagement of the addressee's philosophical pretensions, presented here as a mere cover for self-indulgent hedonism (see further below).

This short invective attack on Piso's morally dubious dining companions has been the subject of much discussion amongst scholars, since Gustav Friedrich first suggested in 1908 that "Socration" should be understood as a pseudonym for Philodemus, the Epicurean philosopher and protégé of Caesar's father-in-law, L. Calpurnius Piso.[3] The identification has been challenged, but is widely accepted amongst scholars both of the Catullan corpus and of Philodemus,[4] and points to a degree of antagonism on Catullus' part towards Piso and his retinue and indeed towards Epicurean philosophy in general. Such a hostile attitude might appear rather surprising in a writer whose outlook on life appears in some respects so consonant with Epicurean values: Catullus' privileging of *otium* and personal friendship, his bitter tirades against the corruption of public life and general dissatisfaction with the *mos maiorum*, his rejection of traditional poetic forms with their celebration of civic values in favor of an aesthetics of *lepos* and *venustas*, all have their analogues in contemporary Epicurean thought. Nevertheless, closer consideration of the Catullan corpus, and particularly of the marked echoes of Philodemus and his fellow-Epicurean poet Lucretius, suggests that ultimately the poet abnegates any kind of philosophical commitment; the poems' substitution of an idealized *amor/amicitia* for the traditional aristocratic valorization of status and achievement in the public sphere parallels but does not, in the end, converge with the philosophical comradeship enjoyed by Philodemus and his "faithful companions" (ἑτάρους ... παναληθέας, *Ep.* 27.5 = *AP* 11.44.5) or the untroubled seclusion in the "citadel of the wise" advocated by Lucretius (2.7–8).[5]

---

[3] Friedrich: 1908, 228. Space precludes discussion of the prosopographical problems surrounding the identification of Catullus' Piso, on which see Syme: 1956, Nisbet: 1961, 180–182 and Wiseman: 1969, 38–40. Worth noting, however, is the dramatic date of Catullus 28, on Veranius' and Fabullus' unprofitable provincial service under Piso, and therefore presumably of the closely connected poem 47, which would be close in time to the delivery of Cicero's *Against Piso* (55 BC). It is difficult to believe that a contemporary audience familiar with Cicero's speech would not have thought immediately of Calpurnius Piso and Philodemus when confronted by an attack on the philosophically named sidekick of a Piso whose uncontrolled appetites extend to sexual and gastronomic excess.

[4] Most recently Thomas: 1994, Sider: 1997, 23–24 and Cairns: 2003, 181–183 (Shapiro: 2014 argues that there is no decisive evidence for the identification and prefers to see both addressees as stock types; but see n. 3). Given the association between Epicureans and pigs attested (e.g.) by Cic. *Pis.* 37 (*Epicure noster ex hara producte non ex schola*) and Hor. *Ep.* 1.4.16 (*Epicuri de grege porcum*), it seems best to take Porcius, too, as a pseudonym, though it is more difficult to identify a likely candidate (Cairns: 2003, 184–187 suggests Plotius Tucca; Thomas: 1994, 152, less plausibly, Lucretius).

[5] Notwithstanding the superficially similar sentiment of Catullus 31.7–8 *o quid solutis est beatius curis,* | *cum mens onus reponit?* ("Oh what is more blissful than release from care, when the mind lays aside its burden?"). The release from care envisaged in this poem is clearly presented as something temporary, even fleeting: As he emphasizes elsewhere (68.34–35), Catullus is truly at home amid

Whether Catullus himself "was" an Epicurean, as argued at length by
Pasquale Giuffrida, is something that we can never know, though it is my
contention in what follows that nothing in the poems prompts such a
supposition.[6] A question that we can legitimately pose, however, and one
which may prove more fruitful, is how the poet responds to the sociopo-
litical crises of his era, and how much overlap we can find between his
responses and those of his Epicurean contemporaries. Conversely, it seems
worth asking whether the clear parallels between Catullus' invective against
(Porcius and) Socration and Cicero's attacks on Piso and other Epicureans
bespeak a rather conventional hostility towards (Epicurean) philosophy on
our poet's part.

We shall return later in this essay to Catullus 47; but before doing so,
I would like to explore the implications of what is certainly the most
widely recognized Philodemean echo in Catullus. Poem 13, the famous
"anti-invitation" to Fabullus, may be read as a parodic response to
Philodemus, *Epigram* 27 (*AP* 11.44), incidentally the most overtly
Epicurean of all Philodemus' surviving poems:[7]

> Cenabis bene, mi Fabulle, apud me
> paucis, si tibi di favent, diebus,
> si tecum attuleris bonam atque magnam
> cenam, non sine candida puella
> et vino et sale et omnibus cachinnis.   5
> haec si, inquam, attuleris, venuste noster,
> cenabis bene; nam tui Catulli
> plenus sacculus est aranearum.
> sed contra accipies **meros amores**
> seu quid suavius elegantiusve est . . .   10

---

the social and erotic entanglements of the metropolis, with all their attendant *curae*. The tranquillity
of Sirmio can be no more than a brief respite.

[6] Giuffrida: 1950, 89–288. Giuffrida's arguments rest on now long-abandoned notions of Catullan
purezza and *castità*, as well as a somewhat eccentric understanding of Epicurean poetics, and have
been largely discredited in subsequent scholarship (already by Granarolo: 1967, 205–224).
Nevertheless, his central theory that Catullus' ideal of friendship is indebted to the Epicurean
conception of φιλία is still occasionally repeated in modern work on the poet (e.g. Landolfi: 1982
140 and Luciani: 2005, 162). In view, however, of the emphasis Catullus lays on reciprocity,
obligation and *benevolentia* in, e.g., poems 72, 73 and 76, affinities with the traditional *Roman*
code of aristocratic *amicitia* are to my mind far more striking. Cf. Ross: 1969, 80–95, on Catullus'
manipulation of "the (almost technical) terminology of . . . political alliances at Rome" (83), and, for
compelling parallels in the language of Cicero's letters, Fitzgerald: 1995, 128–134. For discussion of
the evidence for the Epicureanism of two of Catullus' contemporaries, namely Caesar and Atticus,
see Volk (Chapter 5) and Gilbert (Chapter 4) in this volume respectively.

[7] On the relationship between the two poems, see esp. Hiltbrünner: 1972, Carilli: 1975, 942–945,
Marcovich: 1982 and Dettmer: 1989.

You'll dine well, my dear Fabullus, at my place in a few days time, by the gods' grace—if you bring with you a good, big dinner, not forgetting a pretty girl, and wine and salt/wit and everything that's amusing. *If*, I say, you bring all this, my charming friend, you'll dine well: For your Catullus' purse is full—of cobwebs. But in return I'll give you pure love(-poetry), or whetever is sweeter and more stylish . . .

Αὔριον εἰς λιτήν σε καλιάδα, <u>φίλτατε Πείσων</u>,
    <u>ἐξ ἐνάτης</u> ἕλκει μουσοφιλὴς ἕταρος
εἰκάδα δειπνίζων ἐνιαύσιον· εἰ δ' ἀπολείψεις
    οὔθατα καὶ Βρομίου Χιογενῆ πρόποσιν,
<u>ἀλλ' **ἑτάρους** ὄψει **παναληθέας**</u>, ἀλλ' ἐπακούσῃ   5
    Φαιήκων γαίης πουλὺ <u>μελιχρότερα</u>.
ἢν δέ ποτε στρέψῃς καὶ ἐς ἡμέας ὄμματα, Πείσων,
    ἄξομεν ἐκ λιτῆς εἰκάδα πιοτέρην.

Tomorrow from the ninth hour, my dear Piso, your friend, beloved of the Muses, calls you out to his humble abode for your annual visit, for dinner in celebration of the Twentieth.[8] If you leave behind your sow's udders and draughts of Chian wine, yet you will see the truest of friends and hear things much sweeter than the land of the Phaeacians. But if ever you turn your eyes our way, Piso, we shall celebrate a richer Twentieth, instead of a modest one.

As indicated above, the structure of Catullus' poem precisely mirrors that of Philodemus' epigram (opening address with the date/time of the dinner;[9] contrasting lines on what the addressee will *not* find on offer and the "much sweeter" figurative "fare" to be provided by the host). But Catullus sends up the alleged modesty of Philodemus' dwelling and the banquet to take place there: *His* speaker is not so much an advocate of *litotes* as, simply, broke, to such an extent that Fabullus must bring the dinner, the drink and even the obligatory *candida puella*. Reading the two poems together, we might understand this as a dig at what could be seen as hypocrisy[10] on Philodemus' part: What begins as an invitation ends as a

---

[8] The phrase εἰκάδα δειπνίζων ἐνιαύσιον has been the source of considerable scholarly controversy: I follow Sider: 1997, 156–158 (cf. Sider: 1995, 46–50), who understands δειπνίζων in its usual sense, "feeding," and takes ἐνιαύσιον to qualify σε rather than εἰκάδα. The reference is to the regular Epicurean gatherings held on the twentieth of the month since the Founder's own day (DL 10.18; further testimonia and discussion in Clay: 1998, 89–90, 97).

[9] The lack of specificity in Catullus' *paucis diebus* is of course part of the poem's humor. We might paraphrase: "You'll get a good dinner one of these fine days, if you're lucky."

[10] Which is not to say that the poem's conclusion cannot also be understood as perfectly orthodox in Epicurean terms: Epicurus warns that even austerity can be taken to excess (VS 63; cf. Diogenes of Oenoanda NF 146), and does not suggest that we should turn down the occasional treat if offered; indeed, the fragments of his letters include requests for "offerings" to supplement his usual meagre diet (fr. 130 U, DL 10.11 = fr. 182 U). Tutrone: 2017 persuasively argues that gratitude (whether

begging letter from Piso's client (or parasite?).[11] Particularly important for our purposes is that what Catullus offers his friend in return for bringing his own dinner is distinctly different from the (presumably) philosophical conversation and companionship on offer at Philodemus' party.[12] *Meros amores* is a disputed phrase, the interpretation of which is only made more difficult when Catullus goes on to connect it with a perfume given to his girl by the gods of love: Without entering into the long-running debate on the question, let me merely suggest that the mysterious *unguentum* may be understood as an emblem of the *venustas* and *urbanitas* that the poet prizes so highly in the literary, social and erotic spheres alike.[13] As a gift of the gods of charm (*Venus/venus*) and desire (*Cupido/cupido*), the perfume may be understood as embodying the smartness and elegance of the dinner party, as well as the affection (*amores*: Compare the end of the previous poem, 12.16–17, where the speaker celebrates his love – *amem* – for Fabullus and Veranius) in which both Fabullus and the *puella* are held, and the elegant love-*poetry* (*amores*)[14] in which this affection is enshrined. Philodemus asserts that the Epicurean φιλία he hopes to share with Piso is friendship in the truest sense (παναληθέας, 5); Catullus in response redefines "unmixed love/friendship" (*meros amores*, 9) in terms of a shared

expressed verbally or through material *beneficia*) was fundamental to Epicurean φιλία; see also Asmis: 2004, 161–176, who points out that both Epicurus and Philodemus himself regard it as entirely proper for the wise person to seek remuneration for philosophical teaching. For the suggestion that Philodemus self-consciously characterizes both himself and Piso as "beggars," see Sider 1995: 49–50.

[11] It has been called into question whether the relationship between Piso and Philodemus should be understood as one of *clientela*; but see Sider 1997: 5–7 (with n. 11), who argues cogently that the terminology of patronage is fully applicable here.

[12] Unlike the majority of commentators, I take the primary reference here to be to philosophical discussion rather than poetic performance: In the context of the reference to true friendship and to Phaeacian pleasures, this seems to me a more natural assumption (Epicurean discourse taking the place of Odysseus' *apologoi*, or perhaps more specifically his notorious speech [*Od.* 9.5–11] on the pleasures of good fellowship and the table). For the comparison between Epicureans and Phaeacians (usually in the mouth of hostile witnesses), see esp. Buffière 1956, 317–322 and Gordon 2012, 38–71: The allegorist Heraclitus, writing in the second or third century AD, labels Epicurus, with his supposed love of sensual pleasure, "the Phaeacian philosopher" (*Alleg. Hom.* 79.2), but – as Gordon shows – the slur clearly goes back much earlier, and Philodemus' epigram can be understood as a response to it. This is not to deny that the epigram also has metapoetic implications: See further below.

[13] For this interpretation of the *unguentum*, cf. esp. Vessey: 1971, Marcovich: 1982, Bernstein: 1985, Dettmer: 1986, Richlin: 1988, 356–358, Gowers: 1993, 229–244; the more graphically sexual interpretations of Littman: 1977 and Hallett: 1978 lack textual support, and have been generally rejected.

[14] For *amores* in this sense, cf. e.g. Virg. *E.* 10.53–54, Ov. *AA* 3.343, *Tr.* 2.361, *OLD* s.v. *amor* 5. This interpretation also helps to explain the concluding joke, since the word *nasus* is used not infrequently as a metaphor for the faculty of critical discrimination (e.g. Hor. *Sat.* 1.4.8, Plin. *NH praef.* 7, Mart. 1.3.6).

possession of chic, stylishness, elegance – qualities that have very little to do with *voluptas* in the Epicurean sense.

We should of course acknowledge in this connection that Philodemus, too, is a poet: Indeed, he draws attention to the fact in the second line of his invitation to Piso, characterizing himself as μουσοφιλής, "beloved of the Muses." Possibly, then, the entertainment that he offers his patron should be taken to include poetry, as David Sider suggests in his commentary on *Ep.* 27.[15] The epigram can be understood on a metapoetic as well as a philosophical level: The elegant simplicity of Philodemus' poems is "sweeter" than the more sumptuous style of Homeric epic.[16] Similarly Cicero – though distinctly backhanded in his compliments – praises Philodemus' verse as *ita festivum, ita concinnum, ita elegans, nihil ut fieri possit argutius* ("so charming, so clever, so elegant that nothing could be neater," *Pis.* 70). Here, then, we might at first glance perceive a certain convergence between Catullus' and Philodemus' poetics: Both express a preference for "light" verse, characterized by its charm or "sweetness" (μελιχρότερα, Philod. *Ep.* 27.6; *suavius*, Cat. 13.10); both perhaps look to Callimachus as a model.[17] Intertextual reminiscences of Philodemus in Catullus' poetry tend to suggest antagonism or perhaps rivalry rather than approval, however, and I suggest that the needling quality of the echoes I am exploring here can be attributed to a hostility on Catullus' part to the Greek poet's Epicureanism, for all the superficial similarities between their literary ideals.

Above all, it is the centrality of both poetry and *urbanitas* to Catullus' writing and the social relations it depicts and facilitates that drives a wedge between him and Philodemus. There is nowadays a broad scholarly consensus that orthodox Epicureanism does not permit its adherents too serious a commitment to the study or composition of poetry: Epicurus himself urged his disciple Pythocles to shun all παιδεία (fr. 163 U), and appears to have decreed that the wise man will not "devote himself to the writing of poetry" or "make a practice of writing poetry" (ποιήματα ... ἐνεργείᾳ οὐκ ἂν ποιῆσαι, DL 10.121 = fr. 568 U);[18] Cicero's Epicurean

---

[15] Sider: 1997, 155–156.

[16] For the relatively uncommon comparative μελιχρότερος in a similarly programmatic context, cf. Callimachus, *Aet.* fr. 1.16; cf. also *Ep.* 27.2–3, where Aratus is praised for his imitation of τὸ μελιχρότατον | τῶν ἐπέων ("the sweetest of the verses") of Hesiod.

[17] Cf. n. 16 above; Catullus invokes Callimachus, as *Battiades*, most explicitly at 65.16 (introducing poem 66's translation of the *Coma Berenices*) and 116.2, but echoes can of course be heard throughout the corpus (see e.g. Knox: 2007).

[18] On the text and interpretation of this phrase, see especially Asmis: 1995, 22.

speaker Torquatus accordingly dismisses literary study as a *puerilis delecta-tio* (*Fin.* 1.72). Philodemus appears, in the fragments of his philosophical writing, to concur with this position, particularly in *On Music*, where the study of music is dismissed as too laborious and as getting in the way of more serious pursuits (*Mus.* 4 cols. 151–152 Delattre); in *On Poems* he denies that poetry can be "useful" or "beneficial," at least *qua* poetry (*Poem.* 5 cols. 25.30–34, 32.17–19 Mangoni). As an inherently *pleasurable* activity, writing or listening to poetry is not to be dismissed out of hand, certainly; but it must take second place to genuinely beneficial activities – in particular, philosophical discussion and study. Sider has argued, with some plausibility, that epigram is thus the perfect literary form for the Epicurean poet, owing to the "appearance of not having required any effort" – the improvisatory quality – cultivated by the Hellenistic epigrammatists.[19]

The contrast with Catullus, who praises the minute and painstaking nine-years' labor of Cinna on his epyllion *Smyrna*, and pours scorn on the Suffenuses and Volusiuses who toss off thousands of lines with casual abandon, could hardly be more marked.[20] The exchange of poems and discussion of works in progress are crucial facets of the social life of Catullus and his *amici* as depicted in the poems; and the reading and writing of poetry has a quasi-erotic charge, strong enough to keep the poet awake all night and longing for more, or to make the listener – like Fabullus in poem 13 – long to become "all nose."[21] The superficial similarity between Philodemus' and Catullus' poetics noted above must, then, be heavily qualified when the two poems are read in their broader contexts. Indeed, as I have already suggested, even within Catullus' response to Philodemus' epigram we can observe a crucial change of emphasis: The layering in Philodemus' poem of the philosophical and the metapoetic, both of which are implicit in the reference to the Phaeacians, is replaced in Catullus' case by a single, if multi-faceted, ideal: There is no separation between the

---

[19] Sider: 1997, 27–28 and 32 (quoted phrase at 32). Cf. Asmis: 1995, 32–33.

[20] Poems 95; 22; 36. Cf. also the ideal of literary "polish" implied by the image of the pumice-finished book-roll at 1.2. This is not to deny that Catullus, who is, after all, as much an epigrammatist as Philodemus, can project an air of ostentatious casualness when it suits him to do so (notably, in the informal and quasi-erotic verse-swapping session recollected at 50.1–6), as CUP's anonymous reader rightly reminds me. Nevertheless, the overall impression that the reader derives from Catullus' collection is of a writer wholly devoted to his craft, for all his self-deprecating insistence on the essential non-seriousness of his themes and life-style.

[21] For exchange of poems and discussion of work in progress, see esp. poems 14, 35, 38, 50, 65 and 68A, and (e.g.) Wray: 2001, 99–106, Stroup: 2010, esp. 72–88; for the erotic charge of poetry, see (in addition to 35 and 50) 16.7–11, with Fitzgerald: 1995, 34–55.

different senses of *meros amores*, and the *venustas* and *cupido* symbolized (on my reading) by the *unguentum* belong equally to the spheres of poetry, *amicitia* and *amor*.

Friendship, Patronage and Politics

If Catullus' conception of *amicitia* is to be contrasted, as I have suggested, with the Epicurean φιλία promised by Philodemus, it is also worth bearing in mind the quite different social dynamics of the two poems. Catullus invites a friend of (presumably) similar social status, whereas Philodemus' poem is, in part, a request for material assistance from a social superior, his patron Calpurnius Piso.[22] I have already suggested that Catullus 13 can be read as a kind of parody of this element in Philodemus' poem; and the relationship between friendship and patronage – both of which are subsumed under the Latin word *amicitia* – seems worth exploring further in each of the two poets. This brings us back to poem 47, with its depiction of Philodemus/Socration and Porcius as disreputable parasites, inexplicably favored by the equally disreputable Piso. We can hear echoes here of the anti-Epicurean polemic of Cicero's *Against Piso*: The *convivium de die*, the dinner-party beginning before the end of the working day, is emblematic of a decadent indolence, of the kind pilloried by Cicero in his attack on Piso's (alleged) self-indulgent hedonism (*Pis.* 22):

> Quid ego illorum dierum epulas, quid laetitiam et gratulationem tuam, quid cum tuis sordidissimis gregibus intemperantissimas perpotationes praedicem? Quis te illis diebus sobrium, quis agentem aliquid quod esset libero dignum, quis denique in publico vidit?[23]

> Why need I mention the banquets of those days, your delight and rejoicing, the utterly unrestrained drinking-bouts you engaged in with your filthy flock? Who ever saw you sober during those days, who ever saw you doing anything befitting a free citizen, who ever saw you in public at all?

---

[22] For a nuanced analysis of the social dynamics of the relationship between Piso and Philodemus, see Tutrone: 2017, 288–290.

[23] Cf. *Pis.* 67, where Cicero lampoons Piso for combining self-indulgence with lack of good taste: In contrast to Catullus (47.5–6), who writes of *convivia lauta*, Cicero denies Piso even the ameliorating gloss of *urbanitas* (*nihil apud hunc lautum, nihil elegans, nihil exquisitum*). The discrepancy can be attributed in part to the different perspective adopted by the two writers: Cicero attacks Piso as a peer, Catullus as potential host/patron, to whose dinners (he and) his friends would *wish* to be invited. For Piso's daytime drinking, cf. also *Pis.* 13, 18 and – for his (allegedly) debauched lifestyle in general – *Red. Sen.* 14–15 and *Sest.* 22–23.

Like Cicero, Catullus has a specific axe to grind here: Poem 47 forms, along with 10 and 28, a kind of miniature invective cycle, in which Piso and Gaius Memmius are attacked for their supposed ill-treatment of their younger protégés, Veranius and Fabullus, and of Catullus himself while on provincial service in Macedonia and Bithynia respectively. The poet and his friends will have formed part of the entourage of junior colleagues and *aides-de-camp*, the *cohors amicorum*, personally selected by the governor from amongst his friends and acquaintances. It is clear that young men undertaking such a posting expected to make a financial profit as well as gain experience of provincial administration, and Catullus' major complaint is that Memmius and Piso have prevented him and his friends from doing so. This high-handed behavior (as Catullus characterizes it)[24] is represented by the poet as a breakdown in the system of patronage, which has been corrupted by the arbitrary favoritism of the *nobiles* and their lack of interest in assisting their juniors: In vividly sexual language (10.12–13; 28.9–13), the speaker complains that he and his friends have been "screwed" by their commanding officers, and poem 28 closes with a bitter outcry against the "noble friends" who have – he claims – abused their privileged position and so disgraced the name of Romulus and Remus.[25] Each of the three poems draws an implicit contrast between the personal friendship that exists between Catullus and his *sodales* – Veranius and Fabullus in 28 and 47, Varus and Cinna in 10 – and the perverted, so-called *amicitia* of a patronage system gone awry. Catullus attests to a sense of exclusion and disempowerment amongst young members of the provincial elite, striving to find a place on the political stage of the metropolis – a stage increasingly dominated, in the mid-50s BC, by the Triumvirs and their partisans.

Whereas Philodemus, in his invitation to Piso, suggests a convergence between two senses of "friendship" (as patronage and as Epicurean φιλία), Catullus sets up an opposition between what we might call the "public" and the "private" aspects of *amicitia*, and tends to privilege the latter. The

---

[24] With, certainly, more than a touch of self-irony (cf. Skinner: 1989; 2001; Nappa: 2001, 87–93). Braund: 1996 argues that the speaker discredits himself to such an extent that the image of Memmius that emerges from the poem is ultimately a positive one: While it is true, however, that preventing one's *cohors* from profiteering might indeed be represented as praiseworthy, the graphically sexual language tells against such a reading.

[25] Cf. 29.23–24 for a similar outcry against Caesar and Pompey (*socer generque*, 24), who have "destroyed everything" through their indulgence of unworthy protégés such as Mamurra.

opening lines of poem 10, for example, seem to align personal friendship
with *otium*, in contrast to the public sphere of the Forum (10.1–2):

> Varus me meus ad suos amores
> visum duxerat e foro otiosum

> My friend Varus, finding me at leisure, took me from the Forum to meet
> his girl . . .

The juxtaposition *e foro otiosum* is pointed: Varus leads Catullus *away from*
the *negotium* of the Forum, inviting him into a private world of love and
friendship. It is, significantly, from this decentered perspective that
Memmius' lack of concern for his *cohors* is denounced.

At the same time, throughout the collection Catullus represents himself
and his *sodales* as an exclusive social circle, access to which is reserved for the
urbani and *venusti*. If Catullus – as he depicts himself – is on the fringes of
the political elite, he is very much at the center of the smart set, a position
from which he is empowered to pronounce on the (un)sophisticated behavior of his peers, and to police the boundaries of the in-group. Characters
such as Asinius Marrucinus (poem 12), Suffenus (22) or Egnatius (39) are
excluded on the grounds of social or literary *faux pas*; Fabullus, Veranius,
Cinna and Calvus are "in." Of course, there is considerable irony in the fact
that betrayal seems as endemic to the personal friendships the poet celebrates
as to the corrupt public world he condemns: Alfenus in poem 30, Rufus in
77 and the unnamed *amicus* of 73 are all denounced as false friends, who –
like Lesbia – fail to keep up their side of the "contract" of mutual *officium*.
Nevertheless, the contrast with Epicurean φιλία, the brotherhood of the
enlightened that is potentially accessible to all, is again marked.

In this connection, Lucretius' dedication of his *On the Nature of Things* to
Memmius offers a particularly instructive comparison.[26] At 1.140–142, in
commenting on the difficulty of expressing the *Graiorum obscura reperta*, the
"obscure discoveries of the Greeks," in Latin verse, Lucretius gracefully
attributes his persistence in his task to his hope of gaining Memmius' *amicitia*:

> sed tua me virtus tamen et sperata voluptas
> **suavis** amicitiae quemvis efferre laborem
> suadet . . .

---

[26] I assume with most Lucretian scholars that the dedicatee of the *DRN* is to be identified with
Catullus' Memmius, the praetor of 58 BC. Hutchinson: 2001, arguing that the poem should be
dated to the early 40s rather than the mid-50s, suggests instead the tribune of 54; but cf. the
rejoinder of Volk: 2010.

> But your virtue and the longed-for pleasure of sweet friendship induce me
> to undergo any toil . . .

It is often assumed that the reference here to *amicitia* amounts – like the
conclusion of Philodemus' epigram – to an appeal for patronage; but
whatever the nature of the historical relationship between Lucretius and
Memmius, it is clearly framed within the poem in terms of Epicurean
ideals. As in Catullus, friendship is represented as something "sweet" –
attractive, desirable (*suavis*: cf. Cat. 13.9–10 *amores | seu quid suavius . . . est*);
but more than that, it is the pleasure (*voluptas*) that Lucretius anticipates
from it that motivates him to write his poem. The pun on *suavis* and
suadet underlines the characteristically Epicurean identification of
pleasure as "the starting point of every choice and every aversion"
(*Men.* 129); moreover, the doctrine that friendship is a pleasure worth
pursuing for its own sake is amply attested in Epicurus' surviving
writings.[27] If, then, it is specifically *Epicurean* friendship that Lucretius
seeks, this is something that will follow, presumably, from Memmius'/
the reader's successful conversion to Epicureanism. Two corollaries
follow: First, that Lucretius' conception of friendship, in contrast to
Catullus', is inclusive – if Memmius figures in part as a kind of stand-
in for the reader-in-general, then the poet may be said to seek the
"friendship" of all of us: Any reader can, and indeed should, become
an Epicurean.[28] Secondly, Lucretius' implicitly professed desire to con-
vert Memmius – to win him as an Epicurean φίλος – has potentially
important consequences for the latter's political activities, alluded to
earlier in the proem.

In his opening prayer to Venus, Lucretius warmly praises Memmius as a
man whom the goddess Venus (apparently a kind of patron deity of the
family)[29] "has always wished to succeed and win honor in all things"
(*tempore in omni | omnibus ornatum voluisti excellere rebus*, 1.26–27), and
who cannot well absent himself from public life "at a time of danger for
our country" (*patriai tempore iniquo*, 1.41–43). But this opening encomium is arguably undermined by – or at least in tension with – what the
poet has to say about political life and in particular competition for status
and office later in the poem.[30] In both the proem to Book 3 and the

---

[27] KD 27, 28, VS 23, 52, 56, 57, 78; cf. also Cic., *Fin.* 1.66, DL 10.10–11, 120.
[28] Cf. Tutrone: 2017, 325–327, and, for the "universalizing tendency" of Epicureanism in general,
Roskam in this volume (Chapter 2).
[29] For the (mainly numismatic) evidence, see Schilling: 1954, 271–272.
[30] For a range of views on these passages and Lucretius' handling of political activity in general, see esp.
Fowler: 1989, Benferhat: 2005a, 81–96, Roskam: 2007a, 83–101, Schiesaro: 2007, McConnell:

account of the origins of government at the end of Book 5, Lucretius attributes the desire for fame and success in the public sphere ultimately to the fear of death. Far from selflessly seeking their country's good – as a Cicero would assert – politicians are motivated, he argues, by a desire for personal security, misguidedly associating power and influence with protection from their fellow-citizens (3.59–64; 5.1120–1122). On Lucretius' analysis, however, political competition is in fact ruinous on both the individual and the collective level. In Book 5 he argues that success in the political rat-race not only involves painful effort and anxiety (*sine incassum defessi sanguine sudent,* | *angustum per iter luctantes ambitionis,* "leave them to weary themselves and sweat blood for nothing, as they struggle along the narrow path of ambition," 1131–1132) but inevitably generates *invidia,* "envy" or "ill-will," which, like lightning, is most prone to strike those who climb highest (1125–1128). So security is much more likely to be achieved by *avoiding* public life altogether: "Better peaceful obedience than the desire to exercise *imperium*" (*ut satius multo iam sit parere quietum* | *quam regere imperio res velle*), as Lucretius provocatively asserts at 1129–1130. The community, too, is adversely affected by competition for status and position: In memorable lines from the proem to Book 3 (68–77), Lucretius argues that the desire for primacy leads inexorably to the carnage of civil war – a line of argument that will have seemed highly topical and, again, provocative during the years of social and political upheaval that preceded the outbreak of hostilities between Caesar and Pompey. But this, too, is the very "time of danger for our country" which was seen to absorb Memmius' attention in the proem to Book 1. In effect, then, Lucretius admonishes his dedicatee that he would do better, both from the personal and from the collective point of view, to withdraw altogether from public life.

In taking Epicurus' injunction against political activity (οὐδὲ πολιτεύσεται [sc. ὁ σοφός], DL 10.119 = fr. 8 U) absolutely at face value, Lucretius seems more radical than many of his contemporaries. Roman Epicureans generally found ways of reconciling their philosophical beliefs with the practice of politics: Piso, Manlius Torquatus, the tyrannicide Cassius, even (indirectly) Cicero's friend Atticus continued to play a

---

2012 and Hammer: 2014, 114–144. Fish: 2011, 76–87, seeks to minimize the negativity of Lucretius' treatment, and to bring it more closely into line with that of contemporary Epicureans, arguing that the target of attack is political *ambition* rather than political activity as such; his analysis of the relevant passages of the *DRN* involves reading decidedly against the grain, however, and is not to my mind persuasive. Contrast Roskam: 2007a, esp. 97–99, for the view that Lucretius "radicalizes" Epicurean doctrine in this area.

prominent role in public life in spite of their professed Epicureanism.[31] Arguably, Epicurus himself leaves room for such a position: He concedes that the wise man will show concern for his reputation (though only so far as to avoid falling into contempt, DL 10.120), and, according to later writers, his injunction against political participation was qualified with an "in the normal course of things."[32] Philodemus, in this context, takes a distinctly different line of approach from Lucretius: Whereas the latter seeks – on my reading – to divert his dedicatee from the public career on which he has embarked, the former adopts the role of philosophical adviser, dedicating his *On the Good King According to Homer* to Piso. Constraints of space preclude a full discussion of Philodemus' treatise here, but it is worth noting that the fragments suggest that overriding themes were justice and ἐπιείκεια – gentleness or reasonableness – as exemplified, for example, by Nestor, or by Odysseus' rule of Ithaca (which, according to Telemachus, was as "gentle [ἤπιος] as a father's," *Od.* 2.47).[33] It is easy to see how Philodemus' injunctions might be viewed as cohering with the Epicurean pursuit of serenity – conciliation is arguably much more likely to foster a quiet life than competitiveness and the desire for preeminence – and it is notable that Piso's actual political policies seem very largely to have accorded with the precepts of his mentor (Nisbet, for example, characterizes him as "moderate and statesmanlike").[34] But Philodemus' prescription for political harmony (or, more precisely, Homer's prescription, on Philodemus' Epicurean reading) certainly diverges sharply from that of Lucretius.

---

[31] See esp. Benferhat: 2005a, 98–169 (Atticus), 173–232 (Piso), 261–266 (Cassius), 266–270 (Torquatus); cf. also Castner: 1988, 16–23 (Piso), 24–31 (Cassius), 40–42 (Torquatus), 58–61 (Atticus); Griffin: 1989, 28–32, and 2001; Sedley: 1997 (esp. 46–47), Benferhat: 2002, D. Armstrong: 2011, 109–116. Momigliano: 1941 goes too far, however, in positing a "heroic Epicureanism" as a motivating factor among the opponents of Caesar (so Griffin: 1989, 29–31; cf. Sedley: 1997, 41); conversely, the view of Castner: 1988 and Griffin: 1989 that philosophical commitment amongst the Roman elite was a relatively superficial matter and had little impact on actions in the public sphere has been widely disputed (esp. by Benferhat: 2005a, but also in the more recent work of Griffin herself). See also Valachova: 2018 and Volk in this volume (Chaper 5), as well as Roskam's essay in this volume (Chapter 2) on the dilemma in *On Ends* of Cicero's Torquatus, who is portrayed as a devout Epicurean and an active politician, and that of Gilbert (Chapter 4), who examines the Epicureanism of Atticus.

[32] Cic. *Rep.* 1.10–11, Sen. *De Otio* 3.2 = fr. 9 U, Plut. *Adv. Col.* 1125C = fr. 554 U; Fowler 1989: 127–128, Roskam: 2007a: 50–56.

[33] See esp. cols. 24, 28–29, 30, 42 Dorandi. On the themes of the *On the Good King According to Homer*, see esp. Asmis: 1991, 23–27. For a brief discussion of Philodemus' role as "philosophical adviser," with further bibliography, see also Fish: 2016, 57–58.

[34] Nisbet 1961, xiv; cf. Griffin: 2001, Benferhat: 2002 and 2005a, 178–210.

The "Epicurean" stance on political participation at the period that concerns us is, then, by no means straightforward; but whether we think in terms of Lucretius' uncompromising rejection of public life or the more "engaged" approach of Piso and Philodemus, Catullus again seems to have only so much in common with either. The disenchanted attitude of the Memmius and Piso poems is not untypical of the collection as a whole: While many of the invective poems are "political" in the sense that their targets are public figures (particularly Caesar and his partisans), their overriding sentiment is one of disgust with the state of civic business in general. A representative example is poem 52, in which outrage at the political advancement of Nonius and Vatinius provokes the rhetorical question *quid est, Catulle? quid moraris emori?* ("What's up with you Catullus? Why prolong your life?," 1,4). Though he has sometimes been regarded as an anti-Caesarian partisan, it is noteworthy (as Yasmina Benferhat sagely observes) that what he professes toward Caesar is not so much hostility as studied indifference.[35] As we have seen, he shows a tendency to follow Lucretius' implicit advice to Memmius, turning his back on the public sphere in favor of personal relationships and literary composition. But these relationships are far from bringing him the ἀταραξία that Lucretius proclaims – something which he, arguably, does not even seek, as we shall see.

It is worth observing, too, that Catullus appears deeply pessimistic about the moral condition of the human race in general, to judge at least from the concluding lines of poem 64. The downbeat coda with which the epyllion ends contrasts the virtue of the Age of Heroes with the moral bankruptcy of the present day (397–406):

> sed postquam tellus scelere est imbuta nefando
> iustitiamque omnes cupida de mente fugarunt,
> perfudere manus **fraterno sanguine fratres**,
> destitit extinctos gnatus lugere parentes,
> optavit genitor primaevi funera nati,
> liber uti nuptae poteretur flore novellae,[36]
> ignaro mater substernens se impia nato

---

[35] Benferhat: 2005b, 139: "Le plus frappant réside sans doute dans l'indépendance manifestée jusqu'au bout par Catulle à l'égard de César" ("The most striking thing is undoubtedly the independence shown throughout by Catullus with regard to Caesar"). See esp. poem 93, *nil nimium studeo, Caesar, tibi velle placere* ... ("I'm none too eager, Caesar, to wish to please you ..."). The tendency in recent anglophone scholarship has been to view Catullus as "profoundly estranged" from Roman public life: see e.g. Nappa: 2001, 85–105, Skinner: 2003, esp. 23–24, 137–142, Konstan: 2007 (quoted phrase at 78).

[36] I follow Goold in printing Maehly's *uti nuptae* with Baehrens' *novellae*, for the MSS *innuptae ... novercae*: For discussion, see Fordyce: 1961, *ad loc.*, and Trappes-Lomax: 2007, 205.

impia non verita est divos scelerare penates.
omnia fanda nefanda malo permixta furore
iustificam nobis mentem avertere deorum.

But once the world was plunged into unspeakable wickedness and all drove justice from their greedy hearts, brothers drenched their hands in brothers' blood; the son ceased to mourn for dead parents; the father longed for the death of his young son, so that he might freely pluck the flower of his new-wed bride; the impious mother, lying with her unknowing son, did not shrink from sinning impiously against the household gods. Everything speakable and unspeakable, thrown into confusion by our evil madness, has turned the gods' just mind away from us.

We can again detect considerable irony here – given that the alleged glories of the heroic age evoked earlier in the poem include the heartless abandonment of the innocent Ariadne by Theseus (52–264), the bloody slaughter of countless Trojans by Achilles (343–360) and the gorily described sacrifice of Polyxena on the latter's tomb (362–364).[37] Nevertheless, it is striking that these closing lines bear a strong resemblance to Lucretius' analysis of civil strife in the proem to Book 3: In particular, the phrase *perfudere manus fraterno sanguine fratres* ("brothers drenched their hands in brothers' blood," 64.399) is similar in both cadence and sense to Lucretius' *crudeles gaudent in tristi funere fratris* ("cruelly, they rejoice in a brother's tragic death," 3.72). Catullus, though, seems to reject, or at least ignore, the Epicurean poet's prescription even while pointedly evoking it. Like many ancient writers and thinkers from Hesiod on, he treats human degeneracy as a tragic inevitability, leaving no room for Lucretius' more optimistic suggestion that – at least on the individual level – escape from this bleak prospect to a life of serenity is a genuine possibility.[38]

vesanus Catullus

Catullus' vehement, even passionate, expressions of affection for male *amici* in such poems as 9, 12, 14 and 50 are complemented by the ideal of *amor*-as-*amicitia* in his relations with Lesbia. Most pithily expressed in the phrase *aeternum hoc sanctae foedus amicitiae* (109.6), this ideal is explored from a variety of angles through the sequence of Lesbia-epigrams culminating in the longer, introspective poem 76. Catullus exploits the

---

[37] For echoes of Lucretius' account of the sacrifice of Iphigenia (1.80–101) in these lines, see Skinner: 1976 and Morisi: 2002; ironic readings of the coda to Catullus 64 include Curran: 1969, Bramble: 1970, esp. 25–29, Konstan: 1977, 82–84 and Gaisser: 1995, 613.

[38] Cf. Morisi: 2002, esp. 187–190.

hallowed ideals of reciprocity, *officium* (75.2), *benevolentia* (72.8, 75.3; cf. 73.1) and – most startlingly – *pietas* (76.2, 26), to recast his admittedly adulterous affair (68.143–146) as a relationship of mutual commitment and more-than-physical affection, analogous to male–male friendship or intrafamilial relations (72.4). Lesbia, moreover, is herself idealized, both in the polymetrics and in the elegiacs. Figured as a goddess (68.70, 133–134), she is beyond compare with other women (43.7–8, 86.5–6), and has, accordingly, inspired a love greater than any woman has ever attracted in the past (87), or (even more hyperbolically) will attract in the future (8.5, 37.12). The speaker's passion for her is assimilated to madness (7.10) or – when things go awry – to an incurable disease (76.19–26).

In various respects, this group of poems also invites comparison with both Philodemus and Lucretius. Intertextual echoes of both poets can be detected in Catullus' Lesbia cycle, though in Lucretius' case interpretation is problematic owing to the impossibility of determining the relative chronology of the two writers. I assume here, for the sake of argument, that Catullus echoes Lucretius rather than vice versa; but an equally good case can be made for Lucretius' poem as the "receiving" text.[39] In any case, the essence of my argument will stand whichever way the intertextual dialogue is understood to proceed: Whether Lucretius takes Catullus as an *exemplum* of the evils of love or Catullus (as I argue here) ostentatiously rejects the Epicurean remedy for his ills, the essential antagonism between the two poets' views on *amor* remains.

In Philodemus' case, the matter seems more clear cut, even if we leave on one side the widely held axiom that Roman writers read the work of their Greek counterparts but not vice versa. I have already noted that Catullus 13 reads as a parody of Philodemus' invitation poem to Piso; and much the same can be said of Catullus 43, which can be interpreted as a similarly antagonistic reworking of another of Philodemus' epigrams, 12 Sider (= *Anth. Pal.* 5.132):

> Ὦ **ποδός**, ὦ κνήμης, ὦ τῶν (ἀπόλωλα δικαίως)
> μηρῶν, ὦ γλουτῶν, ὦ κτενός, ὦ λαγόνων,
> ὦ ὤμοιν, ὦ μαστῶν, ὦ τοῦ ῥαδινοῖο τραχήλου,

---

[39] Majority opinion perhaps leans towards the view that Catullus' is the receiving text, at least in poem 64, where the majority of close verbal echoes are concentrated: see e.g. Grimal: 1978, 258–259, Giesecke: 2000, 10–30; for the opposing view, see Herrmann: 1956 and Biondi: 2003. For Catullan echoes (?) in the finale to Book 4, see Lieberg: 1962, 284–300, Kenney: 1970, 388–390 (= 2007: 324–326), R. D. Brown: 1987, 139–143, Luciani: 2005 and Baier: 2010. A less historicizing approach is advocated by Tamás: 2016, whose notion of "reciprocal intertextuality" (developed in relation to Catullus 64) could be applied productively to the finale to Lucretius 4.

ὦ **χειρῶν**, ὦ τῶν (μαίνομαι) **ὀμματίων**,
ὦ κατατεχνοτάτου κινήματος, ὦ περιάλλων   5
    γλωττισμῶν, ὦ τῶν (θῦέ με) **φωναρίων·**
εἰ δ᾽ Ὀπικὴ καὶ Φλῶρα καὶ οὐκ ᾄδουσα τὰ Σαπφοῦς,
    καὶ Περσεὺς Ἰνδῆς ἠράσατ᾽ Ἀνδρομέδης.

O foot, O leg, O (I'm done for) those thighs, O buttocks, O bush, O flanks,
O shoulders, O breasts, O delicate neck, O hands, O (madness!) those eyes,
O wickedly skillful walk, O fabulous kisses, O (slay me!) her speech.
And if she *is* an Oscan—a mere Flora who does not sing Sappho's verses—
Perseus too fell in love with Indian Andromeda.

(tr. Sider)

Salve, nec minimo puella naso
nec bello **pede** nec nigris **ocellis**
nec longis **digitis** nec ore sicco
nec sane nimis **elegante lingua**,
decoctoris amica Formiani.   5
ten provincia narrat esse bellam?
tecum Lesbia nostra comparatur?
o saeclum insapiens et infacetum!

Greetings, girl with no small nose, no pretty foot, no dark eyes, nor long fingers, nor dry mouth, and certainly none too stylish a tongue, girlfriend of the bankrupt of Formiae! Does the province call you beautiful, and compare my Lesbia with you? O what a dull and graceless age we live in!

Both poems employ the form known as *blason anatomique*, whereby the woman's body parts are itemized and each in turn praised or criticized. Striking in Catullus' poem, though, is the technique of negative enumeration: The girl's nose is *not* small, her foot *not* pretty, her fingers *not* long, and so on. Catullus' poem, in effect, inverts Philodemus': Where the Greek poet exclaims rapturously over Flora's feet, eyes, hands and (notably) speech, Catullus condemns these same features – in the case of his target, the girlfriend of Mamurra (the "bankrupt of Formiae," 5) – for their *in*elegance. True beauty belongs, in contrast, to Lesbia, as any generation not devoid of judgment and wit would immediately see. In contrast, Philodemus pronounces himself content with Flora, for all her lack of sophistication and culture. The reference to Lesbia seems particularly pointed in this context: The soubriquet of Catullus' *puella* is of course evocative of Sappho – the most famous "woman of Lesbos" – the very poet of whom Philodemus' Flora is said to be ignorant.[40]

---

[40] The adjective *insapiens* (8) is perhaps similarly loaded: Ironically, it is the philosophical Philodemus who turns out to be "unwise," while Catullus implicitly arrogates to himself preeminence in

What is it, then, that Lesbia has and Mamurra's girlfriend lacks? An answer is suggested by another poem that employs the *blason anatomique* structure, poem 86:

> Quintia formosa est multis. mihi candida, longa,
>   recta est: haec ego sic singula confiteor.
> totum illud formosa nego: nam nulla venustas,
>   nulla in tam magno est corpore mica salis.
> Lesbia formosa est, quae cum pulcerrima tota est,   5
>   tum omnibus una omnis surripuit Veneres.

> Many think Quintia beautiful. To me, she's fair-skinned, tall, stands well: I grant her these qualities, listed off like that. But I totally deny her that word "beautiful": For she's no style, no grain of salt/wit in all that tall body. Now *Lesbia* is beautiful: Not only is she utterly lovely, through and through, but she's robbed all other women of all their charm.

Catullus checks off Quintia's qualities, in a way that recalls the lists of body parts in poem 43 and Philodemus' epigram on Flora, but he denies that they add up to "beauty": Quintia lacks the "grain of salt," the indefinable sparkle, and the charm (*venus*) that Lesbia uniquely possesses. Again, the poem virtually reverses the sentiment of Philodemus' epigram: Whereas Flora's physical qualities outweigh her lack of culture, Lesbia's desirability is founded on something very like the *urbanitas* that Catullus values in his male *amici*.[41]

Catullus' intertextual engagement with Philodemus' poem may be seen as symptomatic of a broader contrast in outlook between the two poets. In general, it seems fair to say that Philodemus' fairly numerous erotic epigrams largely complement the pragmatic attitude adopted in *Epigram* 12, and fall into line with Epicurean doctrine on love and sex, as expounded most fully by Lucretius in the finale to *On the Nature of Things* Book 4, where romantic love (or, in Epicurean terms, obsessive desire for an individual sex-object) is unambiguously condemned as a disturbing delusion. Prostitutes are recommended as suitable partners for casual, no-strings sex (4.1071), though Lucretius does perhaps admit a kind of

---

sapientia (in the etymologically primary sense of "good taste" [*OLD* s.v. *sapio* 5]?). (I owe this point to Alison Keith, in discussion at the 2018 Symposium Cumanum.)

[41] For *sal* as a desirable male quality, cf. 12.4 and 14.16, where the reading *salse* (*G*) is to be preferred to *false* (*OR*); cf. also the *sal* that Fabullus is to bring with him to the dinner of poem 13 (5), which may be understood both literally and metaphorically (as suggested by the placement of the word between *vino* and *omnibus cachinnis*). For *venus(tas)* in male *amici*, cf. 13.6 *venuste noster*, and 3.2, 22.2.

de-romanticized partnership based on habit and a realistic assessment of the woman's qualities as an acceptable alternative (4.1190–1191, 1278–1287).[42] Philodemus, admittedly, does not stick consistently to these principles, and at times portrays himself as unable to resist his desire even when he knows it will lead only to grief (*Ep.* 13),[43] or as rejecting the easily available ἑταίρα in favour of the cloistered virgin (*Ep.* 11). So, too, in the first epigram (in Sider's numeration), Philodemus disclaims any understanding of his own passion for Xanthippe, in terms closely echoed by Catullus in the famous *odi et amo* (poem 85): Catullus' *nescio* is particularly reminiscent of the enjambed οὐκ οἶδα at the beginning of line 4 of Philodemus' poem. But elsewhere Philodemus' stance seems more closely in line with Epicurean doctrine: Like Horace (who, indeed, quotes him in this context, *Sat.* 1.2.120–122), Philodemus ridicules those who spend a fortune on adulterous affairs with married women when cheap, casual sex is freely available (*Ep.* 22), and several other epigrams depict dealings with prostitutes or ἑταίραι. If Sider[44] is right to see philosophical coloring in the Xanthippe poems, we might even understand this as an instantiation of the de-romanticized marital or quasi-marital relationship apparently approved by Lucretius at the very end of Book 4: Xanthippe is perhaps depicted as Philodemus' wife, depending on how the textual problem at 7.5 is resolved,[45] and seems to be connected with the theme of misspent youth and its end in *Epigrams* 4–6. Here, Philodemus hails the onset of middle age with its greying hair as the "age of understanding" (συνετῆς . . . ἡλικίης, *Ep.* 4.4, 5.4) and bids farewell to the "madness" of his youth (μανίη, *Ep.* 4.8; cf. 5.2 ἐμάνην), when he indulged himself in wine and women. In *Epigram* 4, the Muses are asked to mark a coronis – or, perhaps, to mark Xanthippe *as* the coronis – signalling the end of his μανία. We can perhaps detect the traces of a narrative trajectory in Philodemus' poetry, according to which the hot passions of youth depicted in such epigrams as 11 and 13 are abandoned as a result of maturity and philosophical enlightenment (if that is the implication of the "loftier thoughts"

---

[42] For different assessments of the tone and implications of these lines, see esp. R. D. Brown: 1987, 371–372 and Nussbaum: 1994, 185–186.

[43] Sider: 1997, 110, accepts the MSS attribution to Philodemus; Gow-Page and others assign this epigram to Meleager, on the basis of the name Heliodora, which appears in several of Meleager's epigrams.

[44] Sider: 1987; 1995; and 1997, 33–36.

[45] Sider prefers the reading φιλεράστρι' ἄκοιτις (a scribal correction in MS *P*) to Schneider's φιλεράστρια κοίτη (for the MS κοίτης). For discussion, see Sider: 1997, 89–90.

envisaged at the end of *Ep.* 5). Xanthippe, on Sider's reading, figures as a fellow-Epicurean, a worthy partner for the philosophically enlightened poet (and we should remember that Epicurus admitted female as well as male disciples to his school). At the same time, the poet declares a preference for the casual liaison (*Ep.* 22; cf. *Ep.* 17.5–6): Whether or not we choose to see a tension here with his apparent devotion to Xanthippe, this stance appears to be in keeping with Epicurean orthodoxy.

Catullus' poetry too has its narrative aspect, and again the contrast with Philodemus is striking. Where Philodemus disclaims the μανία of youth, Catullus appears to welcome the frenzy of his passion for Lesbia, referring to himself as *vesanus Catullus*, "crazed" or "frenzied Catullus" (7.10), urging Lesbia to "live and love" (5.1) and refusing to be content with even an infinite number of kisses. As we have seen, he celebrates his devotion to her in terms borrowed from the lexicon of male *amicitia* and aristocratic obligation, and pursues an adulterous relationship in preference to the casual liaisons recommended by Horace and Lucretius. Even when things go awry between the lovers, Catullus cannot rid himself of his painful feelings for her, which wrack him like a disease (76).

It is in this last respect that intertextual connections with Lucretius seem particularly marked: The cycle of obsession, disillusion and disgust is memorably portrayed at *DRN* 4.1058–1140, where Lucretius asserts that the initial drop of Venus' sweetness leads inevitably to "chill anxiety" (1060), jealousy and regret (1133–1140), and the natural desire for sex becomes a feverish madness, a festering wound that grows worse from day to day. Lucretius ridicules male idealization of women who are in reality just as flawed as any other, and the use of absurd pet-names to conceal (or even celebrate) their faults (1153–1170). Notable here is the phrase *tota merum sal,* literally "pure salt" (1162), applied by the deluded lover to a woman of small stature: Both the phrase and the context resonate with Catullus' idealization of Lesbia in poem 86. Catullus, then, seems a prime example of the obsessive, romantic love which Lucretius attacks. If, as suggested above, we assume that Catullus is responding to Lucretius rather than vice versa, we can again read the intertextual relationship as one of self-conscious antagonism on Catullus' part. The idealization of *amor* as a more-than-physical passion for one, exceptional individual, and as a mutual commitment analogous to male–male *amicitia*, is the precise inverse of Lucretius' denunciation of emotional commitment in favour of a casual, or at most non-passionate, liaison.

Catullus seems again to recall Lucretius, somewhat sardonically, in poem 76, where he admonishes himself of the need to free himself from his *longus amor* (13–14):

> **difficile est** longum subito deponere amorem?
> **difficile est**, verum hoc qua lubet efficias

> Is it hard to lay aside a lasting love all at once? It's hard—but you must do it somehow!

The emphatically repeated – and somewhat prosaic – phrase *difficile est* is used by Lucretius in a similar context (4.1146–1150):

> nam vitare, plagas in amoris ne iaciamur,
> non ita **difficile est** quam captum retibus ipsis
> exire et validos Veneris perrumpere nodos.
> et tamen implicitus quoque possis inque peditus
> effugere infestum, nisi tute tibi obvius obstes ...

> To avoid becoming entangled in the snares of love is not so difficult as to escape those very nets, once trapped, and to break the strong knots of Venus. And yet, even after you have become ensnared and entangled you might escape the danger, if it were not that you stand in your own way ...

In what follows, Lucretius makes it clear that the remedy for the lover's difficulties is simply to stop deluding himself and see his beloved as she really is (4.1171–1191). Catullus, in effect, rejects the prescription: Clear-eyed understanding of Lesbia's "true" character (cf. 72.5, *nunc te cognovi*) has failed to cure him of his passion, and indeed inflamed his desire all the more (72.5, *impensius uror*), so that all he can do now, in a very un-Epicurean move, is to call upon the gods to rescue him from his predicament (76.17–26). Catullus' Lesbia-cycle, then, both confirms and challenges Lucretius' analysis of romantic love: Idealization is followed by disillusion, just as the Epicurean warns; but it is not clear that for Catullus this invalidates the ideal of *amor-amicitia* proclaimed in poem 109; nor – he implies – is it as easy to extricate oneself from the "snares of love" as Lucretius (and, in a slightly different way, Philodemus) suggests.[46]

Conclusion

I return, in closing, to poem 47 and its invective assault on Socration/Philodemus. Philip De Lacy shows, in an important article, that Cicero's

---

[46] Luciani's (2005, 158) assertion that poem 109 represents the fruits of a "maturation psychologique" and embodies "l'idéal d'une volupté stabilisée, qui ... ressemble fort à l'ataraxie vantée par Lucrèce" does not seem to me to be borne out by the text of either poem.

invective against Piso relies heavily on the conventional clichés of anti-Epicurean polemic, many of which can be traced back to Epicurus' lifetime.[47] I suggest that the same goes for Catullus. Porcius and Socration are represented as greedy and unscrupulous parasites, and their patron as a shameless lecher. Similarly, Epicurus and his earliest followers are regularly accused by hostile witnesses of preaching indulgence in the grossest physical pleasures, and of servile flattery towards the politically powerful for their own selfish ends.[48] Catullus' characterization of Piso and his protégés coheres, I have argued, with a tendency throughout the collection to adopt a resolutely unphilosophical – or even anti-philosophical – stance: Intertextual echoes of both Lucretius and Philodemus are suggestive of antagonism rather than sympathy or philosophical alignment. There are, to be sure, points of convergence between the three poets; but ultimately these serve only to point up the markedly different ways in which the Epicurean poets, on the one hand, and the urbane neoteric, on the other, react to the turbulent times in which all three lived and wrote.

---

[47] De Lacy: 1941.

[48] For the former charge, see e.g. DL 10.6–7, Cic. *Nat. D.* 1.113; for the latter, DL 10.4–5, Athen. *Deipn.* 7.279f. Cicero similarly depicts Philodemus as an *adsentator*, too concerned with his own advantage to correct Piso's crude misunderstanding of Epicurean *voluptas* (*Pis.* 70). As Marilyn Skinner (1979, 141) argues, Catullus also draws on the stereotypical figure of the parasite in New Comedy; his use of comic models may be seen, however, as complementary to the element of anti-Epicurean polemic (cf. Damon: 1997, 235–251, for the suggestion that Cicero's portrait of Philodemus can itself be situated within a tradition of caricaturing philosophers as parasites, which can be traced back to Middle Comedy).

PART II

Epicurus and Lucretian Postures

CHAPTER 7

"Love It or Leave It": Nature's Ultimatum in Lucretius' On the Nature of Things (3.931–962)

*Elizabeth Asmis**

Near the end of Book 3 of his poem *On the Nature of Things*, Lucretius personifies Nature and has her issue an ultimatum (3.931–962). Responding to the complaint of humans that they must die, she rebukes her plaintiffs, as though defending herself in a court of law: Either you have experienced pleasure in the life you have lived so far, in which case "why don't you withdraw like a satisfied banqueter?"; or you have taken no pleasure, in which case "why don't you rather put an end to life and toil?"

This ultimatum has traditionally offended readers by its harshness.[1] Why does Lucretius take this turn? He started his poem with a seductive picture of Venus as sole governor of nature (1.21), bringing joy through the renewal of life in the springtime. Subsequently, he addressed the first great fear identified by Epicurus, fear of the gods, by showing that the gods have nothing to do with the governance of the universe: The nature of things does it all, consisting of nothing but atoms and void. Then, in Book 3, Lucretius takes on the second great fear of Epicureanism: the fear of death. Epicurus called death "the most frightening of evils."[2] Following him, Lucretius argues in detail that "death is nothing to us," for there is nothing of us left to experience anything.

Like Epicurus, however, Lucretius well recognizes that there is more to the fear of death than simply the fear of an afterlife. There is also the fear of being deprived of pleasures that one might still have had. To put it another

* This paper is much indebted to the advice I received from the editors of this volume, as well as from audiences at the University of Notre Dame and in Chicago. Special thanks are due to Constance Meinwald and Julie Ward for their acute observations and criticisms. Unless otherwise noted, all citations henceforth will be from Lucretius' *On the Nature of Things*.

[1] The tradition may be traced to Martha: 1896, who quotes the entire ultimatum as primary evidence for his view that true Epicureanism is "triste et sévère" (143). He assigns to the ultimatum a "dureté méprisante" (149). More recently, Warren: 2004 calls the second part of the ultimatum "incredibly harsh" (136).

[2] *Men.* 125: τὸ φρικωδέστατον ... τῶν κακῶν ὁ θάνατος.

way, death seems like an evil because it takes away goods that we look forward to having. In recent decades, scholars have given much attention to this so-called problem of deprivation, and the Epicureans have been widely accused of not having a satisfactory answer.[3] Still, they did address it, and Lucretius elaborated the Epicurean position in new ways. Nature's ultimatum is part of his answer, and this is where Nature stops being nice.

This chapter seeks to show that Nature's ultimatum serves as a way of reinforcing a message that Lucretius has been developing from the beginning of his poem: This is the necessity of accepting the natural conditions of our existence as a prerequisite for the attainment of happiness. Through the ultimatum, Lucretius now formulates this message as a threat: If you do not accept my conditions, Nature warns, you might as well be dead. At the same time, Nature mitigates her threat by showing that the conditions themselves are not harsh. In fact, she has provided us with everything we need to attain happiness within a lifetime. There is nothing to complain about; instead, we ruin our lives of our own will by complaining about what we lack. In sum, Nature does not deprive us, for she has made it possible to flourish fully within the limits she has placed on us.

I shall begin by giving a brief sketch of the ultimatum and raising a number of questions. Next, these questions will be addressed by considering, first, Nature's audience and, second, Nature as speaker. As speaker, Nature reveals the truth about herself. I divide this truth into two parts: Nature's bounty and the sameness of the natural order of things. Nature's case hinges on both the opportunities she has provided and their everlasting sameness. Instead of ever yearning for something new, therefore, we must focus at every time on renewing our pleasure in the present. After returning to the other questions raised initially, I conclude that, through Nature's ultimatum, Lucretius displaces the problem of deprivation from Nature to us: Instead of being deprived, we deprive ourselves by failing to accept the natural order of things.

---

[3] Nagel: 1970 (reprinted in 1979) initiated a vigorous discussion of the problem of deprivation, that is, the "natural view that death is an evil because it brings to an end all the goods that life contains" (1979, 1–2; cf. 1986, 224–225). Luper-Foy: 1987 attacked the Epicureans vehemently for being as indifferent to life as to death. Against Luper-Foy, Rosenbaum: 1989a pointed out that the Epicureans had a positive attitude toward life; he also emphasized the need to appreciate the "revisionistic" character of Epicurus' philosophy (1986, 220). Others who have discussed the Epicurean position on deprivation are: Silverstein: 1980; Mitsis: 1989; Striker: 1989; Annas: 1993, 344–350; Sanders: 2011; and Warren: 2004, esp. 199–212. Lucretius' so-called symmetry argument has been especially prominent in these discussions; see further Warren: 2014.

An Overview and Some Questions

Nature zeroes in on the issue immediately by addressing her plaintiff as a "mortal" (*mortalis*, 3.933). At issue is the traditional complaint of humans: They are doomed to unhappiness because they are mortal instead of immortal. Nature responds by going on the offensive. Directing her attack at "one of us" (*alicui nostrum*, 3.932), she gives her opponent just two choices (3.935–945): Either go to your death satisfied with what you have enjoyed; or, if you have not enjoyed anything, you might as well put an end to your life. In the remainder of the ultimatum (3.946–962), Nature develops her attack by distinguishing between two ages among her detractors: There is the person who is still at the height of his powers and wants more life (3.946–951); and there is the old person, who has become frail and bewails his impending death. Nature heaps abuse on the latter for having missed out on all the pleasures of life (3.952–962). The final words "it is necessary" (*necessest*, 3.962) hammer in the necessity of accepting death.

Nature's speech is likely to strike the reader as not only abusive but also logically defective. In the first place, how sound is her initial disjunction between two kinds of plaintiffs at 3.935–945? The first type is described as one who has enjoyed his previous life (3.935) and has not wasted "all advantages" (3.936–937). This results in a very wide range, from those who have enjoyed life as a whole to those who enjoyed just a little of it. Everyone in this range is said to be "stupid" for not departing like a "full banqueter" (3.938). This entire group is then opposed to those who have not enjoyed anything about their life and hate it (3.940–941). Why does Nature not distinguish an intermediate category (those who have partially enjoyed life and partially disliked it) between two extremes (those who enjoyed life and those who hated it)?

Further, Nature gives no consideration whatsoever to circumstances outside a person's control. Apart from one's vulnerability to disease and violence, there are serious obstacles to acquiring the right kind of education. Lucretius has been stressing all along that we are deeply imbued with false beliefs that make life miserable for us. Epicurus said that it is never too late to engage in philosophy; everyone should engage in it whether young or old (*Men.* 122). Clearly, however, not everyone has the opportunity to attain philosophical enlightenment, and a longer life may provide it. Young persons deserve special consideration on this score, besides missing out on many other opportunities. Lucretius' personified Nature omits any mention of young people. This is made all the more conspicuous by her division of her opponents into those who are still at the height of their powers and those who are already frail with old age. If she exempts the young from her attacks, why does she not do so explicitly? In general, it seems entirely reasonable for any person, young or old, to want to enjoy some pleasure if she has had none, and to want to enjoy more if she has had some. Why does Nature insist on the need to give up these aims, even to the point of giving up life altogether?

By contrast, Philodemus takes a much more complex approach in his treatise *On Death*. He mentions young people a number of times. We "think" of them, he says, as "unfortunate" (δυστυ[χ]εῖς, 14.1) in dying early; and he regards it as reasonable to desire extra time "to be filled (πληρωθῆ[ναι], 14.6–7) with goods."[4] He also credits Pythocles, a student of Epicurus, for already having achieved a huge amount by the age of eighteen; and he recognizes that a "youth" (μειράκιον, 13.9) can get himself "unstinting" (ἄφθ[ον]α, 13.9–10) goods, so as to have lived "more" than those who have lived ever so many years without enjoyment.[5] Further, Philodemus states that it is "natural" for someone who is capable of making philosophical progress to "feel a stab/prick" (νύττεσθαι) at being snatched away by death.[6] Likewise, he says, people feel a "most natural sting" (φυσικώτατον δηγμόν) about leaving family members without their protection.[7] Lucretius' Nature says nothing whatsoever about "stings." What accounts for this difference?

Nature's Audience

Nature's ultimatum has rightly been linked to a Cynic tradition of diatribe.[8] But what is the philosophical point? As I shall argue, Nature has two main reasons for being so harsh. The first concerns her audience. Although Nature says she is addressing "one of us," she is not addressing just anyone. She has a particular target: the type of person who laments "too much." "You," she says, "indulge too much in lamentations that are diseased" (*nimis aegris | luctibus indulges*, 3.933–934). Likewise, the old person "laments more than is right" (*lamentetur ... amplius aequo,*

---

[4] All references to *On Death* are taken from Henry: 2009.   [5] *Ibid.*, cols. 12.34–13.13.
[6] *Ibid.*, col. 17.32–36.
[7] *Ibid.*, col. 25.2–10. See D. Armstrong: 2004 on the variety of pangs or "stings" mentioned by Philodemus in *On Death*. Another example is the "sting" of anger, as discussed by Philodemus in his treatise *On Anger*. Anger is inevitable for all humans, and we feel it as a pain; but we must keep it within bounds, so as to suffer only a sting (D. Armstrong: 2008 and Asmis: 2011). I agree with D. Armstrong: 2008 that "stings" are fully realized emotions.
[8] Wallach: 1976 discusses the Cynic influence in detail.

3.953).[9] Nature directs her remarks at those who transgress the boundary of what is healthy or right. They are in the grip of a disease that Lucretius himself diagnoses a little later as "so great a bad desire for life" (*mala . . . vitai tanta cupido*, 3.1077). Underlying their complaints, therefore, is an excess desire for life.

As so often in Lucretius' poem, we need to bring into consideration a background of theory that Lucretius does not mention explicitly. Epicurus divided desires into natural and unnatural; and he further subdivided natural desires into necessary and natural only.[10] This results in three kinds of desire: natural and necessary; natural and unnecessary; unnatural and unnecessary. The third kind is said to be "empty," for although it aims for pleasure it results in an excess of pain over pleasure. Lucretius' "bad" desire for life belongs to the last, "empty" group. By contrast, Philodemus' "stings" are natural, as he says, for they remain within the boundary of a natural desire for life. We naturally feel a pang, under certain circumstances, when confronted by death. Lucretius' Nature does not reject such pangs; she does not mention them because she directs her attack against excess lamentation.

Epicurus made two further kinds of distinction, which help to explain what is so "bad" about an excessive desire for life. Finally, he subdivided natural and necessary desires in turn into three kinds: necessary for happiness, necessary for bodily comfort and necessary for life itself.[11] Examples of the last category are the desire for food and drink. Importantly, this does not make the desire for life itself a necessary desire. A desire for life is indeed hypothetically necessary (to use Aristotelian terminology), for it is necessary for happiness and bodily comfort, but it is not necessary in itself. The desire for life must come to a stop when confronted by the necessity of death. This makes it a natural desire, bounded by the necessity to yield to death. If it exceeds this boundary, it becomes both unnecessary and unnatural.

The other additional distinction concerns the nature of pleasure. We desire life with a view to attaining its goal, which is happiness, and this consists in pleasure. Epicurean pleasure, however, differs from what we usually think of as pleasure. Epicurus divided it into two kinds: katastematic and kinetic.[12] Very briefly, the former consists of an absence of pain and belongs to the stable condition of a sensory organ or the mind; the

---

[9] So Heinze: 1897, 176: "Hier wird nur das Übermass der λύπη verworfen" ("This is the rejection only of excessive grief").

[10] *Men.* 127–128, KD 29 and U 456.   [11] *Men.* 127.

[12] See DL 10.136 and Cicero *Fin.* 1.37–39 and 2.6–18. Wolfsdorf: 2013, 147–163, provides a useful introduction to the controversies. I agree with Wolfsdorf, as argued previously by Diano: 1940, that kinetic pleasure always supervenes on katastematic pleasure.

latter consists of a movement, or stimulation, of a sensory organ or the mind. To this division, Epicurus added the unique view that the absence of pain is the height of pleasure; kinetic pleasure merely varies the pleasure without increasing it.[13] It follows that, whereas the desire for katastematic pleasure is necessary, the desire for kinetic pleasure is unnecessary. As such, the desire for kinetic pleasure is either natural or unnatural. If natural, it merely varies the pleasure, without adding anything or taking anything away from it; if unnatural, it must be avoided because it results in an excess of pain over pleasure.

The first main reason, then, that Nature is so harsh is that she is addressing people who lament "too much." All transgress the natural boundary of desire. In particular, those who have enjoyed some pleasure fail to be grateful for what they have already attained. As for those who have enjoyed no pleasure, they might as well not go on, for, as will become clearer, they have willingly shut themselves off from having any pleasure in the past.

Nature as Speaker

This brings us to the second main reason for Nature's harshness. It lies in her own role as speaker of the truth about the nature of things. In short, Nature speaks the truth about herself. This is an objective truth, applying to the nature of the universe and everything in it. By nature, Nature tells us, all things are always the same, bounded forever by the same limits. Nature herself cannot change these limits. Within these limits, however, she has provided an abundance of things that we can enjoy. The harshness of Nature's words emphasizes the fixity of these limits, together with her generosity.

Nature's Abundance

I shall first discuss Nature's abundance before turning to the sameness of the order she has established. This benefit needs to be put in context. Lucretius already devoted most of Book 3 to showing another benefit, which is of the utmost importance: the dissolution of the human being at the time of death. By removing a life after death, nature removes the source of a terror that, as Lucretius puts it, leaves no pleasure pure, but "suffuses everything with the blackness of death" (3.38–40). Nature alludes to this

---

[13] KD 3; cf. 2.16–22.

benefit in her ultimatum when she tells her plaintiff to "take with a serene mind a sleep without care, you fool" (3.939, cf. 962).[14]

To this after-death benefit, Nature adds the power to live a life "worthy of the gods" (*dignam dis*, 3.322). Along with inner faculties, as crowned by reason, this requires some external resources. In her ultimatum, Nature refers to these resources as "advantages" or "benefits" (*commoda*) that have been "heaped up" (*congesta*), as it were, into a sieve in the case of those who fail to enjoy them (3.936–937).[15] She also refers to them as "prizes of life" (*vitai praemia*, 3.956). They are not in themselves pleasures; rather they are sources of pleasure, which it is up to us to enjoy.

Lucretius shows us the abundance of these advantages throughout his poem. Family life is a major benefit: Replete with kisses from wife and children and protected by prosperity (*factis florentibus*), it bestows "so many prizes of life" (*tot praemia vitae*, 3.894–899). The products of the crafts are another large fund of prizes of life: They consist in part of things that are useful, such as ships and agriculture, and in part of "delights" such as paintings and poems (5.1448–1456). Greatest of all, Epicurus' discoveries are "prizes" (*praemia*, 5.5) that illuminate the "advantages of life" (*commoda vitae*, 3.2). In addition, Lucretius' poem overflows with depictions of sensory sources of pleasure. Among them, Lucretius singles out acts of sexual intercourse as "advantages" (*commoda*, 4.1074) conferred on us by our sense of touch. In all of these cases, the advantage becomes void if it is contaminated by false opinions.

Overall, this abundance may be divided into two kinds: natural occurrences and craft products or arrangements, as devised by humans. Nature is directly responsible for the former. In an extended sense, she may also be regarded as responsible for both, for she has equipped humans with the inner powers and external resources to develop the crafts and arrange our lives for the best. In either case, Nature presents herself as a kind of cosmic craftsman when she declares that she cannot "devise or invent" any source of pleasure beyond what she has already devised (3.944). This self-portrait is indebted to a long philosophical tradition. Strictly speaking, Epicurean

---

[14] See also 3.904–911 for a contrast between the sleep of death and the unreasonable mourning of those left behind.

[15] The image of the sieve recurs in Lucretius' list of torments, traditionally imputed to the underworld, which Lucretius takes to represent the torments of the life we live. In that passage (3.1003–1010), Lucretius compares the abundance of advantages to the delights that the seasons bring to us throughout the year; cf. 6.20–21. The use of *commoda* (also used by Lucretius at 3.2, 4.1074 and 6.19) suggests the Stoic notion of "advantages" (εὐχρηστήματα, translated as *commoda* by Cicero at *On Ends* 3.69).

nature does not devise anything, for she lacks purposes. Still, by personifying Nature as a craftsman, Lucretius is able to emphasize not only that nature operates in ways that are useful to us, but also that we should be grateful for these benefits. Nature's repeated warning not to let things pass by *ingratum/ingrata* (3.937, 942 and 958), a term that signifies both "unenjoyed" and "without gratitude," implicitly demands such gratitude. This is the correct attitude to Nature's governance, instead of wailing.

There is a precedent for this portrayal of Nature in Epicurus' own extant writings:

> χάρις τῇ μακαρίᾳ φύσει, ὅτι τὰ ἀναγκαῖα ἐποίησεν εὐπόριστα, τὰ δὲ δυσπόριστα οὐκ ἀναγκαῖα.

> Thanks be to blessed Nature, because she made what is necessary easy to obtain (εὐπόριστα) and what is hard to obtain not necessary.[16]

We do not expect the device of personification from Epicurus, nor the divinization that clings to "blessed." It seems he let go, in this case, of his more prosaic self. What prompts his exhortation is the basic ethical tenet that it is naturally easy to satisfy one's necessary desires. Elsewhere, Epicurus says that it is easy to obtain (εὐπόριστα) what is "natural," thereby enfolding the entire range of natural desires.[17] It turns out that we should be grateful to nature for making it easy not only to obtain the height of pleasure, namely, the absence of pain, but also to vary our pleasures with an abundance of kinetic pleasures.

Lucretius rounds out Epicurus' conception of what is "easy to acquire" by the notion of an "abundance" (εὐπορία) of sources of pleasure. Philodemus touches on this abundance when he says that even a young person can enjoy "unstinting" goods (*On Death*, col. 13.9–10). There is, however, a limit to this abundance. As Lucretius argues explicitly in Book 5 in opposition to the notion of divine providence, there is much about the natural arrangement of things that is harmful to humans. Citing numerous examples of hardships, including premature death (*mors immatura*, 5.221), he declares that the nature of things "is endowed with such great fault" (*tanta stat praedita culpa*, 5.199). To confirm the charge, he offers the memorable image of a baby, lying naked on the ground,

---

[16] fr. 469 U. At KD 21, Epicurus claims that the person who "has learned the limits of life knows that what removes pain that is due to deficiency is easy to obtain," as is "that which makes one's whole life complete (παντελῆ)." On the complete life, see below, n. 30.

[17] *Men.* 130: τὸ μὲν φυσικὸν πᾶν εὐπόριστόν ἐστι, τὸ δὲ κενὸν δυσπόριστον. At KD 15, "natural wealth" is said to be "easy to obtain."

"filling the place with funereal wailing, as is right (*aequum*) for someone who must pass through such great evils in life" (5.225–226).

In her ultimatum, by contrast, Nature admits of no blame. How can these two views be reconciled? Behind the Epicurean view, there lurks, I think, a traditional myth: Homer's story of Zeus' two jars, one full of good things, the other filled with bad things, from which Zeus either bestows a mixture of good and bad, or else bestows only bad things (*Il.* 24.527–533). Challenging this myth, Lucretius' Nature insists there are good things, and plenty of them. There is no reason to wail, for humans are naturally endowed with the ability to take their fill of them. What justifies Nature's focus in her ultimatum is that she wants to pull her plaintiffs away from their absorption in what is wrong and to guide them toward a recognition of what is right.

The Natural Sameness of Things

I turn now from Nature's abundance to the sameness of her arrangements. Lucretius introduces this theme in his attack on the sort of person who has wasted all sources of enjoyment so far: Why don't you, she says, just put an end to your life (3.943)? There is a precedent for this piece of advice, too, in Epicurus' extant writings (*Men.* 126–127). Epicurus first attacks one piece of common wisdom – that a young person should live well and an old person die well – by saying that life is not only "welcome" (ἀσπαστόν) but demands the same care in both cases. Then he turns to a saying of Theognis, which he calls "much worse." This is that it is good not to be born, "but if born, to pass as quickly as possible through the gates of Hades." Epicurus responds: If the speaker really means it, why doesn't he leave life? There is a hint that since he has not done so already, he is attracted by life, just like everyone else.

Lucretius takes over the sentiment, but adds an explanation (3.944–995):

> Nam tibi praeterea quod machiner inveniamque,
> quod placeat, nihil est; eadem sunt omnia semper.

> For there is nothing else I can devise and invent that will please you; all things are always the same.

Nature first presents herself, as already mentioned, as the author of all our pleasures. But what does she mean by adding "all things are always the same"? One interpretation, which comes to mind immediately, is: *For you*, given your attitude, things will always be the same, for *you* will always continue to waste whatever source of pleasure comes your way. The upshot is: There is nothing more I can do for you, so why don't you just end your life? On this interpretation, Nature is speaking a truth about the subjective experience of her plaintiff: *For him*, things will always be the same.

There is, however, another possibility. Instead of describing a subjective attitude, Nature is declaring an objective truth about the natural order of things. "All things," she says, "are always the same," for this is how I have arranged all things. This is a universal arrangement, encompassing the universe as a whole and including pleasure as part of the whole. It follows that, unless her plaintiff changes his attitude, he will indeed always be dissatisfied. This is a consequence, however, of what Nature is saying. What she is stating directly is an objective reason for changing one's attitude: Since the arrangement of pleasures (along with everything else in the nature of things) is always the same, it is up to the plaintiff to accept this sameness, instead of always expecting things to be different.

Lucretius emphasizes the fixity of the natural order from the very beginning of his poem, where he first credited Epicurus with discovering the following (1.75–77):

> ... quid possit oriri,
> quid nequeat, finita potestas denique cuique
> qua nam sit ratione atque alte terminus haerens.

> ... what can arise, and what cannot, and for what reason there is, in short, a limited power for each thing and a deep-set boundary stone.

Repeated three more times in the rest of the work, these lines serve as a kind of physical leitmotif for Lucretius' poem.[18] By nature, the development of things is always confined within the same boundaries. As Lucretius makes clear in the second occurrence of the lines, this sameness applies to kinds of things: Each created thing is generically always the same, having the same boundaries of what it can and cannot do, together with a fixed life-time. Lucretius illustrates this truth rather whimsically by the sameness of spots that differentiate the various kinds of birds (1.584–590):

> Denique iam quoniam generatim reddita finis
> crescendi rebus constat vitamque tenendi,
> et quid quaeque queant per foedera naturai,

---

[18] The lines are repeated verbatim at 1.594–596 and at 5.88–90, as well as 6.64–66 with a substitution of *quid queat esse* for *quid possit oriri*. Lucretius also refers to the boundary stone at 2.1087 (*depactus terminus alte*), together with the explanation that it distinguishes kinds of things from one another.

> quid porro nequeant, sancitum quando quidem extat,
> nec commutatur quicquam, quin omnia constant
> usque adeo, variae volucres ut in ordine cunctae
> ostendant maculas generalis corpore inesse. . .

Further, since there is a limit of growth and the preservation of life for things according to their kind and it is ordained by the pacts of nature what each kind can do and cannot do nor does anything change but that all things are so constant to the point that all the various birds in order show that there are generic marks in their body . . .

Lucretius here refers to the arrangements of nature as "pacts" (*foedera*). Like the political pacts that humans make with one another, these natural pacts distribute powers to each kind of thing within fixed limits.[19] Unlike political pacts, however, these natural pacts cannot be broken; and, while they can be ignored, they will nevertheless always endure.

To return to the ultimatum, Nature is so insistent that "all things are always the same" that she repeats the message, with elaboration, in what she says next (3.946–949):

> si tibi non annis corpus iam marcet et artus
> confecti languent, eadem tamen omnia restant,
> omnia si perges vivendo vincere saecla,
> atque etiam potius, si numquam sis moriturus.

If your body is not already withering with years and your limbs do not yet languish from being used up, yet all things remain the same, if you should live on to outdo all generations or even more, if you should never die.

Nature now singles out the sort of plaintiff who is still at the height of his powers and still has some time left to live. Suppose now that he could live longer – much longer, and even forever. All things would still remain the same (especially if he were to live forever). At this point, it seems to me the subjective interpretation recedes into implausibility. The repetition of "all things," together with the extension of their sameness to infinity, suggests ontological concreteness rather than a personal attitude. We now see the plaintiff as an observer, confronted by the objective sameness of all things for all time, rather than merely as a sufferer wrapped up in his own subjective misery. The sameness of things does indeed condemn to unending misery those who do not recognize it as a source of pleasure. For those

---

[19] The "pacts (*foedera*) of nature" are mentioned also at 2.302 and 5.310; cf. 5.57. Specific examples of natural "pacts" are the relationship between the irrational soul and the mind (3.416) and the power of the magnet to attract iron (6.906–907). See further Asmis: 2008, 141–149.

who do, however, it offers a path to happiness. There is nothing inherently distressing about the natural sameness of things, nor is it inevitably boring (as commentators tend to suggest), but it provides an opportunity to enjoy life to the fullest.[20] Just as the gods enjoy to the fullest the infinitely extended sameness of their lives, so it is possible for humans to enjoy fully the finite sameness of their lives.

Nature rises to a height of invective in the final section of her ultimatum. She now returns to the theme of a full life by adding the example of an old person, who has become feeble. He has "gone through all the prizes of life" by letting them slip past him (3.956–960):

> omnia perfunctus vitai praemia marces;
> sed quia semper aves quod abest, praesentia temnis,
> inperfecta tibi elapsast ingrataque vita,
> et nec opinanti mors ad caput adstitit ante
> quam satur ac plenus possis discedere rerum.

> You are withered, having gone through all the prizes of life. But because you always yearn for what is absent, you have contempt for what is present and your life, incomplete, has slipped away from you without enjoyment and death has come to stand unexpectedly at your head before you can depart sated and full of things.

Paradoxically, the old man's life is incomplete, even though he is on the brink of death. This is an appeal to Epicurus' conception of a "complete" life. In opposition to the conventional view of a biologically complete life, Epicurus identified a complete life as one for which "the mind has reasoned out the limits of corporeal pleasure and removed the fears concerning eternity."[21] Such a life, Epicurus adds, does not require an infinite time; nor does this sort of person go to his death, whenever it is ready for him, in such a way as to either "flee" pleasure or consider anything "lacking from the best life." A finite period contains "equal pleasure" as an infinite time.[22] It follows that the prolongation of pleasure, after one has achieved a complete life, adds nothing to one's pleasure.[23] The reason, as mentioned earlier, is that all we need in order to obtain the

---

[20] Bernard Williams: 1973 offers an interesting perspective on boredom in an influential article called "The Makropulos case: reflections on the tedium of immortality." Here he takes the story of a woman singer who took an elixir of life and lived to the age of 342, with the consequence of becoming utterly bored: "In the end," says the woman, "it is the same, singing and silence" (82); and she puts an end to her life. Williams argues that, given the woman's personal characteristics, things would end up being always the same so as to become unbearably boring. On the Epicurean view, as I try to show, boredom afflicts those who do not know how to enjoy pleasure.

[21] KD 20.   [22] KD 19.   [23] Cicero *Fin.* 2.87–88; cf. *Men.* 126.

maximum of pleasure is the absence of pain, or katastematic pleasure, for both body and mind.

Lucretius avoids going into these details. Instead, he supplies the basic reason why a person has not achieved a complete life: He has let slip by his opportunities. Here, again, he is following Epicurus, who warned against always deferring one's enjoyment.[24] Lucretius, however, goes further: He underpins Epicurus' ethical injunction with an argument derived from his physics. He shows what is wrong about letting go of one's opportunities by having Nature argue that things are always the same. Just as the man in his prime is forever looking for what is new, so the old man is forever seeking what is absent. Both ignore the natural sameness of things by fleeing forever toward what is different.

In short, Nature berates humans for refusing to take their place in the order she has established. Lucretius later sums up this message in his own words in his conclusion to Book 3. Straining to make his meaning clear, he declares (3.1080–1084):

> praeterea versamur ibidem atque insumus usque
> nec nova vivendo procuditur ulla voluptas;
> sed dum abest quod avemus, id exsuperare videtur
> cetera; post aliud, cum contigit illud, avemus
> et sitis aequa tenet vitai semper hiantis.

> We are situated in the same place and are forever within it, nor is any new pleasure hammered out by a continuation of life. But while we yearn for what is absent, this seems to surpass all the rest; afterward, when it happens, we yearn for another, and an equal thirst for life holds us with our mouths forever agape.

The first verse is noteworthy for the density of meaning. *versamur* has a wide range of meanings, including "dwell," "live," and "are situated." In addition to suggesting placement, it has the connotation of being active. *ibidem*, "in the same place," picks up the spatial sense, as does *insumus*, which reinforces the idea of being contained in a place. The second verse reiterates Nature's claim that she cannot devise any new pleasures; the verb *procuditur*, "hammered out," suggests her role as a craftsman. By nature, all pleasures have already been hammered out as a condition for our having a place within the world.

---

[24] VS 14: σὺ δὲ οὐκ ὢν τῆς αὔριον ⟨κύριος⟩ ἀναβάλλῃ τὸ χαῖρον· ὁ δὲ βίος μελλησμῷ παραπόλλυται καὶ εἷς ἕκαστος ἡμῶν ἀσχολούμενος ἀποθνῄσκει ("You, who are not <master> of tomorrow, put off enjoyment. Life is destroyed by deferment, and each of us dies by not providing himself with leisure").

The entire summary confirms, in my view, the objective reading of Nature's insistence that all things are always the same. Objectively, we are always situated in the same place in the natural order of things, so as to have always the same powers to enjoy the same pleasures. Humans ignore this truth by yearning forever to step beyond these boundaries, with the result that we are forever dissatisfied. This is to run away, as it were, from our present, unalterable situation to an empty realm of fancy.

Lucretius offers a visual image of this very situation at 3.1053–1075, prior to the cited summary. He imagines a person who is so burdened by the fear of death that he keeps wanting to "change his place" (*commutare locum*, 3.1059).[25] Bored with life in his urban mansion, he rushes off to his country villa; and once he gets there, he immediately yawns and either falls into a deep sleep or rushes back to the city. Behind the literal change of place lies a deeper yearning. As Lucretius explains, what this person really wants is to escape his own diseased self. Not realizing, however, what ails him, he is forever caught in a futile frenzy to put his own self behind him. The right way to live, Lucretius implies, is to be grounded in one's natural condition, taking advantage of the pleasures that are available within these boundaries. The sameness of nature is a kind of haven, or home, where one must stay put in order to live a full life.

If this is right, what makes Nature so harsh is that she is dealing with run-aways, as it were, who fail to recognize that she has provided for them a place, which is always the same, where they may attain full happiness. Their life has fixed boundaries, but these boundaries enclose a space that is full of opportunities for happiness. Although the conditions are always the same, the place is not boring; rather, it flourishes with opportunity. What is devastating, on the other hand, is the frustration that comes from trying to escape it.

---

[25] See 3.1057–1059 and 1068–1070:

> ut nunc plerumque videmus
> quid sibi quisque velit nescire et quaerere semper
> commutare locum, quasi onus deponere possit.
> . . .
> hoc se quisque modo fugit, at quem scilicet, ut fit,
> effugere haut potis est, ingratis haeret et odit
> propterea morbi quia causam non tenet aeger.

. . . as we now generally see people not knowing what each wants and always seeking to change place, as though one were able to put down a burden . . . In this way, everyone flees himself; yet he clings unwillingly to himself, whom he cannot, in fact, escape, and hates himself because, in his illness, he is unable to see its cause.

Conclusion

How does this help with the problems I noted earlier? Here, I can offer only a bare sketch. First, there is the disjunction between those who have enjoyed their previous life, whether in part or as a whole, and those who have had no enjoyment. Like Epicurus, Lucretius has no patience with those who lament a life of no enjoyment: They are simply irrational. There remain those who have enjoyed life, even if only in part, yet mourn their death. They, too, are fools, for they failed to transform the pleasure they had into a full banquet, or a complete life. At bottom, all these complainers are alike; for whatever pleasure they had leaves them dissatisfied.

Further, Nature appears to ignore the difficulty of rooting out false opinions, as well as the special problems confronting young people. One way to respond is to appeal to Epicurus' distinction among three types of causes: Some things, he says, happen by "necessity," others by "chance" and others by "our own responsibility."[26] Epicurus called chance "unstable" (ἄστατον); he also said that chance furnishes "starting-points for great goods and evils." In her ultimatum, Nature focuses on one type of necessity: the fixity of the natural order of things, with special attention to the limits of pleasure. Epicurus' description of chance as "unstable" marks a contrast with this stability. Lucretius' Nature ignores chance, not because it does not exist, but because it falls outside her realm as an everlastingly fixed arrangement of the universe. Instead, she pairs personal responsibility with the necessity of her arrangement of things in order to impress on us our responsibility for accepting our place within the natural order of things.

One may object that Nature has arranged things in such a way as to give enormous scope to chance and, furthermore, has made humans unduly weak, both physically and intellectually. Still, she might argue, she has conferred on us both the inner strength and the external resources we need in order to use chance as a starting-point for good things, instead of letting it defeat us. There

---

[26] *Men.* 133–134 (Hessler); cf. fr. 375 U. The text in *Men.* is unfortunately faulty: <ἀλλὰ γίγνεσθαι κατ' ἀνάγκην ἃ μὲν πάντων> ἀγγέλλοντος, ἃ δὲ ἀπὸ τύχης, ἃ δὲ παρ' ἡμᾶς ... τὴν δὲ τύχην ἄστατον ὁρᾶν ... ἀρχὰς μέντοι μεγάλων ἀγαθῶν ἢ κακῶν ὑπὸ ταύτης χορηγεῖσθαι ("But he reports that, of all things, some come to be by necessity, others by chance, and others by our responsibility ... chance is unstable to look upon ... yet starting-points for great goods or evils are furnished by it"). I accept the sense of Hessler's supplements in 133, although I do not see the need for inserting πάντων; see also Verde: 2013. As Hessler: 2012, 307 points out, the clause introduced by διὰ lists the reasons for rejecting the determinism of fate. At 134, I accept Lewy's emendation of βέβαιον in place of MSS ἀβέβαιον. In the same passage, Epicurus also rejects the necessity that consists in "the fate (εἱμαρμένη) of the physicists." What makes him reject this kind of necessity is its incompatibility with personal responsibility; see Morel: 2013.

are exceptions: As Seneca attests, there is no necessity to put up with necessity; one is always free to make an end to life.[27] This is a different kind of necessity from the necessity of natural limits; and it appears to be viewed as rare.[28] As for the special problem of youth, neither Epicurus nor any other source specifies the amount of time that a person needs to achieve a complete life.[29] What is needed, in the first place, is a period of learning, then a period of living with happiness.[30] In principle, there seems to be no reason why a person might not be so gifted as to achieve a complete life while still young; but this would likely be difficult.[31] This difficulty would help to explain why, in her speech, Nature neither exempts young people nor singles them out for attack. There is no reason for anyone to bewail the prospect of death; but the middle-aged and the old are especially culpable for doing so.

This brings us to the problem of deprivation in general, as it applies to anyone at all, young or old, wise or fool. Granted that it is natural for a person to desire life, as attended by pleasure, how is it not a deprivation to have death cut off pleasure? Bernard Williams held that the desire for life is categorical, as opposed to the type of desire that is conditional on being alive.[32] On the Epicurean view, the desire for pleasure fits the latter category. In addition, however, the desire for life is itself conditional in the sense that

---

[27] Seneca *Ep.* 12.10 (U 487): "there is no necessity to live in necessity" (*in necessitate vivere necessitas nulla est*); see also VS 9 and 44, as well as Cic. *Fin.* 1.62.

[28] Englert: 1994 emphasizes the rarity of such exigencies. Morel: 2000 takes them as "externes de la nature et des hommes" ("external to nature and to human beings") (82), as exemplified by political or social constraints (85–88). He also lists them (2013, 173) as one of three types of necessity recognized by Epicurus.

[29] Cicero (*Fin.* 2.87–88) glosses Epicurus' "finite" time by "short" and "moderate" but the brevity may be understood simply in contrast with infinite time. Sanders: 2011, 227 takes Philodemus' remarks on Pythocles at *On Death*, cols. 12.34–13.2, as evidence that one can attain wisdom at a "relatively early age"; but Philodemus does not say so explicitly.

[30] Warren: 2004, 130–135 raises the question of whether a complete life requires a "certain finite duration" or whether it is achieved "as soon as the highest state of pleasure is reached"; and he assigns scholars to both sides. He himself thinks that the former interpretation is more likely. In my view, a complete life necessarily happens over a period of experiencing life, for the Epicurean goal of life is a process of living with pleasure, which necessarily occupies a stretch of time. As Warren notes (150–151), Philodemus provides evidence for the first option at *On Death* col. 19.1–3: νῦν [δὲ σ]οφῶι γενομένωι καὶ ποσὸν | χρόνο[ν ἐ]πιζήσαντ[ι] τὸ μέγιστον ἀγα|θὸν ἀπε[ί]ληπται ("As it is, when he has become wise and lived on for a quantity of time, he has obtained the greatest good"). Here, as elsewhere (cols. 3.34 and 13.3), Philodemus refers to the finite stretch of happiness as ποσὸς χρόνος, "a quantity of time." In my view, the perfect tense of ἀπε[ί]ληπται marks the completion of a period of happiness. Likewise, a stretch of time is presupposed at col. 38.14–16 for "having obtained what is able to bring about complete self-sufficiency for a happy life"; after this period of self-sufficiency, every day is an added bonus.

[31] So Warren: 2004, 134 and 154. If, as Annas: 1993, 349 has suggested, one needs to have a plan for one's whole life in order to achieve a complete life, the odds do seem stacked against a young person. In Striker's (1989, 327) view, "a very short life could not possibly be complete."

[32] Williams: 1973, 85–88.

one must yield to the necessity of death. It is futile to desire life beyond its natural boundary. Lucretius' Nature shows how to live within this boundary: One must avail oneself of one's present opportunities so as to reach the goal of a complete life within a finite period.[33] The person who does so accepts death, whenever he is confronted by its necessity, with gratitude for what he has had. By contrast, the person who has wasted his opportunities rejects death, lamenting his demise as a deprivation.

Given one's natural desire for life, then, how is it possible to put a limit to it. Thomas Nagel's distinction between a subjective and an objective point of view underscores the difficulty, but also suggests an answer. Taking a subjective view, we view death as an evil because it deprives us of goods that we might still have had; taking an objective view, we see ourselves as a contingent, dispensable part of the world, needing to give up goods. This results in a clash, Nagel believes, which cannot be fully resolved.[34] The Epicureans claim that it can be resolved by the victory of reason, which takes an objective point of view, over desires that are merely subjective. Lucretius puts Nature on the scene to demand this victory: While harsh to those who refuse to yield to reason, she holds out the promise of a fully contented life to those who recognize themselves as they really are – as a part of nature. The pangs that Philodemus mentions are a sign of the clash, but they are overcome in the end by a rational recognition of the objective conditions of our existence.[35]

---

[33] Some scholars have objected that the Epicurean arguments on death serve to make us indifferent not only to death but also to life by depriving us of any reason to prolong life; so Williams: 1973, 83–84, Silverstein: 1980, 409–410 and Warren 2004: 202–212. As Warren puts it: "The Epicureans appear to offer no significant positive reason for wishing to continue to live, beyond mere inertia" (210). This applies, in Warren's view (211), equally to those who have achieved a complete life. As I have argued, the Epicurean is motivated by the desire for pleasure for as long as he lives, subject only to the condition that he must give it up when it is necessary to die. He loses nothing by giving up the desire; but this does not make him indifferent to life for as long as there is no necessity to die (as demonstrated by Epicurus' own death).

[34] Nagel: 1970 (reprinted in 1979); 1979, 196–213; and 1986, 208–231. Nagel writes in his 1970 article, as reprinted at 1979, 9–10: "A man's sense of his own experience . . . does not embody [the] idea of a natural limit," such as that of mortality, which is "normal to the species." He concludes at 1986, 231: "The objective standpoint may try to cultivate an indifference to its own annihilation, but there will be something false about it; the individual attachment to life will force its way back even at this level."

[35] Metrodorus (VS 47) goes so far as to celebrate this victory as an act of "spitting upon life," worthy of a triumphal song. This attitude casts light, I think, on Philodemus' remarkable description of the person who has achieved the self-sufficiency of a happy life as someone who henceforth, for the rest of his life, "walks about laid out for burial" (ἐντεταφιασμένος περιπατεῖ, *On Death*, col. 38.17–18), taking advantage of each single day as an eternity. It was customary to dress a corpse in ceremonial outfits that were indicative of one's highest achievements, such as an honorary crown (see Cicero *Leg.* 2.60, Lucian *Luct.* 11–12 and Hope: 2009, 72–73). Thus, we are not to see this person as one of the "walking dead," but as someone flourishing at the height of happiness, while prepared for the necessity of death.

Finally, what does Nature have to do with Venus? As Monica Gale and others have shown, Lucretius creates myths of his own to counteract the pernicious myths of the past.[36] He starts his poem by putting Venus on the scene to represent the joy of life. Death is a different matter. When he comes to the topic, Lucretius again offers an anti-myth: Unlike traditional deities, his personified Nature is immovable, both in the sameness of the conditions she has established and in the demand that we accept her conditions. This personification complements the image of Venus we saw initially; for the limits she has placed on our existence are laden with all the pleasures we need to live life to the fullest.

[36] See Gale: 1994.

CHAPTER 8

Kitsch, Death and the Epicurean

Pamela Gordon [*]

The exhortation *carpe diem* – a hackneyed counsel offered along with instructions to pour the wine – reduces Epicureanism to a trite saying. Similarly cloying is a platitude lampooned by Lucretius: "Brief is this pleasure for us insignificant humans; soon it will have passed, and we can never call it back" (*brevis hic est fructus homullis; | iam fuerit neque post umquam revocare licebit*, 3.914–915). These trivializations are not merely simplifications of a serious philosophical position. Rather, as I shall explain, "Epicurean" platitudes are profoundly anti-Epicurean. To put it another way: From its inception, Epicureanism was fundamentally opposed to kitsch. This essay explicates that anti-kitsch stance and explores how Lucretius combats kitsch, even as kitsch was enthusiastically circulated in other Roman contexts in the form of Epicurean objects and clichés. My concern is the ethical rather than the aesthetic ramifications of kitsch, and my primary focus is the revelation of Epicurean thanatology in the third book of *On the Nature of Things* that is often described as a diatribe against the fear of death. I offer my reading not as a replacement of that apt identification, but as a supplement. My argument is that the most vehement strains of Lucretius' diatribe against the fear of death are a polemic against kitsch, and that this polemic intersects with a broader Epicurean tradition of frank criticism.

Rather than starting with a definition of kitsch and a defense of my anachronistic use of a modern concept, let me open with a simple Epicurean pronouncement most likely culled from a larger work: "Against other things it is possible to find security, but when it comes to death we human beings all dwell in an unwalled city," (Πρὸς μὲν τἆλλα δυνατὸν ἀσφάλειαν πορίσασθαι, χάριν δὲ θανάτου πάντες ἄνθρωποι πόλιν ἀτείχιστον οἰκοῦμεν, VS 31). In its original context, the metaphor of the defenseless city may have been complex enough to reveal Epicurus'

[*] I owe heartfelt thanks to Tess Cavagnero, Mike Pope and the editors of this volume.

specific cultural location as he wrote in proximity to the Athenian Acropolis and the Long Walls. But the isolation of the metaphor as it has survived magnifies its blunt representation of the vulnerability of all human life. The starkness of the image is an Epicurean stand against kitsch. I use the term kitsch as it appears in Milan Kundera's novel *The Unbearable Lightness of Being*, in which the narrator asserts that "kitsch is a folding screen set up to curtain off death."[1] Kundera's metaphor is more useful than a dictionary entry, and in the course of this essay I will supplement Kundera's sweeping declarations on the essence of kitsch with further elucidations.

Putrefaction

Before examining the confrontation with kitsch in *On the Nature of Things*, it is necessary to take a closer look at Kundera's account of kitsch. Kitsch, he writes, is a word born in Germany "in the middle of the sentimental nineteenth century."[2] Since then it has been used to describe paintings of Elvis on velvet, bad poems about sunsets and drawings of large-eyed kittens. But by focusing on what he sees as the fundamental urge that creates kitsch, Kundera returns us to a deeper import of the word:

> Behind all the European faiths, religious and political, we find the first chapter of Genesis, which tells us that the world was created properly, that human existence is good, and that we are therefore entitled to multiply. Let us call this basic faith a categorical agreement with being.[3]

For Kundera, this "categorical agreement with being" requires a refusal to acknowledge the existence of excrement.[4] Thus Kundera's narrator in *The Unbearable Lightness of Being* describes the ideal he calls kitsch as "the absolute denial of shit, in both the literal and the figurative senses of the word; kitsch excludes everything from its purview which is essentially unacceptable in human existence."[5] In a world of kitsch, no one eliminates and nothing rots.

Ways of thinking that require kitsch, and the various shapes in which kitsch appears, are of course not universal or timeless, and readers may

---

[1] Kundera: 1984, 253. Compare Kundera: 2006, 51: Kitsch is "a rosy veil thrown over reality." On the moral, rather than exclusively aesthetic, ramifications of kitsch, see Bielskis: 2018, who stresses that kitsch is formative: "It makes people pursue banal dreams."
[2] Kundera: 1984, 248.   [3] *Ibid.*, 248.   [4] Kundera is in some ways indebted to Broch: 1933.
[5] Kundera: 1984, 248.

reasonably protest that I am rashly coopting a term designed for a critique of modern culture. Nonetheless, my hypothesis is that for Lucretius, kitsch is the absolute denial of putrefaction. To refuse to acknowledge putrefaction is to deny that everything is mortal, that the nature of things is larger than human existence and that "the entire world can be felled with a shocking, resounding crash" (*succidere horrisono posse omnia victa fragore*, Lucr. 5.109). This is why Lucretius refers so directly to the decomposition of the body in his most trenchant and sarcastic attacks against kitsch in the third book of *On the Nature of Things*. To some extent, moreover, Lucretius' repudiation of kitsch may be understood as the impetus behind the harrowing description of the plague at the conclusion of the epic.[6]

One sign of Lucretius' unflinching stare at death appears in the "vivid and repellent picture of the wriggling mass of white maggots" that are one of Lucretius' demonstrations that a soul cannot survive the destruction of the body intact.[7] For Lucretius, some particles of the soul remain in the decaying flesh (3.717–721):

> sin ita sinceris membris ablata profugit,
> ut nullas partis in corpore liquerit ex se,
> unde cadavera rancenti iam viscere vermes
> expirant atque unde animantum copia tanta
> exos et exanguis tumidos perfluctuat artus?

> But if it has departed and fled forth with its component parts so intact that it has left in the body no particles of itself, how do corpses exhale worms from flesh already grown putrid, whence comes all the great mass of living creatures, boneless and bloodless, that surge through the swelling limbs?[8]

The gleeful wordplay of *viscere vermes* ("from flesh ... worms") expresses latent inevitability. Like Lucretius' well-known *ignis/lignis* puns (1.905, 1.907, 1.912 and 2.386–387) that capture the idea of wood (*lignis*) containing atoms capable of making fire (*ignis*), the phrase *viscere vermes* signals that flesh yields inexorably to worms. The poet follows this with an image of souls hunting for new homes among the maggots, "an especially outré example" of Lucretius' use of a sarcastic *reductio ad absurdum* of an opposing explanation (3.727–729).[9]

After describing the finality of death and the mortality of the soul, Lucretius sums things up with frank Epicurean wisdom: "Therefore death is nothing to us" (*Nil igitur mors est ad nos*, 3.830), and he explains

---

[6] I will explore Lucretius' presentation of the plague in a future essay.   [7] Kenney: 2014, 168.
[8] In this essay I quote Rouse's Loeb translation (as revised by Smith), with slight modifications.
[9] Kenney: 2014, 168.

dispassionately that death is so final that it is as though we had never been born "once immortal death has taken away mortal life" (*mortalem vitam mors cum inmortalis ademit*, 3.869). But then we have an abrupt change of tone. As E. J. Kenney writes of lines 870–893, "this is the point where the diatribe-satirist takes over"[10] (3.870–875):

> Proinde ubi se videas hominem indignarier ipsum,
> post mortem fore ut aut putescat corpore posto
> aut flammis interfiat malisve ferarum,
> scire licet non sincerum sonere atque subesse
> caecum aliquem cordi stimulum, quamvis neget ipse
> credere se quemquam sibi sensum in morte futurum

> Accordingly, when you see a man resenting his fate, that after death he must either rot with his body laid in the tomb, or perish by fire or the jaws of wild beasts, you may know that he rings false, and that deep in his heart is some hidden sting, although himself he deny the belief in any sensation after death.

The essential word *indignarier* ("to resent") connotes irrational indignation and childish whining, and reappears when Lucretius adds that the complainer "resents that he was born mortal" (*indignatur se mortalem esse creatum*, 3.884). Servius Sulpicius Rufus uses the same term to describe misguided resentment "of us manikins" in a letter to Cicero after the death of Tullia (*Fam.* 4, 5, 4; 248 SB, March 45 BC). The letter avoids Lucretius' graphic clarity, but the implication is clear: Death and decay are compulsory conditions, and protestations are futile.

When used in reference to the human body, the term *putescere* has shock value, as does its English cognate "putrefaction." The phrase *corpore posto* (3.871) probably connotes placement in a grave, and *putescat* (3.871) could serve as a matter-of-fact reference to the decomposition of the interred body after a conventional funeral. Nonetheless, the word *putescat* conjures up the notion of defilement and a body's resultant disgusting odor and appearance.[11] The word *putescere* is at home in the context of abandoned corpses, as when Cicero describes a body ignominiously left out to rot (*Tusc.* 1.102) and Horace describes what happens to the dishonored Ajax when burial is denied (*cur Ajax putescit*, *Sat.* 2.3.194). Comparison with Diogenes of Oenoanda's reference to rotting flesh is instructive, and both he and Lucretius may have had a common source. Diogenes of Oenoanda writes that he does not fear Hades or shudder at the

---

[10] *Ibid.*, 188.
[11] Lucretius also uses *putescere* when he describes how the body "rots away" after it is "ripped" from the soul (*convulsi conque putrescunt*, 3.343).

thought of the putrefaction (μύδησις) of the body (fr. 73 Smith). Elsewhere μυδάω and μύδησις (relatively infrequent words) appear in medical treatises to describe necrosis, ulcerated flesh and infected eyelids (Aret. *CD* 1.4; Galen 14.770; HP *VC.* 15). Significantly, Sophocles uses μύδησις in the context of the horrific exposure of the body of Polynices, the state of which compels the guards to sit up wind (Soph. *Ant.* 410). Lucretius' reference to "birds and beasts" (*volucres . . . feraeque*, 3.880–883) brings to mind the "classic fate of the unburied corpse in literary allusion from Homer onwards."[12] Whether conceived as oblivion or as rotting flesh, death is nothing to the Epicurean. Lucretius stresses the absurdity of the fear of mistreatment after death with the stark image of an impossibility: The deceased standing by in horror as he witnesses his own defiled corpse (3.879–883).

misero misere

Lucretius' blunt references to worms and the decomposition of the body compel the reader to face the stark reality of death. With each elaboration of the theme, the reader sheds another false fear and clings less tightly to commonplace beliefs in immortality. But if his concern is kitsch that obscures the inescapable finality of one's own death, why does Lucretius focus such harsh and unsympathetic attention on the lamentations of the bereaved? Here it is important to keep all of Book 3 in view. After ridiculing the fear of the mistreatment of one's own corpse, Lucretius asserts that one may as well be afraid of being disposed of in a conventional manner: being set on fire, piled over with heavy earth or – a reference to embalmment – being suffocated with honey (while already dead). But then Lucretius shifts abruptly to a vignette of mourners bewailing the death of a young father. The scene offers a brief but vivid picture of the bereft home, wife and children. The lampoon of these grief-stricken mourners displays a sarcasm that seems to many readers particularly gratuitous, misdirected and even cruel (3.894–899):

> "Iam iam non domus accipiet te laeta neque uxor
> optima, nec dulces occurrent oscula nati
> praeripere et tacita pectus dulcedine tangent.
> non poteris factis florentibus esse tuisque
> praesidium. misero misere" aiunt "omnia ademit
> una dies infesta tibi tot praemia vitae."

---

[12] Kenney: 2014, 190. Kenney accepts in part Feeney's (1978, 6) assertion that "birds and dogs, not birds and beasts, are the classic eaters of corpses."

"No longer now will your happy home give you welcome, no longer will your best of wives; no longer will your sweet children race to win the first kisses, and thrill your heart to its depths with sweetness. You will no longer be able to live in prosperity, and protect your own. Wretched man, wretchedly taken!" they say, "one fatal day has robbed you of all these prizes of life."

Two aspects of this passage are parodic. First, the allusion to the happy home is expressed in overly sentimental language. In another time and place, the children would be emerging from the gate of the proverbial picket fence. Second, grief is expressed here in markedly maudlin tones. The words *optima* ("the best") and *dulcis* ("sweet") are typical epithets on sepulchral monuments, and the colloquial phrase *misero misere* ("wretched . . . wretchedly") sounds especially mawkish, as does *una dies infesta* ("one hateful day").[13] Kenney aptly stresses the "scornful echoes of the clichés of mourning," but protests that Lucretius' "implicit rejection of the natural concern of a man for what will happen to his family when he dies, though of a piece with his scornful rejection of all conventional mourning, denies a basic human need."[14] To further emphasize Lucretius' apparent lack of human understanding, Kenney adds that the concern for survivors, when expressed by Homer's Hector as he parts forever with Andromache, "forms part of one of the most moving episodes in all literature."[15] But perhaps this is the point: Although nothing in Lucretius' language suggests a lampoon specifically of the *Iliad*, Lucretius may be mimicking clichéd imitations.

Tobias Reinhardt has argued that the shift in perspective from the readers' fear of their own deaths to the topic of mourning the death of someone else is due to Lucretius' determination to keep the focus on irrational fear. He notes the following: "What Lucretius is doing is trading one argument for the other, offering us an argument that is actually pertinent only to a particular kind of grief and to the fear of *being dead*."[16] For Reinhardt, Lucretius is aware that a parent's fear of dying young, and leaving the children defenseless, is a rational fear – when viewed from the perspective of a parent's wish to protect a child. Such a fear might reasonably trouble a living parent. But the novice Epicurean reader is not yet equipped to comprehend the full Epicurean response to that reasonable fear, so Lucretius needs the reader to focus single-mindedly

---

[13] Kenney: 1971, 205, calls Lucr. 3.898–399 "deliberately banal."   [14] Kenney: 2014, 193.
[15] Kenney: 2003, 193, citing Hom. *Il.* 6.456–465.
[16] Reinhardt: 2002, 293, emphasis in original.

on the simple argument that the dead have no concerns. A parent who no longer exists cannot miss the children. Reinhardt is right to examine how Lucretius steers the reader's philosophical progress as the books of the epic unfold. But his explanation is not entirely satisfying as an answer to the question of why Lucretius satirizes grief. Why does the poem turn so abruptly to a send-up of lamentation for someone whose passing might reasonably distress us: A man who has left behind his young family? Here too, a consideration of late twentieth-century explorations of the concept of kitsch is illuminating. When its broadest trajectory is read as a polemic against kitsch, the coherence of Lucretius' attack on the fear of death becomes clearer. In *Kitsch and Art*, Thomas Kulka writes that "[t]he success of kitsch depends on the universality of the emotions it elicits."[17] Their spontaneous response to a kitschy work of "art" pleases its consumers, but so does their awareness that they are responding in the right way, the way that everyone else responds. Here Kulka quotes Kundera's well-known concept of the second tear:

> Kitsch causes two tears to flow in quick succession. The first tear says: How nice to see children running on the grass.
>
> The second tear says: How nice to be moved, together with all mankind, by children running on the grass!
>
> It is the second tear that makes kitsch kitsch.[18]

In the second tear there is an element of self-congratulation, but also a pleasure in this manifestation of universality. Continuing his own exploration of the definition of kitsch, Kulka writes: "It breeds on universal images ... Since the purpose of kitsch is to please the greatest possible number of people, it always plays on the most common denominators."[19] For Kulka, three conditions are essential. First, kitsch displays objects or concepts that are "highly charged with stock emotions." Second, the subject matter must be immediately and effortlessly recognizable. Third, "kitsch does nothing substantial to enrich our associations relating to the depicted objects or themes."[20] Although his focus is on the visual arts, and the examples he cites are conventionally pleasing (puppies, kittens, cute children), Kulka's observations are relevant to the stock phrases indulged in by Lucretius' lugubrious mourners of the prematurely departed father.

The mourners, Lucretius continues, ought to add that the dead have no yearning for the pleasures whose loss they lament (3.900–901). Taking

---

[17] Kulka: 1996, 27.   [18] Kundera: 1984, 251.   [19] Kulkas: 1996, 27.   [20] *Ibid.*, 37–38.

another tack, the mourners continue with a reference to the endless sleep of the deceased, which contrasts with their own anguish (3.904–908):

> "tu quidem ut es leto sopitus, sic eris aevi
> quod super est cunctis privatus doloribus aegris;
> at nos horrifico cinefactum te prope busto
> insatiabiliter deflevimus aeternumque
> nulla dies nobis maerorem e pectore demet."

> "Yes, you, as you now lie in death's quiet sleep, so you will be for all time that is to come, removed from all distressing pains; but we beside you, as you lay burnt to ashes on the horrible pyre, have bewailed you insatiably, and that everlasting grief no time shall take from our hearts."

Again, the language mocks the commonplaces of sepulchral monuments and formal lament. Of the three-word line, *insatiabiliter deflevimus aeternumque* (3.907), Kenney writes: "The effect of this verse on the cultivated Roman ear cannot have been other than grotesque."[21] David West points out that *insatiabiliter* ("insatiably") occurs elsewhere in Lucretius only in a description of swine enjoying a roll in the muck (6.978). He also reminds us that these lines are spoken in the voice not of Lucretius, but of unenlightened mourners: "Surely these pathetic rhetorical figures and astonishing rhythms are meant as sarcastic caricatures of the mawkish clichés used by such *stulti* and *baratri*."[22] Noting the pompous and pretentious tone, Barbara Wallach identifies these lines as a parody of a now lost genre of consolatory literature that would have resonated with Lucretius' Roman readers.[23] Kenney also points out the triteness of *aeternumque . . . maerorem* ("everlasting grief").[24]

Continuing his lampoon, Lucretius describes maudlin drinkers who philosophize in clichés and lament their own deaths: "Brief is this pleasure for puny humans; soon it will be gone, nor can we ever call it back" (*brevis hic est fructus homullis; | iam fuerit neque post umquam revocare licebit*, 3.914–915). As though, Lucretius retorts, they think the worst thing about death is that they will be thirsty (3.916–918). Not all theoretical considerations of kitsch are germane to my reading of Lucretius, and I reiterate that foregrounding the anti-kitsch impulse of Epicureanism is not the only way to read Lucretius' diatribe against the fear of death. But relevant here is Jason Wirth's observation that "humor and irony are lethal to kitsch."[25] Or, as Kulka formulates it: "Kitsch is indeed totally incompatible with

---

[21] Kenney: 2014, 195.   [22] West: 1969, 29.   [23] Wallach: 1976, 50.
[24] Kenney: 2014, 196. See also Lattimore: 1942, 243–246.   [25] Wirth: 2015, 127.

even the mildest form of questioning; that is, with irony."[26] Mildness is not Lucretius' métier, and his oblique irony often surges into sardonic contempt as he questions conventional responses to death.

Lucretius does not, however, condemn grief itself, nor does he present human sorrow as something contemptible. His strenuous critique of the irrational fear of being dead is not a full exposition of Epicurean theory and practice regarding the proper attitudes toward death. We know from Philodemus of Gadara's *On Death*, for example, that Epicurean theory could countenance the fear of the consequences for the survivors of one's own premature death as a rational cause for disquiet.[27] Rather, in the vignettes of the departed father and the maudlin drinkers, Lucretius' focus is on the way that kitsch – the image of the stereotypically sweet children, the maudlin lamentation, the pseudo-philosophy, the falseness – diverts our attention from the reality of the unwalled city.

The clichéd lamentations for the young father have something in common with the inapt tombstone erected for the character Tomas in *The Unbearable Lightness of Being*: "HE WANTED THE KINGDOM OF HEAVEN ON EARTH."[28] Asserting the heir's right "to express his father's life in his own vocabulary," the erstwhile estranged son chose the phrase despite his awareness of the incongruity with Tomas' own world-view.[29] The disparaging ending to this section of the novel, while not closely applicable to Lucretius, stresses the incongruousness between the reality of death and the mourners' hackneyed response: "Before we are forgotten, we will be turned into kitsch. Kitsch is the stopover between being and oblivion."[30]

A Parallel from Philodemus

Epicurean candor obliterates kitsch. Sometimes Lucretius stages a direct confrontation, as when he emphasizes putrefaction or gives a voice to a personified Nature who addresses not just Memmius or the implied reader, but all humanity (3.933–934):

> "quid tibi tanto operest, mortalis, quod nimis aegris
> luctibus indulges? quid mortem congemis ac fles?"

---

[26] Kulka: 1996, 97.   [27] Sanders: 2011, 230. Cf. also Chapter 7 of Asmis in this volume.
[28] Kundera: 1984, 276.
[29] Similarly, Marie-Claude's commemoration of the deceased Franz, "A RETURN AFTER LONG WANDERINGS," exemplifies kitsch not only because of its trite religiosity but also because both Marie-Claude and the reader know that Franz died detesting her (*ibid.*, 276).
[30] *Ibid.*, 278.

"What ails you so, O mortal, to indulge overmuch in sickly lamentations?
Why do you groan aloud and weep at death?"

But as I have argued, parody also leads to clarity. Pertinent here is a poem
by Philodemus that I would also identify as an Epicurean critique of
kitsch. The male speaker in *Epigrams* 3 addresses Xantho, who is described
with a string of hyperbolic praises. She is "formed of wax" (κηρόπλαστε, 1),
an inscrutable compliment unless it refers to her doll-like quality, a sense
confirmed when she is equated to "a beautiful statue of the double-winged
Pothoi" (διπτερύγων καλὸν ἄγαλμα Πόθων, 2). Two adjectives sound
pedestrian in translation – "with the face of a muse" (μουσοπρόσωπε, 1)
and "with perfumed skin" (μυρόχροε, 1) – but the fact that for us they are
hapax legomena suggests that they would have sounded comically inflated or
even bizarre. That suspicion is heightened by the only other attestation for
the adjective "double-winged" (διπτερύγων), which occurs elsewhere as a
descriptor for mosquitoes (Meleager 33). Next we have a plea that she sing a
"sweet" maudlin song (*Epigrams* 3, 4–7 Sider = *AP* 9.570):

> ψῆλόν μοι χερσὶ δροσιναῖς μύρον· "Ἐν μονοκλίνῳ
>   δεῖ με λιθοδμήτῳ δή ποτε πετριδίῳ
> εὕδειν ἀθανάτως πουλὺν χρόνον·" ᾆδε πάλιν μοι,
>   Ξανθάριον, ναί, ναί, τὸ γλυκὺ τοῦτο μέλος.

Pluck for me with your delicate hands a fragrant song: "In a solitary rocky
bed made of stone I must surely someday
Sleep a deathlessly long time." Yes, yes, Xantharion, sing again for me this
sweet song. (Trans. Sider 1997)

Some scholars see a disjunction between the composer of this epigram and
Philodemus as an Epicurean scholar. Thus Philip Merlan asks: "Is this the
same Philodemus who quoted the tetraphramakos, with its 'Death is
nothing to us?'"[31] But the answer is an emphatic "yes" when we read
these couplets as the words not of Philodemus "himself," but as the
ironically misguided words of his insufficiently Epicurean persona. Not
all readers hear the repeated ναί, ναί as a maudlin refrain, but Sider is right
to adduce the repetition in "No longer, no longer will your happy home
give you welcome"(*iam iam non domus accipiet te*, Lucr. 3.894).[32] The
male speaker in the epigram espouses an outlook on death that is as suspect

---

[31] "Ist das derselbe Philodem, der die Tetrapharmakos mit ihrem 'Tod is ungefährlich' zitert?" Merlin:
1967, 490.
[32] Sider: 1997, 70–71.

as his exaggerated praise of Xantho, which has something in common with Lucretius' ridicule of the language of lovers (4.1160–1169).[33] Xantho, however, plays the role of the candid Epicurean who simultaneously deflates the would-be lover's schmaltzy language and his extravagant reference to the sleep of death. Rather than complying with his request to sing the sentimental lyrics, Xantho rebukes him with a parody of the song (*Epigram* 3, 8–9 Sider):

> οὐκ ἀΐεις, ὤνθρωφ', ὁ τοκογλύφος; ἐν μονοκλίνῳ
> δεῖ σὲ βιοῦν αἰεί, δύσμορε, πετριδίῳ.

> Don't you understand, man, you accountant you? You must
> live forever, you wretch, in a solitary rocky bed! (Trans. Sider 1997)

Her use of the vocative ὦ ἄνθρωπε (ὤνθρωφ', 7) marks her response as a philosophical exhortation, or more generally as a notice to the addressee that he should stay aware of his human limitations. As examples of this usage in Epicurean contexts, Wolfgang Schmid cites Diogenes of Oenoanda's "O fellow human being" (fr. 3, col. 3.9 Smith; ὦ ἄνθρωπε) in his address to potential readers of his epigraphical invitation to Epicureanism, and "O mortal" in Nature's speech, quoted above (Lucr. 3.933–934).[34] Thus, in what Schmid aptly calls a "philosophical palinode," Xantho, as Sider puts it, offers a blunt Epicurean corrective in order to "bring him back to his Epicurean senses."[35] The song he had requested refers to death illogically and histrionically as a "deathlessly long" sleep in a redundantly stony, rocky tomb, a conceit she ridicules by heightening the illogicality: If he is asleep, he must be perpetually alive in this poetically embellished tomb.[36] Sider hears a similarity between Xantho's reproof and Nature's "chiding tones," but I would put a strong stress on Xantho's parodic tone.[37] If we had more of Epicurus' extensive corpus, we would know whether he too sometimes lampooned commonplace misconceptions and conventional platitudes.

---

[33] Compare Lucretius' disparaging *chariton mia* ("one of the graces," 4.1162) as used as a term of endearment by a delusional lover.

[34] Schmid: 1984 also cites P. Oxy. 2.215 (*de cultu deorum* = Epicurus 11 CPF, ed. Obbink).

[35] Schmid: 1984, 274. Sider: 1997, 67

[36] Lucretius also mocks the conventional equation between death and sleep. Commenting on a mourner who laments the "sleep" of the deceased, Lucretius writes: *illud ab hoc igitur quaerendum est, quid sit amari | tanto opere, ad somnum si res redit atque quietem, | cur quisquam aeterno possit tabescere luctu* ("Of such a speaker then we may well ask, if all ends in sleep and quiet rest, what bitterness there is in it so great that one could pine with everlasting sorrow?," 3.909–911).

[37] Sider: 1997, 69.

Epicureanism into Kitsch

In *On Ends*, Cicero tells a story about a stroll around Athens with some erudite companions. Among them is Cicero's friend Atticus, who had a serious interest in Epicureanism and might – perhaps with qualifications – be called an adherent.[38] As they walk, an array of monuments and locales remind them of the Greek past. When they pass the Garden, Atticus remarks: "I could not forget Epicurus if I wanted to; my confrères have his image not only on plaques, but even on their drinking cups and rings" (*nec tamen Epicuri licet oblivisci, si cupiam, cuius imaginem non modo in tabulis nostri familiares, sed etiam in poculis et in anulis habent*, 5.3). Atticus acknowledges that he frequents the Garden, but adds an indication of his disinclination to revere the long-gone founder: "As the old proverb says, *I remember the living.*" A defense of my argument that Epicureanism was profoundly anti-kitsch requires that I acknowledge the proliferation of Epicurean accoutrements. In other words, I must acknowledge Epicurean kitsch. One person's art is another's kitsch, but I would assert that a ring depicting a philosopher qualifies as the latter, and the touch of amusement I hear in Atticus' remark suggests he would agree.

Several rings and intaglios depicting busts of Epicurus in profile have survived, and are presumably examples of the objects Atticus refers to.[39] Bernard Frischer counts six rings: five gems catalogued in Richter's *Gems of the Greeks and Romans*, and a gold ring.[40] To these Frischer tentatively adds a gem in Munich and I would add a glass gem at the British Museum.[41] Richter identified the miniature portraits through their resemblance to sculptures of Epicurus, and the appearance of the inscription "Epicurus" on one (a Carnelian ring). In addition, Richter catalogs two gems that might represent Metrodorus. Sadly, the dates and provenance of these apparently first- to third-century objects are not known. Before concluding that Epicureans in particular were assiduous ring-wearers, it is important to note that Richter also catalogs other relevant rings, including two depicting Aristotle and fourteen depicting Socrates. Thus, material philosophical kitsch was by no means uniquely Epicurean.

---

[38] See Gilbert's examination of Atticus' Epicureanism in this volume (Chapter 4).

[39] Listed in the catalogues as rings are items 438 bis (Richter: 1971) and British Museum: 1917, 0501.1636. The surviving intaglios were presumably settings for rings. Any of these objects may have been used as seals, perhaps on letters or wherever security was wanted.

[40] Frischer: 1982, 87 n. 1. Richter: 1971 (numbers 438, 438bis–441). The gold ring is British Museum: 1917, 0501.1636.

[41] Brandt et al.: 1968, number 361; and British Museum: 1923, 0401.798.

It is hard to know what sort of plaques or "tablets" (*tabulis*) Atticus has in mind, but Pliny the Elder also records with disdain that Epicureans among his contemporaries "bear portraits of Epicurus around with them, both privately and abroad" (*Epicuri voltus per cubicula gestant ac circumferunt secum, NH* 355). Pliny's remark is in some ways inscrutable, and he may mean that people wear or carry (*gestant*) Epicurus' portrait literally around their bedrooms (*per cubicula*) and also parade it around publicly (*circumferunt secum*). Disparagement is certainly implied, as the remark occurs in the context of Pliny's complaint that instead of preserving wax models of themselves and recent ancestors (on display in the home and ready to carry in funeral processions), his contemporaries buy expensive works by foreign artists and "prize the likenesses of strangers" (*alienasque effigies colunt, NH* 355). After describing their ostentatious picture galleries, he adds that "the same people" display portraits of athletes in their "anointing rooms" (apparently where they and their guests prepare for exercise), and – in the passage quoted above – pictures of Epicurus in their private rooms (or specifically in their bedrooms). Here he takes a passing swipe at Epicureans, grumbling that they also observe Epicurus' birthday and the traditional gathering on the twentieth of every month, but his general complaint is the broader collecting habits of his contemporaries. This brief tangent on Epicurean traditions implies that he views both the portraits and the festivals as indicative of excessive devotion to Epicurus.

As for the Epicurean cups, none has survived. But perhaps Lucretius refers obliquely to such paraphernalia when he describes the maudlin drinkers' laments for the brevity of the lives of "puny humans" (3.914–915; mentioned above). In these verses, Lucretius moves from his critique of commonplace complaints about death to prefacing his imitation of the drinkers: "People also do this when they recline and hold out their cups and wreath their brows" (*hoc etiam faciunt ubi discubuere tenentque / pocula saepe homines et inumbrant ora coronis*, 3.912–913). At first sight the poor saps who bemoan their future deaths seem to represent any inebriated, cup-holding, late-night philosophizers. The "eat, drink, and be merry" conceit pre-dates Epicurus, but in the context of *On the Nature of Things*, are these fools wayward Epicureans?[42] Kenney takes these lines as evidence for the prevalence of a trivialized Epicureanism in Republican Rome. In his view, Lucretius is describing how drunken inhibition brings out irrational beliefs hidden beneath an Epicurean veneer.

---

[42] For the conceit, see Athenaeus' attribution of the similar sentiments to the fourth-century BC comic poet Amphis (Athen. 336c K–A).

Commenting on Lucretius' harsh response, Kenney concludes: "The situation is piquant: The real Epicurean arraigns the false."[43] Admittedly, even if Kenney is right about the drinkers' pretentions to Epicureanism, their cups are not necessarily emblazoned with portraits of Epicurus. Frischer points out, however, that a cup from Boscoreale that depicts Zeno (the Stoic) mocking Epicurus supports the assumption that cups decorated with Epicurus' image did exist, "since parody pre-supposes a serious model."[44] Like a coffee mug purchased in a museum shop, an Epicurus cup might be either cheesy or tasteful, depending upon the owner's sensibilities. But Cicero's account of the conversation as the friends pass the Garden suggests that Atticus detects cheesiness.

It would be interesting to explore whether certain formulaic refrains displayed on Roman funeral monuments were commonly perceived as Epicurean sentiments and whether Lucretius would mock them. Examples include jingles such as *non fui, fui, non sum* ("I was not, I was, I am not") and *balnea vina venus* ("baths, wine, sex").[45] But for now, I turn to Horace, who discerned the potential for kitsch in what I would cautiously characterize as the spoken equivalent of an Epicurean ring or cup: quasi- or pseudo-Epicurean slogans, prime among them the well-worn exhortation *carpe diem*. Although some readers take seriously the philosophical discourse of the *carpe diem* ode (*Odes* 1.11), I would describe Horace's proffering of the philosophical mottoes in *Odes* 1.11 as the devious maneuvers of an unreliable narrator. W. S. Anderson has described in detail how this works: The male speaker (perhaps to be understood as Horace's persona) engages discourse presented with gravity in other odes: the harsh weather outside, the advice to cut short hopes for the future, the injunction not to ask about troubling matters and the invitation to enjoy the wine instead.[46] Anderson demonstrates how these motifs are presented mechanically along with other clichés in *Odes* 1.11 by a half-avuncular and half-predatory speaker who is impatient to have sex with the justifiably wary Leuconoe. As Anderson points out, even the meter of the ode is suspect: "The speaker emerges as a person of clipped and perfunctory argument, who gets trapped, particularly by the choriambs, and exposed as a man of ready phrases and trite slogans." Six of the thirteen relentlessly repetitive metrical units (all choriambs) sound particularly glib: *scire nefas;*

---

[43] Kenney: 2014, 197.   [44] Frischer: 1982, 88.
[45] For the former, see *CIL* 8, 3463, and variants discussed by Lattimore: 1942, 83–85. For the latter see *CE* 1318, *CE* 1499 and variants discussed by Kajanto: 1969.
[46] Anderson: 1992.

ut melius; *quidquid erit*; *vina liques*; *dum loquimur*; *carpe diem* ("it is wrong to know"; "so much the better"; "whatever will be"; "strain the wine"; "while we are [merely] talking"; "harvest the day"; *Odes* 1.11.1–8). Here the rhetoric of other odes sometimes identified specifically as *"carpe diem* odes" is "reduced and essentially parodied, to work for the patent purposes of seduction."[47] While Anderson does not mention Epicureanism in his insightful essay, *carpe diem* is not merely *philosophical* language, but is specifically *Epicurean*. The agricultural metaphor *carpe* ("harvest or pluck") must be a direct echo of Epicurus' similar-sounding καρπίζεται ("harvest"; "enjoy the fruits of"), which may have appeared more aphoristically in other sources but has survived in Epicurus' *Letter to Menoeceus*, where we read that the wise person chooses and "enjoys the fruits not of the longest time, but of the sweetest time" (χρόνον οὐ τὸν μήκιστον ἀλλὰ τὸν ἥδιστον καρπίζεται, *Men*. 126). Nonetheless, in *Odes* 1.11, Epicurus' reference to the harvesting of time has turned into trite "Epicurean" moralizing. But although Horace was likely not a card-carrying (or *ring-wearing*) Epicurean, his sardonic conjuring of Epicurean kitsch does not preclude an appreciation for authentic Epicurean wisdom. His send-up may be as much a self-parody as a lampoon of hackneyed Epicureanism.

Why was Epicureanism so easy to reduce to a slogan or to an object that can be worn on a finger or held in the hand? Any philosophical school could attract ill-informed practitioners or be subject to parody, but Epicureanism presents a special case. Although he was an Epicurean-friendly reader, Don Fowler found Epicureanism "austerely and challeng-ingly simple." In Epicureanism as a scientific philosophy he saw "a strong aspiration" toward "the one true story." Epicureanism's urge to explain all of reality as a result of the movements of atoms, its "constant aspiration to reduction," led to a "thinness and clarity of the message." But for Fowler, Lucretius' *On the Nature of Things* represents a fundamental departure from early Epicureanism. Whereas Epicurus was a reductionist, Lucretius' rich language suggests "multiple approaches to the world."[48] Fowler sensed a tension between Epicurus and Lucretius that renders the latter's epic "as deeply un-Epicurean as it is deeply Epicurean."[49] I agree with Fowler about the richness and complexity of Lucretius' presentation of Epicureanism, but the question of whether Epicurus' approach is in fact

---

[47] Anderson: 1993, 120. Davis refers frequently to "CD odes" (i.e. *carpe diem* odes), e.g. Davis: 1991, 146. Note also the title of West: 1995, which does not discuss *Odes* 1.11 in detail: *Carpe Diem: Horace Odes I.*

[48] Fowler: 2002, 442. [49] *Ibid.*, 443.

reductive lies outside the scope of this essay. Nonetheless, one result of the potential "thinness and clarity of the message" is that Epicureanism could be condensed to simple slogans and clichés, or even to one word. Cicero and Seneca routinely reduce the entire philosophy to "Pleasure" (*Voluptas*), and Marcus Aurelius chose as his label for Epicureanism the single word "Atoms."[50] Others gave Epicureanism a two-word title: One of Lucilius' characters calls it "Effluences and Atoms," and Cassius (a friend to the Garden) counters Cicero's hostile summation affirmatively with the Greek pair "Pleasure and Tranquility."[51]

With the formulation of the *Principal Doctrines*, Epicurus may have begun this process himself. His followers sometimes expanded the *Principal Doctrines*, so that the text preserved by Diogenes Laertius (usually considered canonical) differs from the *Vatican Sayings* and the version displayed by Diogenes of Oenoanda. But sometimes faithful followers reduced the doctrines to the tetrapharmakos, the four-fold remedy for human suffering found in a text by Philodemus: "The gods do not concern us; death is nothing to us; what is good can be easily obtained; what is bad can be avoided" (PHerc. 1005, col. 4.9–14). Could this be kitsch? The potential is there, but my sense is that these statements possess a clarity that prevents them from sinking to the realm of irredeemable kitsch.

Conclusion: Anti-Kitsch as Frank Criticism

When we read the diatribe against the fear of death as a polemic against kitsch, we can see more clearly that Lucretius is not presenting a full course in Epicurean thanatology, but is instead leading the reader through the first steps by stripping away the conventional clichés that occlude reality. The process involves the potential pain Lucretius refers to when he writes that Epicureanism may first seem "rather bitter" (*tristior*, 1.944), causing most people to "recoil" (*abhorret*, 1.945). Though ultimately liberating, both the message and its delivery can be harsh, and Lucretius' metaphorical honey softens the bitterness of the medicine, but does not coat the whole. Lucretius' reference to the initially bitter taste of Epicurean teaching resonates with a particular mode of therapeutic Epicurean instruction described in *On Frank Criticism* (PHerc. 1471), Philodemus' fragmentary epitome of lectures delivered by his teacher Zeno of Sidon. We know from

---

[50] Abundant examples in Cic. *Fin.* and Sen. *Vit. Beat,* and Marcus Aurelius *Med.* 4.3, 6.24, 7.32, 7.50, 8.17, 9.28, 10.6, 11.18.
[51] Lucil. 820 W. Cic. *Fam.* 15.19.2 = SB 216.

this work that Epicurean advice and correction could be "mild" (μέτριον) or "harsh" (σκληρόν) and "bitter" (πικρόν), depending on circumstances such as the error being addressed, the status of the speaker and the fortitude of the hearer.

I take some aspects of Lucretius' diatribe against kitsch as a manifestation of the more bitter type of Epicurean frank criticism. Lucretius' treatment of death had begun by candidly appealing to the readers' reason, carefully laying out the proofs of the mortality of the soul and the Epicurean assertion that "death is nothing to us." Then, progressing from the appeal to reason to language that stirs the emotions, Lucretius' tone ranges from quiet persuasion to harsher frankness, with his descriptions of putrefaction and the vignette of the father and his orphans being the most bitter. Philodemus was careful to specify that even the bitter mode of frank criticism must not include sarcasm and derision (*On Frank Criticism* fr. 23.1–4; cf. 37; 38), and perhaps he would not praise Lucretius' diatribe. But Lucretius seems to employ varying degrees of mildness and bitterness depending on whether his target is Memmius or an unspecified, implied reader. When he addresses Memmius directly, he is as deferential as Philodemus advises a teacher to be when instructing someone of higher social status. When Lucretius gives Nature the opportunity to speak, he tempers the rebuke by remarking that she might justly censure "someone of *us*" (3.932). Lucretius also softens the blow by rhetorically presenting Memmius with the opportunity to rebuke *himself* (3.1024–1026):[52]

> Hoc etiam tibi tute interdum dicere possis:
> "lumina sis oculis etiam bonus Ancu" reliquit,
> "qui melior multis quam tu fuit, improbe, rebus."

> This thought also you may at times address to yourself: "Even good Ancus has closed his eyes on the light, he who was better than you, unconscionable man, in many ways."

But the most hypothetical of Lucretius' implied readers do not require deference or the gentler types of frank criticism such as the approaches Philodemus recommends for the instruction of the most vulnerable. Like the theoretical mourners and other fools *within* Lucretius' epic, the implied readers will not crumble under the teacher's harsh reprimands. Meanwhile, the actual readers of *On the Nature of Things* are out of the

---

[52] If the singular second-person pronouns do not refer specifically to Memmius, Lucretius is giving the opportunity to the implied reader. Philodemus' *On Frank Criticism* demonstrates that self-disclosure and mutual correction were essential aspects of Epicurean education (e.g. frr. 39–42 and, apparently, fr. 53).

direct path and are thus insulated from the sting of harsh criticism. Nonetheless, Lucretius' diatribe against the fear of death does not allow any of its actual or implied addressees to take refuge in platitudes and false assurances. To deny that our metaphorical city has penetrable walls – to pretend that human lives are not dispensable in the great scheme of things – and to bemoan the eventuality of one's own death ... this is kitsch.

CHAPTER 9

Page, Stage, Image: Confronting Ennius with Lucretius' On the Nature of Things

Mathias Hanses

Introduction

Manuscripts containing the works of Quintus Ennius (239–169 BC) appear not to have survived much beyond the fourth century AD,[1] so scholars interested in the *disiecti membra poetae* ("limbs of a scattered poet," Hor. *Sat.* 1.4.62) have long been focusing on later authors who engaged with his oeuvre. That group includes the late-Republican writer Lucretius, whose Epicurean poem *On the Nature of Things* is steeped in archaic language and metrical constructions reminiscent of Ennian poetry. It also contains a prominent reference to the earlier poet's views on the afterlife (1.112–135). In revisiting the intertextual connection between the two authors in this paper, I do not seek to contest the typical conclusion that Ennius ranked next to Homer and Empedocles among those literary predecessors whom Lucretius revered but with whose worldview he often disagreed.[2] Rather, I will reassess a number of familiar points of contact between the two writers in Book 1 of *On the Nature of Things* – which is where Lucretius first sets up his poem's sustained allusive conversation with Ennius – in pursuit of a twofold thesis.

Throughout, I cite the fragments of Ennius from Goldberg and Manuwald: 2018. I also follow their editorial practice of using the numbering of Skutsch: 1985 when referring to the *Annals* and Manuwald: 2012 for the tragedies. Quotations from Lucretius are based on the OCT edition. For all other authors, I follow the Teubner. Translations from the Latin and Greek are my own. My sincere thanks go to Erin M. Hanses and Jason Nethercut for their helpful suggestions and bibliographical assistance, to Katharina Volk for commenting on a much earlier version of this paper and to Sergio Yona and Gregson Davis for including my contribution in this volume.

[1] See Suerbaum: 2002, 139–142, for a survey of the evidence.

[2] See, e.g., Kenney: 1970, 309; Harrison: 2002, 2; Gale: 2007, 61. Taylor: 2016 is more nuanced, noting that when it comes to tragic (i.e., mythological) material, Lucretius does not in fact discard the content of Ennius' poetry entirely. Rather, he tends to play competing versions of a story against each other. A particularly thorough discussion of Ennian allusion in Lucretius is Nethercut: 2012. See also Nethercut: 2014 and 2018, esp. 79–82. For tragedy in Lucretius, see also Schiesaro: 1990, 111–122; Fowler: 2000: 138–155; Marcović: 2008; and Cowan: 2013.

First, I posit that in those passages where Lucretius is known to engage with Ennius – not just in the discussion of life after death, but also in the encomium of Epicurus (1.62–79), the sacrifice of Iphigenia (1.82–101) and the brief narration of the Trojan War (1.464–482) – the Epicurean poet repeats more key terminology from his Ennian source passages than has previously been recognized. The depth and number of these references to Ennius suggest that throughout Book 1, Lucretius tends to contest not just common worldviews in a general sense, but common worldviews as expressed – more specifically – by Ennius. This thorough engagement with Rome's first "national" poet shows that Ennius' compositions provided more than engaging accounts of classical mythology and vivid narrations of historical events on which to hinge Roman identity. Rather, the cosmology of his poetry could count as religion or even philosophy.

Second, I posit that Lucretius' need to refute Ennius is so urgent because the earlier poet's works continued to be included at the Roman *ludi* and hence contributed to the spectators' mass-indoctrination in what, to an Epicurean, would constitute a harmful ideology. In an attempt to counter this potentially detrimental effect, Lucretius alludes specifically to those parts of Ennius' epic and dramatic output that, as writers from Cicero to Aulus Gellius consistently report, remained popular in recitations and revival performances. What is more, where Lucretius describes mythological events in particularly Ennian language and imagery, his versions correspond closely to the same stories' portrayal in the visual arts. This phenomenon hints at a rich cross-pollination between stagings of Ennius' works and depictions of classical myth in Roman painting. In engaging with both at the same time, Lucretius provides his readers with a guidebook on how to deconstruct commonly held misconceptions wherever they encounter them, be it in their studies of classical literature, while attending Ennian performances in the theater or while glancing at pictorial representations of mythological scenes on the walls of Roman houses.

Pyrrhus and Epicurus

Lucretius' engagement with Ennius begins well before he actually mentions the older poet in Book 1 (at line 117). After the opening hymn to Venus (1.1–43) and an initial explication of the vocabulary he will be applying to atoms (1.49–61), Lucretius introduces the reader to his idol, Epicurus (1.62–79). The philosopher remains unnamed, but it is commonly understood that he is the Greek man who, back "when life lay

foully on the earth, oppressed by heavy superstition" (*foede cum vita iaceret |
in terris oppressa gravi sub religione*, 1.62–63), first dared to look up at the
sky (*primum Graius homo mortalis tollere contra | est oculos ausus*, 1.66–67)
and challenged the reign of *religio*. His intellect "proceeded far beyond the
burning walls of the world" (*extra | processit longe flammantia moenia
mundi*, 1.72–73) and brought back actual knowledge of what can and
cannot happen, and thereby dispelled irrational fears of the gods and
brought us closer to ἀταραξία.

In this context, the phrase *Graius homo* – used to describe Epicurus at
1.66 – connects back to, and establishes a firm intertextual connection
with, Ennius' *Annals*.[3] The sixth book of this epic narrated Pyrrhus'
campaign against Rome, and it seems to have made its author's admiration
for the Hellenistic king readily apparent.[4] Ennius describes the Epirote
invader as "from the highest stock" (*a stirpe supremo*, fr. 166 Sk) and as
"a vigorous man ..., a Greek man with a Greek father, a king" (*navos
repertus homo, Graio patre, Graius homo, rex*, fr. 165 Sk). Throughout the
rest of the book, which foregrounded its martial interests from its very
first lines,[5] Ennius explored what such terms as *virtus* ("manly valor"), *vis*
("force") and *vincere* ("to be victorious") come to mean when they are
applied to a general who famously won every battle but at such a cost that
he might as well have lost. It is this key vocabulary that, I posit, was of
particular interest to Lucretius. In Ennius, Pyrrhus is said, for example,
to have dedicated an inscription in the temple of Jupiter in Tarentum,
which noted that "men who previously were undefeated, best father of
Olympus, I have defeated with force in battle and I have, in turn, been
defeated by the same men" (*qui antehac | invicti fuere viri, pater optume*

---

[3] Bailey: 1947, 2.609 notes the phrase's Ennian origin but does not explore this observation further.
Gale: 1994, 72–74 posits a different intertext, suggesting that *primum Graius homo* reflects
Empedocles' description of Pythagoras (fr. 129.1). For Empedocles in Lucretius, see more
generally Sedley: 1998, 15–34 and Garani: 2007. Harrison: 2002, 8–11 explores similarities
between Epicurus and Pyrrhus as contemporaries and fellow "invaders" of Italy. Nethercut:
2012 adds that in putting Ennian language to "un-Ennian" uses, Lucretius might be making
Epicurus resemble an epic hero like Hector, Achilles or Odysseus (72, 96 and 143–147).
Additional allusions to Book 6 of Ennius' *Annals* feature in Lucretius' fifth book, on which see
Gale: 2009, 201 and Nethercut: 2012, 95–102.

[4] For Book 6 of the *Annals* and its function as a Pyrrhus encomium, see, e.g., Suerbaum: 1995;
Fantham: 2006; and Fabrizi: 2012, 119–150. Goldberg: 1995, 101–102; Elliott: 2013, 167–169;
and N. Goldschmidt: 2013, 160–161, discuss the book's afterlife in Vergil. Goldberg and
Manuwald: 2018, 1.198–214 collect and contextualize the fragments.

[5] A fragment from *Annals* 6 notes the composition's intent "to unfurl the edges of vast war" (*ingentis
oras evolvere belli*, fr. 164 Sk). For its placement at the start of the book, see Skutsch: 1985, 328–329.
Farrell: 2008, 17 n. 21 remains skeptical.

Olympi, | *hos ego vi pugna vici victusque sum ab isdem,* fr. 180–182 Sk).[6]
Words derived from *vincere* (*in-victi . . . vici victusque*) here alternate and
alliterate with forms of *vir* ("man," hence *virtus*) and *vis* in an evaluation
of the paradox that is a Pyrrhic victory. The source that contains the
fragment (Oros. *Hist.* 4.1.14) goes on to say that, when asked "why he
called himself defeated although he had won" (*cur se victum diceret qui
vicisset*), Pyrrhus responded "truly, if I win another time in this same
manner, I will return without a single soldier to Epirus" (*ne ego si iterum
eodem modo vicero sine ullo milite Epirum revertar*). Presuming this
wording echoes the king's presentation in the *Annals*, it seems that
vocabulary derived from *vincere* (*victum . . . vicisset . . . vicero*) predomi-
nated not just in the fragment itself, but also in its immediate
surroundings.[7]

As far as Ennius' use of the term *virtus* is concerned, it also stands at the
center of Pyrrhus' assertion that he has no interest in riches but wants to
challenge the Romans in the area of "manly valor" (*virtute experiamur,*
fr. 187 Sk.). Those who retain their *virtus* will be spared, even if they end
up captured (*quorum virtuti belli fortuna pepercit* | *eorundem me libertati
parcere certum est,* fr. 188–189 Sk.). The sentiment serves not only to
praise the king's own manliness, but also to declare his martial *virtus* more
important than the decisive kind of victory that so famously eluded him.[8]

In repeating the epithet *Graius homo,* then, from Ennius' depiction of
Pyrrhus, Lucretius evokes memories of the earlier poem but proceeds to
paint an altogether different picture of what constitutes a Greek hero. In
particular, he employs the same key vocabulary that Ennius had used in
the *Annals* but re-purposes it for a celebration of the human mind.[9] The
world's depressing state awakens Epicurus' *virtus,* but, in notable contrast
to Ennius' Pyrrhus, his is a *virtus* of the intellect (*acrem* | *irritat animi
virtutem,* 1.69–70). Similarly, the phrase "the vigorous force of [Epicurus']
mind prevails" (*vivida vis animi pervicit,* 1.72) is as alliterative as the
Ennian source passage it recalls, and it relies on the same terminology
(*vis . . . per-vicit*). Yet the philosopher's victory, unlike Pyrrhus', is never in

---

[6] For the complicated history of this fragment's attribution to Ennius, see Skutsch: 1985, 344–346
and Fantham: 2006, 566.

[7] In addition to the examples adduced here, fr. 167 Sk. likewise centers on the verb *vincere.*

[8] Compare, e.g., Suerbaum: 1995, 38, who calls this fragment "programmatisch."

[9] Cf., e.g., West: 1969, 57–63 and Buchheit: 1971, who examine the passage's triumphal language.
Gale: 1994, 117–128 considers Lucretius' militaristic similes and metaphors borrowings from
Homeric and Ennian epic.

doubt. Indeed, his *victoria* raises all of us up to the sky (*nos exaequat victoria caelo*, 1.79).[10]

Lucretius thus issues a challenge to traditional conceptions of heroism as propagated, in particular, in the sixth book of Ennius' *Annals*. Since Cicero refers to the Ennian Pyrrhus' aforementioned speech on the subject of *virtus* as "those famous [words]" (*illa praeclara*, *Off.* 1.38),[11] it seems that access to the text would have been readily available to Lucretius' readers.[12] Yet that is not to say that they would have necessarily studied the poem in a scroll. After all, Latin epics were also recited at the Roman *ludi* in the first century BC,[13] and Aulus Gellius still witnessed a public reading from Book 6 of the *Annals* as late as the second century AD.[14] The event occurred when "there was rest on a certain day at Rome in the forum from business" (*otium erat quodam die Romae in foro a negotiis*) amid a "certain happy celebration of a festival" (*laeta quaedam celebritas feriarum*, Gell. 16.10.1). It seems likely, therefore, that Lucretius' readers would have encountered Ennius' views on *virtus*, *vis* and *vincere* at official celebrations of city-wide holidays. On these occasions, anyone steeped in *On the Nature of Things* would have been ready to critique the *Annals'* use of the relevant terms, and to advance the counter-model provided by Epicurean philosophy. This multi-mediality of Ennian reception – occurring, as I contend it would have, both through reading and through performance – is particularly relevant to the next section, where I discuss an intertextual connection that relies even more directly on non-written media.

Iphigenia

Having completed the encomium of Epicurus, Lucretius segues into his famous description of the sacrifice of Iphianassa/Iphigenia. The account of Agamemnon's ritual murder of his daughter on what she thought was to be

---

[10] At Sil. *Pun.* 12.411, the god Apollo remarks that Ennius "will raise leaders up to the sky" (*attollet ... duces caelo*). If that line is based on Ennius' own poetry, then Lucretius' *nos exaequat victoria caelo* might constitute another reversal of Ennian language (and priorities) in the younger poet's description of Epicurus.

[11] Cf. Elliott: 2013, 167–169.

[12] For Ennius' role in Roman education, see Bonner: 1977, 213, 215 and 223; N. Goldschmidt: 2013, 17–28.

[13] For early public performances of Ennian epic at the *ludi Romani*, see Wiseman: 2015, 63–70. For similar recitations of the works of Vergil in the theater, see Tac. *Dial.* 13.2; Donat. *Vit. Verg.* 26; Serv. *Ecl.* 6.11.

[14] For the placement of the relevant fragment in Book 6 of the *Annals*, see most recently Goldberg and Manuwald: 2018, 1.202–203.

her wedding day – meant to ensure the Greek fleet's passage out of the Bay of Aulis – constitutes a prime example of Lucretius' thesis that superstition in the guise of reverence will sway people toward terrible deeds (*tantum religio potuit suadere malorum*, 1.82–101 at 101). The passage has also long been recognized as richly intertextual.[15] Depending on their respective backgrounds and interests, different modern critics have foregrounded certain allusions at the expense of others, as would no doubt have been the case among the varied readership(s) of the Roman Republic. There are, for example, clear echoes of the *parodos* of Aeschylus' *Agamemnon* in Lucretius' focus on the pollution incurred through human sacrifice, the theme of a wedding perverted into a funeral and in the fact that, as in the *Oresteia*, Iphigenia has to be carried to the altar and actually dies (rather than being replaced with a deer and spirited away by Diana at the very last second). In particular, Aeschylus' Agamemnon notes the horror of "soiling a father's hands with streams of a young woman's blood right by the altar" (μιαίνων παρθενοσφάγοισιν | ῥείθροις πατρώιους χέρας | πέλας βωμοῦ, Aesch. *Ag.* 209–211). Similar language recurs in Lucretius' lament that "at Aulis, the leaders of the Greeks, the first among the men, foully soiled the altar of Diana with the blood of a young woman, Iphigenia" (*Aulide ... Triviai virginis aram | Iphianassai turparunt sanguine foede | ductores Danaum delecti, prima virorum*, 1.84–86).[16]

To these Aeschylean resonances has been added the observation that in Euripides' *Iphigenia at Aulis*, the young woman "was first to call [Agamemnon] father" and to "attach [her] body to [his] knees" (πρώτη σ᾽ ἐκάλεσα πατέρα ... | πρώτη δὲ γόνασι σοῖσι σῶμα δοῦσ᾽ ἐμόν, Eur. *IA* 1220–1221). In Lucretius, Iphigenia is "silent with fear" and, "having fallen to her knees, she sought the ground. And it did not help the miserable woman at such a time that she had been first to bestow the name of father on the king" (*muta metu terram genibus summissa petebat. | nec miserae prodesse in tali tempore quibat | quod patrio princeps donarat nomine regem*, 1.92–94).[17] Based on the similarities between these passages, Barnaby Taylor (2016, 145–150) has argued that Lucretius alludes to competing dramatic versions of the myth, including some where

---

[15] In addition to what I adduce below, Furley: 1970, 62 and Gale: 1994, 72 discuss echoes of Empedocles' fr. 137, which describes a father sacrificing an animal that – due to metempsychosis – used to be his son. Cf. also Gale: 2007, 64 and 67.

[16] For Lucretius' varied allusions to the *Agamemnon*, see Perutelli: 1996; Harrison: 2002, 5; Panoussi: 2009, 20–25; Nethercut: 2012, 126; and Taylor: 2016, 147.

[17] See Bailey: 1947, 2.614–615; Nethercut: 2012, 126–127; and Taylor: 2016, 147–148, for this and potential further echoes of Euripides' *Iphigenia at Aulis*.

Iphigenia is saved (as, apparently, she was in Euripides' *IA*) and others where she is not (e.g., Aeschylus' *Agamemnon*). In doing so, Lucretius endorses the latter in an attempt to "correct" or rationalize the former and underlines the true horror of the event.

This argument is convincing, but it is nevertheless necessary to account more fully than Taylor does for Stephen Harrison's (2002, 4–6) observation that the passage's entire style is markedly Ennian, even and especially at the start (the episode's first lines, 1.84–86, are quoted above). This suggests that the main – though certainly not the only – author whose work Lucretius employs to exemplify the noxious beliefs on display in many tragedies is Ennius. Harrison himself points to the use of *indugredi* at 1.82 as reminiscent of Ennius' favored term *induperator*; to the archaic genitives *Triviai* (1.84; the noun also occurs in Ennius' fr. 171 M.) and *Iphianassai* (1.85); to Ennius' phrases *duxit delectos* (fr. 331 Sk.) and *delecti viri* (fr. 89.5 M.), which fuse into Lucretius' *ductores . . . delecti* (1.86); and to the fact that the construction *prima virorum* (1.86) in its combination of a neuter plural with a genitive is recognizably Ennian as well.[18] To these linguistic echoes, I would add that Iphigenia wears an *infula* at 1.87–88. This noun describes the headband of a priestess, particularly a Vestal Virgin,[19] which reinforces the passage's specifically Roman ring. In turn, the phrase *muta metu* at 1.92 is not attested in Ennius, but its alliteration does contribute to the passage's archaizing tone and recalls the earlier author's penchant for this stylistic feature. Most importantly, the phrase used to describe Iphigenia's murder (*aram . . . turparunt sanguine*, 1.84–85) is lifted directly out of Ennius' *Andromacha*, where – looking back to the night she was captured – the titular character uses the same words to describe the slaughter of Priam at the altar of Jupiter (*aram sanguine turpari*, fr. 23.17 M.).[20] Occurring as it does at the outset of the Lucretian episode, and providing a summary of it, the quote sets an emphatically Ennian tone for Lucretius' entire narration of the sacrifice. Other intertexts are certainly active as well, but the reader has to pass through Ennian Latin, as it were, in order to reach them.

A further example of this latter phenomenon is provided by an additional echo of Ennius' tragedies that has, to my knowledge, not previously been discussed. As the sacrifice begins, Lucretius' Agamemnon stands

---

[18] Compare fr. 84 Sk. (*infera noctis*) and fr. 264 Sk. (*caeli vasta*). *Pace* Taylor: 2016, 147 with n. 40, who finds that the construction mirrors Greek syntax.

[19] Cf. Bailey: 1947, 2.614.

[20] For this observation, see also Jocelyn: 1967, 251; Harrison: 2002, 6; Goldberg: 2000, 56–57; Panoussi: 2009, 39–41; Nethercut: 2012, 127–129 and Taylor: 2016, 149–150.

motionless at the altar and is despondent (*maestum ... ante aras adstare parentem*, 1.89), but he does not cry. By contrast, "the citizens shed tears at the sight of [Iphigenia]" (*aspectu ... suo lacrimas effundere civis*, 1.91). Ennius points to this difference between rulers and their subjects in fr. 194 M., likely from his *Iphigenia*: "The *plebs* in this regard is preferable to the king: The *plebs* is allowed to cry, the king is not allowed to do so honorably" (*plebes in hoc regi antestat loco: licet | lacrimare plebi, regi honeste non licet*). Lucretius echoes this Ennian passage in both sentiment and wording (note the correspondence between *lacrimas effundere* and *lacrimare, adstare* and *antestat*). At one step's further remove, one also notices similar lines in Euripides' *Iphigenia at Aulis*, where Agamemnon complains that those of low birth "are allowed to cry readily" (δακρῦσαι ῥαιδίως αὐτοῖς ἔχει, 447) while "to a high-born man these things are wretched" (τῶι δὲ γενναίωι φύσιν | ἄνολβα ταῦτα, 448–449). This similarity between Euripides' and Ennius' lines has given rise to the suspicion that the Roman tragedian's *Iphigenia* may have been based at least in part on the Greek *Iphigenia at Aulis*. Yet while the additional, Euripidean intertext would have been readily detectable to the learned, the road there leads through Ennius' *Iphigenia*.[21]

In alluding to this particular Latin play, and to Ennius more broadly, Lucretius notably does not attack the earlier poet outright. It is apparent from the fragments of the plays as much as from the Ennian language preserved in *On the Nature of Things* that the relevant tragedies would have been critical of Iphigenia's murder as well.[22] Lucretius may – I submit – even be appropriating a voice from within Ennius' own oeuvre. In one fragment from the *Iphigenia*, Achilles complains that "nobody looks at what is in front of their feet, instead they study the expanses of the sky" (*quod est ante pedes nemo spectat, caeli scrutantur plagas*, fr. 82.3 M.). This condemnation of astrological superstition is compatible with Lucretius' depiction of Iphigenia's sacrifice, where excessive contemplation of the supernatural leads to a horrible atrocity. Perhaps, then, the play contained a scene where Achilles rejected his bride-to-be's murder in almost proto-Lucretian terms. Either way, Lucretius uses some of tragedy's own insights against itself. He activates vivid reminiscences of Ennius' plays and uses

---

[21] That Ennius' *Iphigenia* is the main model for Lucretius' account of the sacrifice is the thesis of Harrison: 2002, 4–6, but he does not point out these particular parallels.

[22] See, e.g., Jocelyn: 1967, 251, who discusses the *Andromacha*'s focus on the polluting effect of human sacrifice.

them to undermine the religious beliefs that motivate many of the genre's most memorable characters.

This observation brings us back to the question of how Lucretius' readership would have become familiar with the relevant intertexts. The Iphigenia passage's most overt allusion to Ennian drama occurs in the aforementioned quotation from the *Andromacha* (*aram … turparunt sanguine*, Lucr. 1.84–85 ~ *aram sanguine turpari*, Ennius fr. 23.17 M.). Like Ennius' other works, this play would have been available for perusal in written form, but the tragedies of the Middle Republic also continued to be re-performed with great frequency.[23] In the repertoire of dramatic classics, the *Andromacha* featured prominently. At *Acad.* 2.20, Cicero observes that many are able to recognize this tragedy as soon as the accompanying piper plays his first notes. At *Att.* 4.15.6, he mentions a specific revival of the play at the *ludi Apollinares* of 54 BC.[24] Cicero thus delivers firm evidence that the *Andromacha* was staged in the very decade of the original publication of *On the Nature of Things*,[25] perhaps routinely so. This provides further support for the thesis that, as I posited was the case with Lucretius' earlier reliance on Book 6 of the *Annals*, the Epicurean poet preferred to employ those parts of Ennius' oeuvre that were most readily recognizable from performances at Roman festivals. Elsewhere in *On the Nature of Things*, Lucretius imagines his fellow Romans assembled in a theater and bathed in the varied colors cast off by the awnings that protect the spectators against the sun (4.72–83). He notes that after attending such *ludi*, spectators for days "seem to perceive … the glitter of the varied marvels of the stage" (*videantur | cernere … | scaenai … varios splendere decores*, 4.979–983).[26] In picking his Ennian quotations, Lucretius relies on these lasting memories of dramatic festivals, but he deconstructs the value systems that underlie the shows and provides his readers with a toolkit for confronting the plots the next time they encounter them at the *ludi scaenici*.[27]

To a reader, then, whose first language was Latin, who was well-versed in the Roman classics and/or who attended the *ludi*, Lucretius'

---

[23] Goldberg: 2000 and Manuwald: 2011, 112–113 collect a plethora of evidence.

[24] Cf. also the performances described at Cic. *Sest.* 118–123, where a tragic actor inserts lines from Ennius' *Andromacha* into Accius' *Eurysaces* to make a contemporary point.

[25] Cicero's famous letter about the *Lucreti poemata* (*QFr.* 2.10.3) likewise dates to 54 BC, so perhaps it was even in the very year of this revival that *On the Nature of Things* saw publication.

[26] For further references to the realities of the Roman theater, see 2.416–417, 3.58, 4.296–299 and 6.109–110.

[27] See now also Hanses: 2020, 61–62, 344–349 for similar deliberations regarding Lucretius' engagement with comic performances.

condemnation of the sacrifice of Iphigenia would have conjured especially strong reminiscences of Ennius' Trojan plays (including the *Iphigenia* and *Andromacha*), familiar as they continued to be from the stage. Yet I submit that there would have been a further, non-textual component to a late-republican reader's understanding of Lucretius' Iphigenia passage that likewise relates to the reception of Ennius. It has long been noted that the relevant lines of *On the Nature of Things* correspond closely to the sacrifice's depiction in a fresco from the House of the Tragic Poet in Pompeii (Figure 9.1).[28] In Lucretius, Iphigenia "perceived that her father was standing despondent by the altars and that the servants were hiding the iron on his account" (*et maestum ... ante aras adstare parentem | sensit et hunc propter ferrum celare ministros*, 1.89–90). In the image, Agamemnon likewise sorrowfully veils his head on the left while his daughter looks at him, and a priest conceals a dagger on the right. Furthermore, the young woman's lips are closed in the fresco, which suggests that she is "silent with fear" (*muta metu*, 1.92), and in both painting and poem, "she was lifted up by the hands of men and, shivering, she was brought to the altars" (*nam sublata virum manibus tremibundaque ad aras | deductast*, 1.95–96).

The Pompeian fresco likely stems from the Neronian era,[29] and it therefore postdates Lucretius' poem by about a century. Yet the motif itself harks back to a painting by the fourth-century BC artist Timanthes,[30] variations of which were popular already in the Roman Republic.[31] It strikes me as significant that Lucretius' description of the sacrifice of Iphigenia is simultaneously so rich in Ennian language and so similar to the story's typical depiction in the visual arts. The resemblances suggest that tragic actors could have taken cues from images portraying the sacrifice of Iphigenia. In turn, the myth's visualizations on the walls of Roman houses could themselves be partially informed by dramatic (re-) performances of classic plays, including those of Ennius. We may imagine, for example, that his *Iphigenia* contained a scene where the young woman is carried off stage to be sacrificed while Agamemnon veils his head, or that a different play, like the *Andromacha*, narrated the event (as we know it did the sacrifice of Priam). Witnessing such a moment in the theater could

---

[28] For the fresco, its date, its similarity to Lucretius' description of the sacrifice and its place in the history of the Iphigenia motif, see Hourticq: 1946, 122; Morisset and Thévenot: 1950, 97; Schefold: 1957, 4; Croisille: 1963, esp. 218–219; Peters: 1963, 143; and Bragantini and Sampaolo: 2013, no. 149.

[29] See previous note.   [30] Described at Cic. *Orat.* 74 and Plin. *HN* 35.73.

[31] See in detail Croisille: 1963.

Figure 9.1   *Sacrifice of Iphigenia*, Pompeii, House of the Tragic Poet (VI.8.3), Museo
Archeologico Nazionale di Napoli, inv. 9112. Photo credit: Scala / Art Resource, NY

have influenced a painter, even if he was also imitating Timanthes. Cicero,
for one, hints at such mutual cross-pollinations at *Orat.* 74, where he notes
that in portraying the sacrifice of Iphigenia (*immolanda Iphigenia*), a
painter (*pictor ille*) will portray varied characters in different gradations of
sadness, culminating in Agamemnon with his head veiled (*obvolvendum
caput Agamemnonis esse*) as in the Pompeian fresco, and that similar
observations apply to an "actor" (*histrio*).

   On this reading, Lucretius would be using specifically Ennian language
to activate memories of the tale's portrayal on the Roman stage and in the
visual arts, that is, in different media that exerted a noticeable influence on

each other. For a full appreciation of this triangular relationship, it is significant that the fresco includes Diana on the top right and Iphigenia with a deer on the upper left. The painter has emphasized that the young woman escaped her painful death through the goddess' intervention, as she likely did in Ennius' plays as well, considering his *Iphigenia* was based in part on Euripides' *Iphigenia at Aulis*. In alluding only to the painting's lower register and ignoring the top, Lucretius urges his readers to assume the same kind of "selective ambivalence" (Taylor: 2016, 143–144 and 150) toward the visual arts that they are to bring to bear on tragedy. They are to accept certain parts of the story (i.e., condemnations of the violence inherent in Iphigenia's sacrifice) but reject any supernatural components, because the gods do not in fact meddle in human affairs.

Pergama partu

For a further example of Lucretius' multi-medial intertextuality, we now jump ahead a few hundred lines in Book 1 of *On the Nature of Things*. Moving beyond the prologue and into a more thorough discussion of Epicurean physics, Lucretius first establishes the duality between atoms and void. The next step is to distinguish between *coniuncta* and *eventa*. According to 1.451–454, *coniuncta* are concrete, palpable properties that are inseparably tied to the objects that display them. Stones have weight, fire has heat and water is a liquid because of these elements' specific atomic structures. Everything else is an *eventum*, a mere accident, including "slavery ... poverty and riches, freedom, war, concord, everything else by whose arrival and departure Nature herself remains unimpaired" (*servitium ... paupertas divitiaeque,* | *libertas bellum concordia, cetera quorum* | *adventu manet incolumis natura abituque,* 1.455–457). Even time does not exist independently (1.459) but only in the observation of physical objects. This juxtaposition between *coniuncta* and *eventa* contains an overt value judgment. As Monica Gale (1994, 109–110) has argued, Lucretius declares his own subject matter, *natura*, more lasting and significant than the transitory topics that concern other writers, especially those who focus on epic, tragedy or history.[32] It makes sense, therefore, that he would employ the language of earlier authors in providing an example of one such "insignificant" *eventum*, namely, the Trojan War (1.464–477):

---

[32] For Lucretius' understanding of epic *as* history, see Nethercut: 2014.

denique Tyndaridem raptam belloque subactas
Troiugenas gentis cum dicunt esse, videndumst   465
ne forte haec per se cogant nos esse fateri,
quando ea saecla hominum, quorum haec eventa fuerunt,
irrevocabilis abstulerit iam praeterita aetas.
...
denique materies si rerum nulla fuisset
nec locus ac spatium, res in quo quaeque geruntur,
numquam Tyndaridis forma conflatus amoris
ignis, Alexandri Phrygio sub pectore gliscens,
clara accendisset saevi certamina belli,   475
nec clam durateus Troianis Pergama partu
inflammasset equus nocturno Graiugenarum.

Finally, when they say that the daughter of Tyndareus (Helen) was really
taken and the Trojan peoples were subdued by war, we have to see to it that
they do not by chance make us grant that these things actually exist, since
the irrevocable past has taken away those ages of men to which these events
belong ... What is more, if there had been no matter, nor space and place,
in which each deed is done, never would the fire of love, fanned by the
beauty of Tyndareus' daughter, blazing up in the Phrygian chest of
Alexander (Paris), have kindled the brilliant struggles of savage war, nor
would the wooden horse, unbeknownst to the Trojans, have set Pergamon
(the citadel of Troy) on fire with its nocturnal birthing of Greeks.

Lucretius here flags the presence of various intertexts in the background of
his own composition. After all, the verb *dicunt* (1.465) provides a prime
example of an Alexandrian footnote[33]; that is, it constitutes a self-reflexive
marker of allusivity that encourages the reader to contemplate which
earlier writers may have spoken about Troy. One obvious answer is
Homer, and the adjective *durateus* ("wooden," 1.476, transliterated from
the Greek δουράτεος) indeed underlines Lucretius' debts to this earlier
poet, who had likewise applied the word to the Trojan Horse in his
account of the city's sack (*Od.* 8.493 and 8.512).[34] As far as the metaphor
of the horse's pregnancy is concerned, it also features in Aeschylus'
Agamemnon (ἵππου νεοσσός, "the offspring of the horse," 825) and
Euripides' *Trojan Women* (ἐγκύμον' ἵππον τευχέων, "the horse pregnant
with weapons," 11). These varied Greek intertexts would all have been
readily detectable to the more learned members of Lucretius' readership.

---

[33] The most influential discussion of Alexandrian footnotes is Hinds: 1998, 1–16. For their presence
here and elsewhere in Lucretius, see Nethercut: 2018.
[34] See Nethercut: 2012, 84.

Nevertheless, as was the case in Lucretius' description of the sacrifice of Iphigenia, the passage is again especially rich in the language of Ennian drama. Prior studies have noted the presence of the archaizing noun *Tyndaris* (1.464 and 1.473) to describe Helen, of *Troiugenae* (1.465) to refer to the Trojans and of *Graiugenae* (1.477) to describe the Greeks.[35] Even more notable, because demonstrably based in Roman tragedy, is Lucretius' observation that the Trojan horse "set Pergamon (*Pergama*) on fire with its nocturnal birthing (*partu*) of Greeks" (1.476–477). The words *Pergama* and *partu* are lifted directly out of Ennius' *Alexander*,[36] a play dealing with young Paris' expulsion from Troy and his eventual rediscovery. According to this tragedy "the horse pregnant with armed men has jumped over (the walls) with a huge leap to destroy harsh Pergamon with its birthing" (*nam maximo saltu superavit gravidus armatis equus | qui suo partu ardua perdat Pergama*, fr. 22 M.). This Latin expression of the pregnant-horse motif would likely have been most easily detectable to Roman readers, while its Aeschylean and Euripidean versions would have required a bit of extra intellectual effort. I would add that the above quotation from Ennius' *Alexander* has to be part of a prophecy, since the play was set before the destruction of Priam's kingdom. Accordingly, the relevant lines must belong to Cassandra, who in this same play prophesies the fall of Troy and exclaims with reference to her brother that "the torch is here, is here, covered in blood and fire" (*adest, adest fax obvoluta sanguine atque incendio*, fr. 151a M.).[37] Ennius' *Hecuba* is similarly said to have envisioned "that she was birthing a firebrand, and then she produced Paris, who was the cause of the conflagration" (*haec se facem parere vidit et Parin creavit, qui causa fuit incendii*, fr. 200 M.). In a context already rich in allusions to Ennius, Lucretius is picking up on this fire imagery as well, and his reference to the fire "blazing up in the Phrygian chest of Alexander" (1.474) echoes the *Alexander*'s depiction of Paris as a torch that will destroy the city.[38]

It turns out, then, that we are dealing with a passage that is remarkably similar to the two we have already examined. Lucretius' *Iliupersis* engages with a variety of different intertexts, but Ennian language is especially conspicuous. As before, the lines even contain one clear instance of direct citation (*Pergama partu*, 1.476; compare *Graius homo* at 1.66 and *aram . . . turparunt sanguine* at 1.84–85). It also seems, yet again, that Lucretius has

---

[35] See, e.g., Bailey: 1947, 2.677–679; Nethercut: 2012, 84.   [36] See Bailey: 1947, 2.680.

[37] For this latter fragment's ascription to the *Alexander*, see Jocelyn: 1967, 204–205.

[38] Compare Bailey: 1947, 2.679 and Marcović: 2008. For similar fire imagery in Euripides' Trojan Trilogy, on which Ennius' *Alexander* was partially based, see Scodel: 1980, 78.

Figure 9.2 *Trojan Horse*, Pompeii, House of Cipius Pamphilus (VII.6.38), Museo
Archeologico Nazionale di Napoli, inv. 9010. Photo credit: Mathias Hanses

picked a motif that was popular with theatrical audiences. We admittedly
do not have any direct attestations for performances of the *Alexander* in the
50s BC, but we do know from a letter of Cicero's (*Fam.* 7.7) that a
luxurious revival of an *Equus Troianus* tragedy was put on at the spectac-
ular inauguration of the Theater of Pompey in 55 BC. The show was a
great success with the people (*Fam.* 7.7.2), though the orator himself
disapproved, and it occurred only briefly before the aforementioned stag-
ing of the *Andromacha* in 54 BC. In alluding to the *Alexander*'s narration
of the fall of Troy and the Trojan Horse, Lucretius is thus gesturing
toward a moment that his readers would have experienced in one form
or another at the late Republic's increasingly sensational *ludi scaenici*,
perhaps even on multiple occasions.

The visual record likewise provides parallels to my prior discussion, in
that rediscovered Roman houses on the Bay of Naples have yielded
multiple depictions of the Trojan Horse. Like Ennius' plays, these images
foreground the prophecies of Cassandra, who stands apart on the bottom
left (Figure 9.2) and top left (Figure 9.3) of two early-Imperial Pompeian
frescos, predicting the city's downfall as it is about to occur.[39] In a third,

[39] For these frescos and their interpretation, see Schefold: 1957, 206; Peters: 1963, 78 and 134;
Bragantini and Sampaolo: 2013, nos. 157, 158 and 235b.

Figure 9.3   *Iliupersis*, Pompeii, House IX.7.16, Museo Archeologico Nazionale di Napoli, inv.120176. Photo credit: Mathias Hanses

now badly damaged, from the Villa Arianna in Stabiae, the artist emphasized the horse's "birthing" of enemy combatants through the prominent
inclusion of a ladder.[40] Given the aforementioned consistency in the visual
record from the Republic to the Empire, the frescos – though later than
the works of Ennius and Lucretius – could provide further support for a
triangular connection of reciprocal inspiration between *On the Nature of
Things* on the one hand and memorable portrayals of mythological events
in paintings and in tragedy on the other. In alluding to multiple media at
the same time – which would, in turn, have influenced each other –
Lucretius is instructing his readers on how to respond if they are wowed
by impressive displays related to the Trojan War, be it at the opening of
the city's first permanent theater or in their studies or while glancing at
frescos on a dining-room wall. In the end, the plots portrayed are only
eventa. They are long gone, and they could never have happened in
the first place if it were not for the *rerum natura*. What counts, therefore,
is the philosophical instruction provided by a poem like Lucretius', which
will teach the reader about the far more significant *coniuncta* of
Epicurean physics.

Ennius noster

There is one final way in which Lucretius' Trojan-War episode highlights
its engagement with Ennius, and that is in its use of the archaic verb *cluere*
("to be said to be," "to be reckoned as existing"; cf. *OLD* s.v. *clueo*). Two
occurrences of the word bookend the relevant lines in *On the Nature of
Things*. At the start, Lucretius uses it in his definition of *eventa* and
coniuncta (*nam quaecumque cluent, aut his coniuncta duabus | rebus ea
invenies aut horum eventa videbis*, "for all things that are reckoned to exist,
you will either find them to be properties of these two [i.e., of atoms and
void] or you will see that they are accidents that result from them,"
1.449–450). At the end, *cluere* recurs in Lucretius' assertion that *eventa*
do not exist in the same manner as atoms and void (*nec ratione cluere eadem
qua constet inane*, 1.480). I would suggest that in repeatedly employing
cluere to deny that mere "accidents" such as the Trojan War maintain an
independent presence in the universe, Lucretius inverts Ennius' own use of
the same verb in expressing the hope that his "subject matter and poems
will be reckoned famous broadly among the peoples" (*latos <per> populos*

---

[40] Museo Archeologico Nazionale di Napoli, inv. 9893. See Allroggen-Bedel: 1974, 27–89,
for discussion.

res atque poemata nostra | <... *clara*> *cluebunt*, fr. 12–13 Sk.). Lucretius paraphrases these same lines of the *Annals* in his rejection of Ennius' views on metempsychosis, which I mentioned briefly at the outset of this chapter. Here, he refers to *Ennius noster* as "the one who first brought a crown of perennial foliage down from delightful Mt. Helicon for it to be reckoned famous throughout the Italic tribes of men" (*Ennius ut noster cecinit qui primus amoeno* | *detulit ex Helicone perenni fronde coronam,* | *per gentis Italas hominum quae clara clueret*, 1.117–119). The fact that Lucretius' *clara clueret* echoes the *Annals' cluebunt* is often adduced in tentative reconstructions of the Ennian source passage but has not been factored into interpretations of *On the Nature of Things*.[41] I submit that Lucretius intended the verb to have an Ennian ring, both here and in its recurrence in the Trojan-War episode, thereby undermining the earlier poet through the use of his own vocabulary.

Since I have now mentioned Lucretius' explicit naming of Ennius at 1.117, the surrounding lines can lend themselves to some concluding reflections on the role the earlier poet plays in *On the Nature of Things*. At 1.102–135, Lucretius targets Ennius' eschatological views and, as in the other passages I have examined, uses Ennius' own words against him. For example, Ennius had dismissively referred to a preceding generation of poets (and especially to Naevius) as "fauns and soothsayers" (*fauni vatesque*, fr. 207 Sk.). Lucretius now lumps Ennius himself in with the *vates*, whose "fearmongering words" (*vatum* | *terriloquis ... dictis*, 1.102–103), "superstitions and threats" (*religionibus atque minis ... vatum*, 1.109) will cause people to stray from their commitment to Epicurean philosophy and hence to lose their peace of mind.[42] In particular, Ennius propagates misleading but long-lived (*Ennius aeternis exponit versibus edens*, 1.121) views about the nature of the soul.[43] As a result, there is widespread "ignorance" (*ignoratur enim*, 1.112) as to whether the "soul" (*anima*) is born with the body or, on the contrary, inserted into the body at the moment of birth, whether it perishes together with us at death or "sees the darkness of Orcus and the vast emptinesses" or, finally, whether it "inserts itself in a divine manner into other animals,[44] as our Ennius sang"

---

[41] For example, Gale: 2001 focuses rather on allusion to Empedocles, noting that like *clara clueret*, the poet's name means "eternally renowned."

[42] Cf. Kenney: 1970, 378.

[43] For the related pun on *Ennius* and *perennis* at 1.117–118, see Friedländer: 1941, 20; Snyder: 1980, 31 and 107; Gale: 2001.

[44] Bailey: 1947, 2.621 prefers the translation "beasts other than men," thereby excluding humans from the animal kingdom.

(*an tenebras Orci visat vastasque lacunas,* | *an pecudes alias divinitus insinuet se,* | *Ennius ut noster cecinit*, 1.115–117). The latter claim about the transmigration of souls is puzzling even to Lucretius, especially in light of Ennius' own view that "there do in fact exist Acherusian expanses ... where neither our souls abide nor our bodies, but certain images pale in wondrous ways" (*etsi praeterea tamen esse Acherusia templa* | ... | *quo neque permaneant animae neque corpora nostra* | *sed quaedam simulacra modis pallentia miris*, 1.120–123). Lucretius dismisses this tripartite division – soul, body and a pallid ghost-like image – as distracting from Epicurus' calming insight that our existence ceases with death.

I have been making a case throughout that Lucretius' need to deconstruct Ennius' harmful perceptions arose specifically from the continued inclusion of the latter's works at the Roman *ludi* (shows that, in turn, had an impact on contemporary painting, and vice versa). This argument is also borne out by the passage quoted immediately above. It has not, to my knowledge, been previously emphasized that Lucretius' description of misconstrued ideas about the underworld once again reflects key lines of the popular *Andromacha*.[45] In fr. 24 M., one of this play's characters, perhaps Andromache herself, greets "the Acherusian expanses and the vast depths of Orcus" (*Acherusia templa alta Orci salvete infera*). The fragment is preserved in Varro's *On the Latin Language* (7.6), but Cicero quotes what may be a longer version of the same passage (omitting *salvete*) at *Tusc.* 1.48: *Acheru[n]sia templa alta Orci, pallida leti, nubila tenebris loca* ("the deep Acherusian fields of Orcus, pale places of death clouded in darkness").[46] At 1.115–123, Lucretius is thus reusing at least three (*Acherusia templa ... Orci*) and possibly five words (*tenebris/tenebras ... pallida/pallentia*) from the *Andromacha*'s address to the Acherusian realm of Orcus. It seems, therefore, that the responsibility Lucretius ascribes to Ennius' works for perpetuating harmful ideas about the afterlife connects directly, here as elsewhere, to plays we know to have been frequently performed at Roman festivals. In other words, Lucretius addresses a threat that emanates from the *ludi*, where a dangerous ideology undermines the ἀταραξία of Roman audiences. Lucretius is warning his readers against these perilous beliefs and tells them how to respond the next time they encounter them in their reading or in the theater.

---

[45] Jocelyn: 1967, 256 notes the recurrence of *Acherusia templa* in both passages but does not posit a connection. Prinzen: 1998, 50–58 at 50–51 mentions the parallel briefly. Goldberg and Manuwald: 2018, 2.33–35 speak only of "similar phrasing."

[46] Jocelyn: 1967, 255–256 rejects this suggestion.

Similar observations apply to Lucretius' paraphrase of Ennius' views on the transmigration of souls. When he ascribes to his predecessor the statement that the soul "inserts itself in a divine manner into other animals" ([*anima*] *pecudes alias divinitus insinuet se*, 1.116, see above), he is basing this claim on the first book of the *Annals*, where Ennius maintained that "the race adorned with feathers is in the habit of producing eggs, not a soul … the soul itself comes afterwards from there (i.e., the sky) in a divine manner to the chicks" (*ova parire solet genus pennis condecoratum,* | *non animam … post inde venit divinitus pullis* | *ipsa anima,* fr. 8–10 Sk). We can note here both the overlap in content and the recurrence of *anima* and *divinitus*, a parallel that has not been previously observed. Furthermore, Lucretius' dismissal of Ennius' claim that the soul of Homer came to live in him after a chain of Pythagorean transmigrations, and that the Greek poet's ghost-like *simulacrum* visited him in a dream to explain this development (1.124–126), is well known likewise to be based on Book 1 of the *Annals* (e.g., *visus Homerus adesse poeta*, "the poet Homer appeared to be present," fr. 3 Sk.). The same is true of Lucretius' reference, at 1.117–119, to Ennius' hope that his "subject matter and poems will be reckoned famous broadly among the peoples" (fr. 12–13 Sk.), with which I started this section. All of these paraphrases and quotations engage with the same part of Ennius' epic. Of course, we do not in this case have any evidence testifying to later recitations of the book in question. Yet the plethora of fragments that survive from Book 1 of the *Annals* show beyond a doubt that it too was among the best-known parts of Ennius' works,[47] even though we can no longer tell if it was familiar through public recitations or private reading (or both).

Lucretius thus engages yet again with a part of Ennius' oeuvre that would have been of central importance to the literary, dramatic and artistic scene of late-Republican Rome. The Trojan tragedies (certainly the *Andromacha*, and possibly the *Iphigenia* and the *Alexander* as well) were a staple at the *ludi*'s increasingly impressive shows, which evidenced some cross-contamination with the visual arts. In turn, the *Annals*' book on Pyrrhus would have been comparably well known from public recitations at the same events. Whatever the preferred medium may have been for the distribution of Book 1, it too exerted a formative influence on many Romans' (faulty) understanding of the workings of the cosmos. Lucretius

---

[47] For a recent critical assessment of the fragments relating to the proem of the *Annals*, see Elliott: 2013, 115–117 and 144–151. Goldberg and Manuwald: 2018, 1.108–115 provide ample evidence for the "powerful impression" that Ennius' dream of Homer made on later Roman authors.

engages with these Ennian compositions in greater detail than has been previously shown and confronts them specifically in their capacity as works that communicate ideas of a philosophical, religious and even scientific nature to large audiences.[48] He makes the latter element clear by noting that in Ennius' dream, Homer's ghost proceeded "to expound upon the nature of things" (*rerum naturam expandere dictis*, 1.126). Ennius continued to pass this information on to Lucretius' contemporaries even and especially in the first century BC. This made Ennius an adversary to be reckoned with and a direct competitor in asserting a hold on the understanding of the *rerum natura*. Accordingly, Lucretius equips his readers with the necessary gear to confront Ennius' supposedly harmful ideas wherever they next encounter them, be it in a well-stocked library, at a literary recitation, on the walls of a *domus* or at the late-Republican *ludi*'s exceptionally lavish revivals of classic tragedies.

---

[48] For Epicurean views of scientific or natural phenomena such as the sun, see Gellar-Goad's chapter (10) in this volume.

Lucretius on the Size of the Sun

T. H. M. Gellar-Goad[*]

Scientists do not currently know how big the sun is. In fact, in a certain sense, the size of the sun cannot even be known. Rebecca Boyle: "[T]he task of determining the sun's size is trickier than it might seem because the sun is a roiling ball of plasma with no surface. It's also constantly spewing gas and radiation and magnetism, so the diameter of its 'disk' is constantly fluctuating. But it's easier to measure during an eclipse."[1] That last sentence adverts to the unprecedented, elaborate, high-effort undertaking to measure the sun's diameter during the August 2017 total solar eclipse (see further International Occultation Timing Association 2017). Granted, the uncertainty about the sun's size in twenty-first-century astronomy concerns a scale and precision well beyond the everyday considerations of nonspecialists. The mainstream community of solar-system scholars would agree unanimously and with a high degree of certainty that the sun is larger – much, much larger – than, say, a soccer ball or a human foot.

No such consensus is to be found in the astronomical-astrological thinking of the Hellenistic philosophers and their immediate Greek and Roman successors.[2] As with many concepts fundamental to a modern scientific understanding of the universe, the size of the sun was already a matter of speculation in some ancient philosophy. By the first century BC, however, one school was generally perceived to be an outlier on the question: the Epicureans. It was their contention that the sun is the size that it appears to be, a tenet that provoked the derision of their rivals in philosophy and astronomy, and one that on first view may seem baldly

---

[*] In a chapter that considers the continued difficulties people have grappling with the sun, it's worth recalling the hit They Might Be Giants song "Why Does the Sun Shine?" (1994), whose subtitle and first line went, "the Sun is a mass of incandescent gas." Well, no, it's not. TMBG released a palinode many years later, "Why Does the Sun Really Shine?" (2009), whose subtitle and first line goes, "the Sun is a miasma of incandescent plasma."

[1] Boyle: 2017.   [2] So Barnes: 1989, 31 n. 11; Bailey: 1947, 3.1408.

preposterous. The sun is indeed, after all, much larger than a soccer ball or a human foot; and as Jonathan Barnes shows, ancient astronomers' calculations of the sun's magnitude, even if inaccurate "by at least a factor of 15," were nevertheless "of *roughly* the right order of magnitude."[3] Yet despite many disagreements on orthodoxy and heterodoxy in virtually every field of inquiry, the Epicureans and their critics were in agreement that Epicureans believe the sun to be more or less the size it appears.

This chapter advances a threefold argument. [1] Despite the acrimonious mockery of Epicurus' opponents, his and his followers' claims about the size of the sun mean, as a few modern scholars have suggested, that estimation of the sun's magnitude requires careful evaluation and judgment based on data offered by the senses, including but not limited to sight. [2] The presentation of this issue in Lucretius' *On the Nature of Things* (5.564–613), which scholars have treated as an afterthought although it in fact innovates on Epicurus in the explicit discussion of the sun's heat, uses complicated subordination to underscore stylistically that claims about the sun's size are critically dependent on *sensus* and judgments based thereupon, thus issuing a didactic challenge to the Lucretian speaker's addressee. [3] The assertion that the sun is the size it appears became an Epicurean shibboleth, so to speak – a statement prompting reactions that distinguish Epicureans from non-Epicureans, the cognoscenti from the ignoramuses. I begin by surveying the relevant sources and then considering ancient and modern responses to the Epicurean position. I next proceed to stylistic analysis of the passage in Lucretius and finally connect it to the broader didactic program of *On the Nature of Things*.[4]

The Texts

Epicurus' surviving discussion of the size of the sun appears early in his *Letter to Pythocles* (DL 10.91):

> τὸ δὲ μέγεθος ἡλίου τε καὶ τῶν λοιπῶν ἄστρων κατὰ μὲν τὸ πρὸς ἡμᾶς τηλικοῦτόν ἐστιν ἡλίκον φαίνεται. κατὰ δὲ τὸ καθ' αὑτὸ ἤτοι μεῖζον τοῦ ὁρωμένου ἢ μικρῷ ἔλαττον ἢ τηλικοῦτον τυγχάνει. οὕτω γὰρ καὶ τὰ παρ' ἡμῖν πυρὰ ἐξ ἀποστήματος θεωρούμενα κατὰ τὴν αἴσθησιν θεωρεῖται.

> And the size of the sun and the other stars, in respect to our position, is as big as it appears. But in respect to its own position indeed it happens to be

---

[3] Barnes: 1989, 30; emphasis preserved.
[4] For the text of Lucretius, which will henceforth be cited as *DRN*, I use Bailey: 1947. All translations are my own. I owe thanks to Sergio Yona and Amy "Not Nathan" Lather.

bigger than what is seen or a little smaller or the same size. For so also fires near us, when seen at a distance, are seen in accordance with perception.[5]

On a preliminary, prima facie reading of these lines, Epicurus evidently makes a distinction between the size of the sun "relative to us" (κατὰ τὸ πρὸς ἡμᾶς) and its absolute size or its size "relative to itself" (κατὰ τὸ καθ' αὑτό). David Furley explicates this distinction as "presumably mean[ing] no more than that we have to infer its size from its apparent size."[6] In the former frame of reference, the sun's magnitude is firmly correlated to the function of our senses (τηλικοῦτόν ἐστιν ἡλίκον φαίνεται). In the latter, the sun's absolute size is not stated absolutely, but rather characterized in comparison to its size as we adjudge it based on our sense-perception (μεῖζον τοῦ ὁρωμένου ἢ μικρῷ ἔλαττον ἢ τηλικοῦτον).

The text of Diogenes Laertius includes, between the first and second sentence of this passage, an interpolation with a quotation from elsewhere in Epicurus' corpus: "So also in the eleventh [book of his] On Nature: 'For if,' he says, 'it had lost from its size on account of the distance, it would much more have lost from its bright appearance.[7] For there is no other distance for it more suitable for measurement'" (τοῦτο καὶ ἐν τῇ ια' Περὶ φύσεως: εἰ γάρ, φησί, τὸ μέγεθος διὰ τὸ διάστημα ἀπεβεβλήκει, πολλῷ μᾶλλον ἂν τὴν χρόαν. ἄλλο γὰρ τούτῳ συμμετρότερον διάστημα οὐθέν ἐστι). David Sedley explains the final sentence of this quotation as expressing the unique difficulties of measuring the magnitude of the sun: Epicurus "must mean that you cannot get a better vantage point for viewing the sun's size by moving towards it or away from it. For the size of any terrestrial object . . . one distance is more σύμμετρον than another, because you cannot judge its size if you are too close to it or too far away."[8] The sun is too remote – and roughly equally remote from all parts of the world – for us to be able to change our perspective on it. We cannot, therefore, do the necessary perspective-based reasoning about its size with any more certainty anywhere on earth (an issue to which I return below).

In Lucretius' DRN, the same basic doctrine is expanded to a space of about fifty lines (5.564–613), with more extended treatment of the moon (574–584), stars (585–591) and the immense light and heat transmitted

[5] Similarly Aetius 2.21.5. Late doxographies include a section on the size of the sun, including pseudo-Plutarch, pseudo-Galen, Eusebius, Stobaeus and Theodoretus: See Barnes: 1989, 31 and 31 n. 9; Diels: 1879, 351–352. For a philological analysis of Letter to Pythocles 91, including consideration of textual issues and the interpolation of later scholia, see Verde: 2016.

[6] Furley: 1999, 429; similarly Bailey: 1947, 3.1409 n. 1; Asmis: 1984, 155 and 2009, 98 and 98 n. 23.

[7] I translate χρόα here as "bright appearance" on the recommendation of Algra: 2000, 184 n. 76.

[8] Sedley: 1976, 49; contra Asmis: 1984, 314 n. 66.

by the sun (592–613). The opening of the passage is focused most directly
on the matter of the sun's magnitude (564–573):

> nec nimio solis maior rota nec minor ardor
> esse potest, nostris quam sensibus esse videtur.
> nam quibus e spatiis cumque ignes lumina possunt
> adicere et calidum membris adflare vaporem,
> nil illa his intervallis de corpore libant
> flammarum, nil ad speciem est contractior ignis.
> proinde, calor quoniam solis lumenque profusum[9]
> perveniunt nostros ad sensus et loca fulgent,
> forma quoque hinc solis debet filumque videri,
> nil adeo ut possis plus aut minus addere vere.

The sun's wheel cannot be too much bigger, nor its heat too much lesser,
than it is perceived to be by our senses. Because fires—from whatever
distances they can send out light and blow hot air upon our limbs—lose
nothing from the body of their flames because of these distances, the fire is
no more tapered to the sight. Since therefore the sun's heat and poured-out
light make it all the way to our senses and make places shine, so also the
shape and contour ought to be perceived from down here in such a way that
you could not truly attribute more or less to it.

Epicurus' basic claim is echoed in the first two lines of this passage of
Lucretius. The distinction that Epicurus makes explicitly between τὸ πρὸς
ἡμᾶς and τὸ καθ' αὑτό is implicit in the Lucretian *perveniunt nostros ad
sensus* (571) and *hinc ... debet ... videri* (572). And the Lucretius-*ego*[10]
amplifies the analogy to include earthly fires (a point reprised at lines
586–589, cited and translated below).

A key addition to the Lucretian treatment of this question is the
emphasis on the sun's heat. Epicurus' appeals in his *Letter to Pythocles*,
not simply to sight (θεωρούμενα, θεωρεῖται) but to perception generally,
(φαίνεται, κατὰ τὴν αἴσθησιν) implicitly include the non-visual perception
of heat produced by the sun. In *DRN*, the point is made explicit and
important to the process of determining the sun's size. The visual presentation of the sun, its "wheel" (*rota*), is correlated with its "heat" (*ardor*) in
the passage's opening line (564). Similarly, the light and heat of terrestrial
fires are closely linked (*ignes lumina possunt* | *adicere et calidum membris*

---

[9] Bailey: 1947, 1.460 follows Marullus in moving this line (573 in the manuscripts) to the position
I print here (570).

[10] In this paper I use the terms "Lucretian speaker" and "Lucretius-*ego*" rather than "Lucretius" to
describe what the text's speaker does and says: See Gellar-Goad: 2020 (Chapter 1).

adflare vaporem, 566–567). A few lines later the heat and light of the sun again form a naturally conjoined pair (*calor . . . solis lumenque*, 570).

The Lucretian speaker next asserts that the moon is no bigger than it appears (5.575–578) because objects viewed at a distance (on which see my discussion below) become blurred in appearance before they seem to become smaller (579–581); to the extent that the moon has a "clear appearance" (*clara species*, 582), it must be the size it appears (581–584). Furley assumes that this means that the moon has a "razor sharp" outline and therefore is about a foot in diameter.[11] In line with my interpretation below of the Lucretian position on the size of the sun, I am less confident than Furley. The full moon's outline to viewers on earth – although it seems like a perfect circle – is not in fact razor sharp, since during a total solar eclipse the perceptible "diamond ring" effect is produced by the filtering of the last vestiges of sunlight through the mountains and valleys on the moon's surface.[12]

After covering the moon and stars, the Lucretian speaker returns to the topic of the sun and reassures us that we need not wonder how "this sun of such small size could be able to send out so much light . . . and infuse all things with warm air" (*tantulus ille queat tantum sol mittere lumen,* | . . . | . . . *et calido perfundat cuncta vapore*, 591, 593). The standard of comparison for *tantulus* is not expressed in the text, and I follow Kiempe Algra's interpretation, namely, that the sun is small when compared to the size of the cosmos.[13] Throughout the explanation that follows (*DRN* 5.594–613), the Lucretius-*ego* uses a variety of terms to denote the sun's heat: *vapor*, *ardor*, *fervor* and *aestus* (in the compound *aestifer*). This lexical richness runs parallel to the multiplicity of Lucretian terms for atoms (*primordia*, *principia*, *semina* etc.). In the case of the atoms, James Warren argues that the "range of terms . . . express[es] the importance of atoms by noting the various roles they play."[14] Similarly here, I suggest, the range of terms for solar warmth underscores the importance of heat regarding the puzzle of the size of the sun.

---

[11] Furley: 1996, 125.

[12] See, e.g., Thomas: 2017 and, for the original scholarly explanation, Baily: 1836. Also Romeo: 1979, 18. At any rate, Romeo suggests that certainty about the moon's size is for the Lucretius-*ego* unattainable, because a close-up look (τὸ παρόν) is impossible (12).

[13] Algra: 2001, 34–35 n. 57. The size of the cosmos is not a settled issue: David Konstan, in a September 2020 conference paper ("Gravity and the Shape and Location of the Earth," *Epistemology and Meteorology: Epicureanism and Scientific Debates*, SPIN-SPIDER Online Workshop), asserts that Epicurus conceives of a very small cosmos; thanks to David Konstan for sharing a draft of that paper and further observations with me *per litteras*.

[14] Warren: 2007, 22. And see Pope: 2018b for a provocative reading of Lucretian *semina* as particularly sexual and inseminatory.

Finally, a papyrus of Demetrius Lacon addresses the role of distance in perceived brightness of luminescent objects: "Things falling earthwards always look clearer, while further away things [look] less clear" (αἰεὶ τὰ μὲν ἔνγειον προπείπτοντα [τ]ρανότερα βλέπεται, τὰ δὲ πορρώτερα ἀτ[ρα]νώτερα, PHerc. 1013, col. 12.4–8). In other words, lights dim with distance. This point is introduced within the context of a discussion about the size of the sun, and indeed the title of this work by Demetrius may have been Περὶ ἡλίου μεγέθους. The papyrus is, of course, fragmentary, and the immediate context of the comment is patchy, but the text's basic observation points to the fact that, for the sun, magnitude and intensity are crucial unknowns. Without information about how big and bright the sun is near its very surface, one cannot say with certainty, based on its brightness for earthlings, how far away it is; and, conversely, without knowing how far away it is, one cannot with certainty discern its size from its brightness alone.

Ancient and Modern Doxographies

In Cicero's *On Ends* (1.6.20) we can see a reprise of Epicurus' assertion in his *Letter to Pythocles*: "He [Epicurus] adjudges it [the sun] to be as big as it appears, or a little bigger or smaller" (*tantum enim esse censet, quantus videtur, uel paulo aut maiorem aut minorem*). This accurate if incomplete doxographical statement is immediately preceded by a claim, unsupported by any actual Epicurean writings (so Barnes: 1989, 32), that Epicurus thinks the sun is the size of a human foot: "To Democritus the sun appears to be large, and he is definitely an educated guy, completely learned in geometry, but to *him* [Epicurus] perhaps a foot's length" (*sol Democrito magnus videtur, quippe homini erudito in geometriaque perfecto, huic pedalis fortasse*). Cicero's (mis)representation of Epicurus' view here is one of the milder takes on the Epicurean position that rival philosophers voiced in antiquity. Bailey adduces additional mockery by Cicero at *Academica* 2.26.82 and notes that "[T]he belief of Epicurus … that the sun, moon, and stars are in fact the same or nearly the same size as we see them was ridiculed in antiquity as much as by modern critics."[15]

In fact, it was not Epicurus but Heraclitus (generally well-respected by later ancient philosophers) who, according to Aetius 2.21.4, asserted that the sun was "a human foot's width" (εὖρος ποδὸς ἀνθρωπείου). Yet this did not stop the opponents of Epicurean philosophy from regarding as

---

[15] Bailey: 1947, 3.1407.

absurd Epicurus' claim that the sun is the size it appears. Despite the fact that the Epicureans "were not committed to any particular figure" for the sun's size, the ongoing disputes among Hellenistic philosophical schools were not conducive to honest intellectual debate.[16] Epicurean heterodoxy concerning the size of the sun even came to serve as ammunition for Stoic charges of unmanliness, as Pamela Gordon shows.[17] In the end, the philosophical dissension about the magnitudes of celestial bodies could readily be portrayed as a silly and pointless endeavor altogether, as attested most directly by Lucian's comic dialogue *Icaromenippus*.

Scholars of the modern era have puzzled over the Epicurean position on the size of the sun, with some following the literalist reading that characterizes ancient anti-Epicurean reactions; the preponderance of scholars, however, subscribes to one of a number of alternative accounts of Epicurus' meaning.[18] The older, literal-minded view is represented in lapidary form by Jan Woltjer: *novimus Epicurum et Lucretium eiusmodi absurdas doctrinas probare, ad sensuum auctoritatem provocantes* ("we are aware that Epicurus and Lucretius, arguing from the authority of the senses, proffer absurd teachings of this sort").[19] More nuanced and much more recent is the argument of Elizabeth Asmis on the Lucretian version that "the heavenly bodies, since they appear distinctly, are seen by means of very fine eidola that have suffered very little disturbance in traveling over a vast distance, and that therefore present the size of the heavenly bodies approximately as it is 'in itself.'"[20] Furley, meanwhile, holds that Epicurus indeed believes the sun is small and that his insistence on its size is attributable to his adherence to flat-earth theory, the particulars of which would require a diminutive sun.[21]

Yet the matter is more complex than such face-value readings admit. As Barnes points out, "the texts show that, for the Epicureans, the sun was a special case ... and that the theory of its magnitude was grounded in special considerations."[22] One may also recall the problem of being unable to find a more suitable place for "measurement" (συμμετρότερον) of the sun's size based on perspective and distance, a crucial unknown for the resolution of the question. Epicurus' position can as a result be taken to be

---

[16] Barnes: 1989, 33 and Algra: 2000, 186.   [17] Gordon: 2012, 78.

[18] For a doxography of size-of-the-sun scholarship more focused on the related issues of the sun's distance from the earth and the earth's shape, see Bakker: 2016, 236–239. Overview doxographies are found also in Arrighetti: 1973, 527–528 and Delattre and Pigeaud: 2010, 1089–1099 n. 9.

[19] Woltjer: 1877, 126.

[20] Asmis: 1984, 313. Contrast Rudolph: 2011 on the optical theory of Democritus, discussed below.

[21] Furley: 1996; 1999, 421 and 428–429; Bakker: 2016, 239.   [22] Barnes: 1989, 38.

one of aporia, an assertion that the sun's size simply cannot be determined to any meaningful degree of accuracy or precision. Hence, Sedley notes that claims about celestial bodies depend entirely on "appearances" (φάσματα), which are themselves derived from "accidents" (συμπτώματα), and so "we cannot assume their perceptible qualities, such as their colours, their relative sizes and their apparent orbits, to be intrinsic to their true natures rather than mere accidental properties."[23] For Epicurus, the size of objects in the sky cannot be resolved by "visual sense-perception alone" (αὐτὴ ἡ ὄψις), but instead must depend on the Epicurean argumentative methods of ἀντιμαρτύρησις and οὐκ ἀντιμαρτύρησις.[24]

The Epicureans' aporetic stance on celestial dimensions underlies another aspect of their claims about the size of the sun: their opposition to the confident, positivist calculations of astronomers. In part, this Epicurean anti-astronomical sentiment was ideological. Theologically motivated astronomy, such as that espoused by Platonists, ran counter to Epicurus' goal of eliminating superstition.[25] Mathematical astronomy as practiced in Cyzicus by Eudoxus and his school, meanwhile, was in Epicurus' opinion "engendered by faulty observations" and "founded on false principles."[26] This was, in essence, a methodological dispute, with Epicurus objecting that the mathematical astronomers "based their calculations on arbitrary starting points" and that "contrary to what the astronomers want us to believe, we have no means to determine the size of the sun apart from perception, however unclear its data may be."[27] Marco Beretta further suggests that Epicurus was skeptical both of the astronomers' technical capabilities and of their theoretical sophistication when it came to measurements on an atomic scale.[28]

Algra, in my view correctly, brings in considerations of perspective and field of view to shed light on how the sun can be the size it appears without having to be the size of a human foot: "[E]en berg aan de horizon 'lijkt'

---

[23] Sedley: 1976, 40, commenting on PHerc. 1042 col. 3.11–end, PHerc. 154 col. 3.1–2. So also Beretta: 2015, 58. Algra: 2001, 15 similarly points to a logical leap lurking behind the small-sun reading of Epicurus.

[24] Algra: 2000, 183. Compare Konstan: 2020, 9–10 on the role of φαντασία in Epicurean theory of perception and misperception, with the size of the sun as exemplary case.

[25] Barnes: 1989, 41.   [26] Sedley: 1976, 36 and 53 respectively.

[27] Algra: 2000, 187 n. 88 and 187 respectively.

[28] Beretta: 2015, 59; see also *DRN* 4.161–167. Bakker (2016, 258) suggests that the size of the sun was ultimately unimportant to Epicurean philosophers, since otherwise "one would have expected them to take heed of it in other contexts as well, which they did not." Similarly, one might note that Epicurus and Lucretius on the size of the sun do not merit inclusion in Long and Sedley: 1987.

minuscuul in de zin dat hij maar een klein deel van mijn gezichtsveld inneemt. Maar ik kan ook zeggen: 'dat lijkt mij een grote berg,' als ik hem vergelijk met andere referentieobjecten" ("a mountain on the horizon 'looks' minuscule in the sense that it occupies only a small part of my visual field. But I can also say: 'That looks like a big mountain to me,' when I compare it with other reference objects").[29] The difficulty with applying this mountain example to the sun is the lack of such "other reference objects" suitable for putting the sun's size into perspective. There is, as we have noted, nowhere on earth more σύμμετρον than anywhere else for establishing how big the sun is. Again, an amount of aporia on the question is necessitated.

Francesco Verde endorses Algra's view, and further adduces the phrase τὸ φάντασμα τὸ ἡλιακόν found in PHerc. 1013 (col. 21.5–6, "the sun's apparition," Demetrius Lacon again).[30] According to Daniela Taormina, Demetrius "argues that it is the image of the sun that has the size it appears to have,"[31] not the sun itself. Frederik Bakker adds that "the portion of our field of view that is occupied by the sun . . . is proportional to the ratio of the sun's size and distance ... [Thus the Epicureans] refrained from assigning a specific size" to the sun.[32] But Bakker comments elsewhere (2016, 258) that the Lucretian speaker's account of lunar eclipses (*DRN* 5.762–770; cf. Epicurus *Letter to Pythocles* in DL 10.96–97) implies that the sun is larger than the earth. So regardless of the sun's true size, the Epicureans seem not to have contended seriously that it was so small as twelve inches in diameter.

I argue that the one consistent message the Epicurean sources themselves communicate is that this question, perhaps indeed irresolvable, at the least creates a tug of war between the fundamental basis for knowledge, namely sense-perception, and the chief means of preventing misconceptions, false beliefs and anxiety – i.e., reasoned judgment based on sense-perception. When it comes to the sun, our observational data is sorely limited. And yet it is the only evidence we can access. At the same time, we can no more accept our first impressions of this sense-data as true than we can take Epicurus' statements in his *Letter to Pythocles* prima facie to mean that he thinks the sun is about as big as his own left foot. Rather, he seems to imply that one must be tentative and judicious in evaluating and hedging our limited information so that we do not reason incorrectly and end up like the fearful, the superstitious and the erotically infatuated.

[29] Algra: 2001, 17.   [30] Verde: 2017, n. 18.   [31] Taormina: 2016, 123.
[32] Bakker: 2016, 236 n. 184.

Complications in Lucretian Language

I further argue that the Lucretian version of the doctrine on solar magnitude uses language and style to underscore the aporetic Epicurean appeal to the senses. Lucretius' passage brings the crucial concept of heat into the discussion, and it expands Epicurus' analogy to terrestrial fires in a way that both complicates and conditions its applicability to the question of the sun's size. This presentation of the fire analogy, in turn, recalls the Lucretian speaker's examinations of perspective, distance and vision in the opening of Book 4 of *On the Nature of Things* (239–268 and 353–363).

The passage in Lucretius that deals with the size of the sun involves a lot of hedging, since every single sentence is hypotactic. The twelve sentences contained in 5.564–613 average 2.5 subordinate clauses each, with as many as six in one sentence (5.585–591), for an average of three subordinations per five lines of poetry. Categories of subordination include causal, conditional, comparative, temporal, relative, noun clause, result and indirect question. Such pervasive hypotaxis confers an acute mark of contingency upon the message of these lines. The subordination and the contingency are particularly intense in the analogy between celestial and terrestrial fires (5.585–591):

> postremo quoscumque vides hinc aetheris ignis;
> quandoquidem quoscumque in terris cernimus <ignis>,
> dum tremor est[33] clarus dum cernitur ardor eorum,
> perparvum quiddam interdum mutare videntur
> alteram utram in partem filum, quo longius absunt;
> scire licet perquam pauxillo posse minores
> esse vel exigua maiores parte brevique.[34]

> Finally whatever fires of the aether you see from down here – inasmuch as whatever fires we see in the lands, so long as their trembling is clear, and their heat is perceived, are indeed sometimes perceived to change their contour little in either direction the further away they are – it is possible to know that they can indeed be only a little smaller or a tad bit bigger.

The sentence begins with a subordinate (relative) clause introduced by *quoscumque*, followed on the next line by a second (circumstantial) and

---

[33] Here I follow Rouse: 1975, 422, in maintaining the reading *dum tremor est clarus* as opposed to Bailey: 1947, 1.462, who follows Diels in printing *dum tremor <et> clarus*.
[34] Bailey: 1947, 1.462, follows Marullus in moving the two final lines (594–595 in the manuscripts) to the position I print here (590–591).

then a third (relative) subordinate clause. The next line brings two further (temporal) subordinate clauses in parataxis with one another. Two lines later there is another relative clause. The main verb does not appear until the penultimate line, only after three verbs and an adjective appealing to our sense-perceptions as observers (*cernimus, cernitur, videntur, clarus*), and that main verb governs a complementary infinitive (*scire*) that itself governs an indirect statement. The overall effect is too contorted and qualified to be taken as a simple declaration of doctrine.

I noted above that the abundance and variety of words for heat in this portion of the poem point to the importance of heat regarding the question of the sun's size, and that by including heat in its presentation of the matter, Lucretius' text appears to innovate on that of Epicurus. Sense-perception is not limited to sight alone, and our sensation of the radiant warmth of the sun (*calor ... | nostros ad sensus*, 5.570–571) furnishes another kind of data for the reckoning of its size. Its immense heat, despite its profound distance from earth – the extent of this distance is less important than the fact that we can get no significant degree closer to it regardless of how high we climb – attests to the considerable magnitude of the sun. Another Roman-era Epicurean, Diogenes of Oenoanda, similarly appeals to the sun's heat in his refutation of a different misconception about the day star: "[Some people] suspect indeed that the sun is just as low in the sky as it appears, even though it is not just as low in the sky. For if it were just as low, then the earth and all things upon it would have to be burned up" (τὸν γοῦν ἥλιον ὑπολαμβάνουσιν οὕτως εἶναι ταπεινὸν ὥσπερ φαίνεται, μὴ ὄντα οὕτως ταπεινόν. εἰ γὰρ ἦν οὕτως, ἐνπυρίζεσθαι τὴν γῆν ἔδει καὶ τὰ ἐπ' αὐτῆς πάντα πράγματα, fr. 8 Ch). If, as the texts suggest, the sun's heat operates analogously to that of terrestrial fires, then Diogenes' argument here, which is couched as a counterfactual, suggests that the sun has considerable magnitude and heat.

It is furthermore remarkable that the Lucretian section on how the sun is able to fill the earth with warmth (5.590–613) is drenched in water imagery (*rigando*, 594; *perfundat*, 595; *largifluum fontem*, 598; *confluit* and *profluat*, 601) and is analogized to a spring irrigating a field (*nonne vides etiam quam late parvus aquai | prata riget fons interdum campisque redundet?*, "also, don't you see how widely a little source of water sometimes irrigates the meadows and streams over the fields?," 602–603). This paradoxical parallelism draws the reader's attention to the thermal properties of the sun and reminds us once more that appearance and actuality are not one and the same. Furthermore, it emphasizes, by opposition, the immediately preceding analogy of stars in the sky to fires on earth.

That previous analogy (5.585–591), which the Lucretian speaker uses to illustrate the principle that cosmic bodies are more or less the size they appear, likewise (as we have just seen) participates in the passage's stylistic and semantic complications. To begin with, the speaker's claim about fires is false if one takes it to mean that fires do not diminish in size with distance. Fires do, in fact, appear to get smaller as one gets farther away from them. Accordingly, it has been attractive to interpret the claim to mean that fires do not appear to get smaller when viewed at a great distance, up until the point that they disappear entirely. This is the argument of both Bailey and Sedley with reference to lights on land as viewed from across a body of water: That they do not appear to get smaller the farther away one gets from them.[35]

This line of reasoning is, in my judgment, flawed for two reasons. First, inasmuch as their evidence is anecdotal and experiential in nature, my own *sensus* does not match the *sensus* of Bailey or Sedley. When I carefully studied city lights growing distant while flying home from a conference, I found a sense-experience analogous not to Sedley's description of distant fires but rather to Sedley's description of distant structures: "[H]ouses seen from an aeroplane 'appear' smaller than they are in the sense that they fill a smaller area of our visual field than usual. It is quite another thing for a house to appear smaller than it is in the sense that we are deceived into believing it to be smaller than it is."[36] Perhaps lights viewed at a distance are simply more difficult to size up with the imprecision of the naked eye. At any rate, the conflict between individual perceptions in this type of situation suggests either an error in judgment based on sense-data, or else that the sensory experiences may not be generalizable, and thus that this interpretation of the Lucretian analogy is incomplete.

The second, more pressing problem is that Bailey's and Sedley's explanations omit the inclusion by the Lucretius-*ego* of the continued perception of the heat as well as the light of fires as a principal condition for the analogy's validity (*dum cernitur ardor eorum*, 5.587; Algra: 2001, 15 and 17, uniquely includes the warmth criterion). The text requires it to be a both/and condition with regard to perceptible light and heat together, and in such a situation the distant-lights hypotheses of Bailey and Sedley are

[35] Bailey: 1947, 3.1409; Sedley: 1976, 50.

[36] Sedley: 1976, 51. Similarly, my own experience with shading my eyes from the sun conflicts with Furley's (1999, 429) comments on the matter: "[W]hen we see a mountain in the distance, it is so small that it can be blocked from sight by the extent of a hand; yet we know, from a close look, that it is enormous. In the case of the sun, the effect is not the same, because the sun is a light, and lights behave differently."

inadequate to account for the syntactical nuances. Matters are complicated further still by the readily observable phenomenon that heat and light dissipate at vastly different distances, and the intensity of the fire affects the transmission of its heat and the character of its light. Even when both light and heat are sensible, the point is still, as Algra notes, that "de grootte *in principe* nog goed kunnen *schatten*" ("*in principle*, the size can still be *estimated* well").[37]

In the end, readers of *DRN* 5.564–613 are left with a question: Given what we know about fires on earth, how big indeed would the sun have to be in order to seem big enough to have such phosphorescent and thermal action at such a distance? For a caution on the limits of the analogy to earthly fires, we need only look to Asmis' point that the Lucretius-*ego* "seems to have held that in most cases there is a difference in presentation between an object and another that resembles it."[38] In principle, the lingering question can be answered only if we can accurately assert the distance between us and the sun – a measurement that was, for Epicurus and his school, unfathomable, given the limits of their empirical science. Once again, the Epicurean/Lucretian position ultimately seems to be one of reasoned aporia.

Size of the Sun as Didactic Challenge

Getting to this state of reasoned aporia is no simple task, as my rumina-tions above indicate. The text of *DRN* presents what can be taken on a simple surface reading to mean that the sun is the size of a soccer ball, a claim that may strike ancient and modern readers alike as patently ridic-ulous. I suggest that the complication and the seemingly questionable wording are part of the point of the passage, a call for us to apply our Epicurean philosophical and critical thinking to a knotty problem. In this respect, the Lucretian presentation of the size of the sun can be compared to the role of hunting imagery throughout the poem (Whitlatch: 2014) or the final-exam interpretation of the plague scene at the poem's end (e.g., Clay: 1983, 257–266). Each of the three constitutes a didactic challenge to the reader, whose successful progression through the Lucretian narrator's didactic plot entails solving the riddle it presents.

A principal element of the response to the solar challenge is to think about optics and perspective when it comes to figuring out the size of the sun. Contrary to Barnes' claim that "there is virtually no evidence on how

---

[37] Algra: 2001, 17; emphases mine.   [38] Asmis: 1984, 155 n. 29.

the Epicureans understood the perception of size,"[39] recent scholarship on perspective in the atomic theory of Democritus gives ample clues for Epicurus' own thinking, which can in turn be confirmed as Epicurean by examination of relevant passages elsewhere in Lucretius' *DRN*. Kelli Rudolph's study of Democritus clarifies the theoretical function of εἴδωλα in the perception of size in relation to distance.[40] Rudolph also explores the importance of Democritus' metaphor of wax impressions for his atomic theory of vision: Because "a wax impression is an isomorphic copy of the original, but never an exact replica" (2011, 79), the eidolic-vision theory of Democritus allows for "epistemic uncertainty in the images we see" (80). Since, according to Democritus, sight consists in the physical reception of physical emissions from viewed bodies, the objects so viewed and visions of them should not be considered identical, because the εἴδωλον of the thing is never the thing itself. For Epicurus and his followers who have adopted Democritean atomism and optics, therefore, visual sensation – though it may (inasmuch as it is a sense-perception) be infallible – requires active cognition in order for sensations to be properly related to and with their sources.[41]

We can verify that some such theory of vision at a distance is in force in *DRN* by considering passages that deal with perspective in the treatment of simulacra in Book 4. The main description of how we are able to judge distance by sight appears at 4.244–255. In essence, the image emitted by the perceived object to the viewer pushes the intervening "air" (*aer*, 247, 251) past the viewer's eyes, and the quantity of the air is directly proportional to the distance between viewer and viewed.[42] That the sun falls into the category of distant objects requiring intentional perspective-taking along these lines is arguably obvious, but is also suggested by the Lucretian speaker's explanation, shortly thereafter in the same book, of the sun's blinding power (4.325–328). According to the Lucretius-*ego*, the sun is endowed with great power even though it is shining from on high (*vis magnast ipsius ... alte*, 326); the sun's simulacra, therefore, as they travel through air (*aera per purum*, 327, a phrase that looks back to the importance of air in 4.244–255), can strike the eyes heavily enough to

---

[39] Barnes: 1989, 37.   [40] Rudolph: 2011, 79 figs. 1–2; 2015, 50; *contra* Nightingale: 2015, 56.

[41] For the Epicurean doctrine of the infallibility of sense perceptions see, e.g., DL 10.31–32; Striker: 1977; Taylor: 1980; Asmis: 1984, 152; Vogt: 2016: *passim*, with further bibliography at 155 n. 1.

[42] This is the "intromission" theory of optics characteristic of the ancient atomists, including Leucippus, Democritus and the Epicureans: See, e.g., Thibodeau: 2016, 133–134 and 138.

harm their atomic compounding.[43] From these lines the reader can determine that the sun is not entirely a special case, but is subject to the same air-based perspectival adjustments as are other observable objects.

The image most often cited by scholars examining the Lucretian treatment of perspective is that of the tower seen from far away (4.353–363), which is square but appears at a distance to be round. According to the speaker's explanation for the apparent roundness of the tower's "angle" (*angulus*, 355), "while the simulacra are moving through a lot of air, the air with constant collisions forces it [the angle] to become dull" (*aera per multum quia dum simulacra feruntur,* | *cogit hebescere eum crebris offensibus aer,* 358–359). As a result, "every angle all at once has escaped our perception" (*suffugit sensum simul angulus omnis,* 360). That the tower appears round does not make it round; that the tower is in reality square does not invalidate our perceiving it as having a round appearance from a distance.[44] The fact that the Lucretian discussion of the size of the sun invokes readers' sense-perception (with *videtur* at 5.565, inter alia) prompts them to think back to the Lucretian discussion of perception at a distance, and to recall from the tower example that data derived from visual perception degrades over distance along with the simulacra themselves. We know intuitively that the sun is farther away than such a tower, and thus we know that we need care in assessing the size of the sun, just as we would in assessing the size (and shape) of a far-off tower.

Finally, there must be perspective-taking on our tactile sensation of warmth as well as on our sight. The heat emitted by a candle, by a bonfire and by a burning building fades away at profoundly different distances – an important piece of evidence in figuring out just how big the sun appears to be. Similarly, the Lucretian speaker's explicit introduction of heat into the Epicurean doctrine on the size of the sun may suggest to readers that they ponder as well the difference in perceived heat transmitted by the sun and the moon, despite the roughly equivalent percentage of the sky they fill – attested by, among other things, the moon's ability to eclipse the sun for terrestrial viewers. Vision alone, it appears, is insufficient for solving the puzzle.

So the implied prompts to remember the role of heat in addition to light, and to apply our understanding of perspective to the question of the size of the sun, amount to another current in the didactic airstream of *DRN*.

---

[43] Pope: 2018a, 207–208, suggests that the lines that follow, 4.329–331, use sexual and ejaculatory imagery in describing the sun's rays.

[44] Cf. Vogt: 2016, 148.

The Lucretian speaker, rather than merely parroting a ruthlessly ridiculed doctrine, instead pulls his student-readers into the process of inquiry. It becomes the didactic audience's task to receive data from sense-perception, and to use lessons learned earlier in the poem (as about perspective and distance, cf. 4.239–268, 353–363) in making correct rational judgments based upon that sense data. Asmis reminds us that for the Lucretius-*ego* "there is no clash between the judgment of the senses and objective reality, because the type of fact that seems to be in conflict with sense perception does not fall within the province of sense perception at all, but belongs to an entirely distinct domain of reality ... judged by reason."[45] As Demetrius Lacon writes of a related solar question, "the sun does not *appear* stationary, but rather it *is thought* to appear stationary" (ο[ὐ] φαίνεται μ[ὲ]ν ὁ ἥλιο[ς ἑσ[τ]ηκώς, δοκεῖ δὲ φαίν[εσ]θαι, PHerc. 1013 col. 20.7–9; cited by Barnes: 1989, 35–36 n. 36). Tricky cases such as the size of the sun, where sense data is incomplete, may require suspension of such reasoned judgment, until enough evidence becomes available to evaluate our hypotheses through the process of ἐπιμαρτύρησις, until which point the opinion must remain a προσμένον.[46]

In the Epicurean and Lucretian account of reality, the senses themselves are infallible. The Lucretian speaker's assertion that the sun is just as big as it is perceived to be by our senses must therefore also be infallible – just as the perception that the sun is bigger when it is close to the horizon at sunrise and sunset must be infallible, without our having to believe that the sun actually changes sizes dramatically during the day. But our interpretation of what exactly that assertion entails about the sun's actual size is a matter of judgment, and as such is fallible and uncertain indeed. As with the argumentation presented by the Lucretius-*ego* throughout the poem, and as with the gripping, awful plague scene at the end of Book 6, we must be keen-scented, relentless and detached from mundane concerns and fears in order to reckon and judge accurately in cosmic matters.

Size of the Sun as Epicurean Shibboleth

The Epicureans did not believe that the sun was the size of a human foot. They distinguished between the sun's actual size and the size of its appearance, the latter of which was the only magnitude measurable from

---

[45] Asmis: 1984, 155.
[46] So Bailey: 1926, 287–288; Romeo: 1979, 12; Taylor: 2016, 142 n. 20, with Epicurus VS 24, DL 10.34, Sextus Empiricus *Against the Grammarians* 7.211–212 and 215–216.

earth with the technology available. In this matter as almost everywhere else, the Epicureans appealed to the truth of sense-perception – with the important caution that discerning reality from appearance requires perception-based judgment, which itself is not guaranteed to be true. In Lucretius' poem, the discussion of solar magnitude adds more detail to Epicurus' original conception, especially with the introduction of the sun's heat into the passage. Complicated style emphasizes how full of hedges and conditioned claims the Lucretius-*ego* is, and his thorny exposition of the doctrine amounts to a didactic challenge that sends readers elsewhere in his work, to ponder perspective and to hunt down a proper understanding of this aspect of the natural world.

By staking out a stance of aporia conditioned by sense-perception and reasoning thereupon, the Epicureans did in fact prove to be less wrong than everyone else. Algra emphasizes that "*all* ancient estimates of the size of the sun, including those put forward by the mathematical astronomers, were false."[47] The failing of ancient mathematical science in estimate-making was pervasive since, Geoffrey Lloyd notes, "an important recurrent phenomenon in Greek speculations about nature is a premature or insecurely grounded quantification or mathematicisation."[48] Epicurus and his school, in avoiding a concrete statement of the sun's size, avoided being concretely wrong, in contrast to Eudoxus and all the rest. The sun passage in *DRN* pushes the reader towards non-commitment rather than risking such a misjudgment.

In closing I argue that the size of the sun is an Epicurean shibboleth. In Epicurus, in Lucretius and in Demetrius, we see the same nostrum repeated, with progressive elaborations that do not fully clarify the basic precept. The persistence of Epicureans in this formulation is not so much the result of reflexive dogma or pseudo-intellectual obscurantism as it is a passphrase, a litmus test. Think like an Epicurean, and you will figure out that the sun's appearance and the sun itself are two related but distinct things with two different sizes; that you must keep the infallible data of the senses, tactile as well as visual, in proper perspective when making judgments about your perception; and that the available data is insufficient to estimate the sun's magnitude to an acceptable degree of confidence (compare Barnes: 1989, 36). Think that Epicureans believe the sun's diameter is a foot, that they are absurd, and you have exposed yourself as un-Epicurean. The first/second-century AD Stoic doxographer Cleomedes, who as Algra points out "nowhere takes account of the Epicurean principle

---

[47] Algra: 2000, 187 n. 88; emphasis preserved.   [48] Lloyd: 1987, 280.

of multiple explanations,"[49] likewise fails this test when he mocks Epicurus' position on the size of the sun.

Thinking like an Epicurean – rather than figuring out the actual size of the sun – is, I suggest, the point of the Lucretian passage on the size of the sun, as it is indeed the fundamental point of Epicurean natural philosophy generally. Constantina Romeo suggests that Epicurus' moral program of liberating humankind from the fear of death motivates his followers' ardent defense of his claims on the sun's size. Since Epicurus presented understanding of the natural and celestial world as essential for a life of ataraxia, "nel momento in cui lo Stoico ritiene di avere dimostrato l'errore di Epicuro nella scienza della natura, sostiene pure che Epicuro non ha dato nessun conforto di fronte alla morte" ("in the moment in which the Stoic [Posidonius] thinks he has shown Epicurus' mistakes in natural science, he also claims that Epicurus has provided no comfort in the face of death").[50] Yet Posidonius has actually failed the test, has misunderstood the stakes of the debate. Precise measurement of the sun's size is not what is at issue for the Epicureans, and so proof of scientific error does not vitiate Epicurus' moral philosophy. The Epicureans pushed back so fiercely against their opponents' (mis)characterizations of Epicurus' position because of the underlying epistemological and phenomenological principles. It does not matter to Epicurean ethics or to ataraxia whether the size of the sun is known. After all, the Epicureans did not even need to affix a certain size to the sun to accomplish their core epistemological objective: to remove anxiety about divine control over cosmological phenomena.[51] What matters, and the underlying reason for this Epicurean shibboleth, is a readiness to use careful reasoning and good judgment to embrace uncertainty about the nature of things without succumbing to the anxiety-inducing fear of death.

---

[49] Algra: 2000, 183.   [50] Romeo: 1979, 17.
[51] On the Epicurean methodology of offering multiple plausible explanations for natural phenomena in situations where a single correct explanation could not be produced, see especially Hankinson: 2013.

Bibliography

Alberti, A. 1995. "The Epicurean Theory of Law and Justice," in Laks and Schofield: 1995, 161–190.

Albrecht, M. von 2003. *Cicero's Style*. Leiden.

Algra, K. 2000. "The Treatise of Cleomedes and its Critique of Epicurean Cosmology," in Erler: 2000: 164–189.

　　2001. *Epicurus en de zon. Wiskunde en fysica bij een Hellenistisch filosoof.* Amsterdam.

Algra, K. et al. (eds.) 1999. *The Cambridge History of Hellenistic Philosophy.* Cambridge.

Allman, D. and M. Beaty (eds.) 2002. *Cultivating Citizens: Soulcraft and Citizenship in Contemporary America.* Oxford.

Allroggen-Bedel, A. 1974. *Maskendarstellungen in der römisch-kampanischen Wandmalerei.* Munich.

Anderson, W. S. 1982. *Essays on Roman Satire.* Princeton, NJ.

　　1992. "Horace's Different Recommenders of 'Carpe diem' in C. 1.4, 7, 9, 11." *CJ* 88: 115–122.

Angeli, A. 1988. (ed.) *Filodemo. Agli amici di scuola (PHerc. 1005). Edizione, traduzione e commento.* Naples.

Annas, J. 1993. *The Morality of Happiness.* Oxford.

Annas, J. and G. Betegh (eds.) 2016. *Cicero's De finibus. Philosophical Approaches.* Cambridge.

Armstrong, D. 2003. "Philodemus, the Herculaneum Papyri, and the Therapy of Fear," in Gordon and Suits: 2003, 17–43.

　　2004. "All Things to All Men: Philodemus' Model of Therapy and the Audience of *De Morte*," in Fitzgerald, Obbink and Holland: 2004, 15–54.

　　2008. "'Be Angry and Sin Not': Philodemus versus the Stoics on Natural Bites and Natural Emotions," in Fitzgerald: 2008, 79–121.

　　2011. "Epicurean Virtues, Epicurean Friendship: Cicero vs the Herculaneum Papyri," in Fish and Sanders: 2011, 105–128.

Armstrong, D. and M. McOsker (eds.) 2020. *Philodemus: On Anger.* Atlanta, GA.

Armstrong, J. M. 1997. "Epicurean Justice." *Phronesis* 42: 324–334.

Arrighetti, G. 1973. *Epicuro, Opere. Introduzione, testo critico, traduzione e note.* Turin.

Asmis, E. 1984. *Epicurus' Scientific Method.* Ithaca, NY.

1990. "Philodemus' Epicureanism." *Aufstieg und Niedergang der römischen Welt* 36.4: 2369–2406.

1991. "Philodemus's Poetic Theory and *On the Good King According to Homer.*" *CA* 10: 1–45.

1993. *The Morality of Happiness.* Oxford.

1995. "Epicurean Poetics," in Obbink: 1995, 15–34.

2004. "Epicurean Economics," in Fitzgerald, Obbink and Holland: 2004, 133–176.

2008. "Lucretius' New World Order: Making a Pact with Nature." *CQ* 58: 141–57.

2009. "Epicurean Empiricism," in Warren: 2009, 84–104.

2011. "The Necessity of Anger in Philodemus' *On Anger,*" in Fish and Sanders: 2011, 152–182.

Auvray-Assayas, C. and D. Delattre (eds.) 2001. *Cicéron et Philodème: la polémique en philosophie.* Paris.

Baier, T. 2010. "Das Irrationale bei Lukrez." *WJA* 34: 97–114.

Bailey, C. 1922. *Lucreti De Rerum Natura Libri Sex,* 2nd ed. Oxford.

1926. *Epicurus: The Extant Remains.* Oxford.

1947. *Titi Lucreti Cari De Rerum Natura Libri Sex. Edited with Prolegomena, Critical Apparatus, Translation and Commentary.* 3 vols. Oxford.

Baily, F. 1836. "On a Remarkable Phenomenon that Occurs in Total and Annular Eclipses of the Sun." *Monthly Notices of the Royal Astronomical Society* 4.2: 15–19.

Bakker, F. 2016. *Epicurean Meteorology: Sources, Method, Scope and Organization.* Leiden.

Baraz, Y. 2012. *A Written Republic: Cicero's Philosophical Politics.* Princeton, NJ.

Barnes, J. 1989. "The Size of the Sun in Antiquity." *ACD* 225: 29–41.

Bees, R. 2004. *Die Oikeiosislehre der Stoa.* Würzburg.

Belliotti, R. 2009. *Roman Philosophy and the Good Life.* Lanham, MD.

Benferhat, Y. 2001. "*Cum Scriberem contra Epicureos*: Cicéron et l'épicurisme dans les *Tusculanes* I–II." *VL* 164: 21–35.

2002. "Plaidoyer pour une victime de Cicéron: Pison." *REL* 80: 55–77.

2005a. *Ciues Epicurei: les épicuriens et l'idée de monarchie à Rome et en Italie de Sylla à Octave.* Brussels.

2005b. "Catulle et les affrontements politico-littéraires à Rome à la fin de la République," in Poignault: 2005, 131–148.

Berry, D. H. and A. Erskine (eds.) 2010. *Form and Function in Roman Oratory.* Cambridge.

Beretta, M. 2015. *La rivoluzione culturale di Lucrezio. Filosofia e scienza nell'antica Roma.* Rome.

Bergsma, A., G. Poot and A. C. Liefbroer. 2008. "Happiness in the Garden of Epicurus." *Journal of Happiness Studies* 9: 397–423.

Bernstein, W. H. 1985. "A Sense of Taste: Catullus 13." *CJ* 80: 127–130.

Bibauw, J. (ed.) 1969. *Hommages à Marcel Renard II.* Brussels.

Bielskis, A. 2018. "On the Genealogy of Kitsch and the Critique of Ideology: A Reflection on Method." *Genealogy* 2.1.9.

Biondi, G. G. 2003. "Lucrezio e Catullo: osservazioni su una *vexata quaestio* (con note sulla interpretazione e la cronologia di Catull. 64 e 68)." *Paideia* 58: 207–234.

Blyth, D. 2010/11. "Cicero and Philosophy as Text." *CJ* 106: 71–98.

Boissier, G. 1897. *Cicero and His Friends.* New York.

Bonner, S. F. 1977. *Education in Ancient Rome.* Berkeley, CA.

Bourne, F. C. 1977. "Caesar the Epicurean." *CW* 70: 417–432.

Boyle, R. 2017. 18 August. "Earth Has the Solar System's Best Eclipses." *FiveThirtyEight.* https://fivethirtyeight.com/features/earth-has-the-solar-sys tems-best-eclipses/.

Bragantini, I. and V. Sampaolo. 2013. *La pittura Pompeiana.* Naples.

Bramble, J. C. 1970. "Structure and Ambiguity in Catullus LXIV." *PCPhS* 16: 22–41.

Brandt, E. et al. 1968. *Antike Gemmen in deutschen Sammlungen, vol 2: Staatliche Münzsammlung.* Munich.

Braund, D. and C. Gill (eds.) 2003. *Myth, History and Culture in Republican Rome: Studies in Honour of T.P. Wiseman.* Exeter.

Braund, D. C. 1996. "The Politics of Catullus 10: Memmius, Caesar and the Bithynians." *Hermathena* 160: 45–57.

Bringmann, K. 2012. "Cicero über seine Philosophica: Zu Überlieferung und Interpretation einer umstrittenen Selbstaussage in Att. 12, 52, 3." *Hermes* 140: 25–36.

Brinton, A. 1988. "Cicero's Use of Historical Examples in Moral Argument." *Ph&Rh* 21: 169–184.

Brittain, C. 2016. "Cicero's Sceptical Methods: The Example of *De finibus*," in Annas and Betegh: 2016, 12–40.

Broch, H. 1933. "Das Böse im Wertsystem der Kunst." *Die neue Rundschau* 44.2: 157–191.

Brown, E. 2002. "Epicurus on the Value of Friendship (*Sententia Vaticana* 23)." *CPh*: 68–80.

Brown, R. D. 1987. *Lucretius on Love and Sex: A Commentary on De Rerum Natura IV, 1030–1287.* Leiden.

Brunt, P. A. 1975. "Stoicism and the Principate." *PBSR* 43: 7–35.

1986. "Cicero's *Officium* in the Civil War." *JRS* 76: 12–32.

1989. "Philosophy and Religion in the Late Republic," in Griffin and Barnes: 1989, 174–198.

Buchheit, V. 1971. "Epikurs Triumph des Geistes." *Hermes* 99: 303–323.

Buffière, F. 1956. *Les mythes d'Homère et la pensée grecque.* Paris.

Cairns, F. 2003. "Catullus in and about Bithynia: Poems 68, 10, 28 and 47," in Braund and Gill: 2003, 165–190.

Cappello, O. 2016. "Everything You Wanted to Know About Atticus (but Were Afraid to Ask Cicero): Looking for Atticus in Cicero's *ad Atticum*." *Arethusa* 49: 463–487.

2019. *The School of Doubt: Skepticism, History, and Politics in Cicero's Academica*. Leiden.

Carilli, M. 1975. "Le nugae di Catullo e l'epigramma greco." *ASNP* 5: 925–953.

Castagnoli, L. 2013. "Democritus and Epicurus on Sensible Qualities in Plutarch's *Against Colotes* 3–9." *Aetia* 3.

Castner, C. J. 1988. *Prosopography of Roman Epicureans from the Second Century B.C. to the Second Century A.D.* Frankfurt am Main.

Chandler, C. 2017. *Philodemus: On Rhetoric, Books 1 and 2: Translation and Exegetical Essays*. Philadelphia, PA.

Chevallier, R. (ed.) 1984. *Présence de Cicéron*. Paris.

Classen, C. J. 2010. "Teaching Philosophy, a Form or Function of Roman Oratory: Velleius' Speech in Cicero's 'De natura deorum,'" in Berry and Erskine: 2010, 195–207.

Clay, D. 1983. *Lucretius and Epicurus*. Ithaca, NY.

1998. *Paradosis and Survival: Three Chapters in the History of Epicurean Philosophy*. Ann Arbor, MI.

Cleary, J. J. and D. C. Shartin (eds.) 1989. *Proceedings of the Boston Area Colloquium in Ancient Philosophy*. Boston, MA.

Cleary, J. J. and W. Wians (eds.) 1994. *Proceedings of the Boston Area Colloquium in Ancient Philosophy, vol. 10*. Boston, MA.

Cosenza, P. 1996. "La dimostrazione della non eleggibilità dell'ingiustizia nella *Rata Sententia* XXXIV di Epicuro," in Giannantoni and Gigante: 1996, 361–376.

Cowan, R. 2013. "Fear and Loathing in Lucretius: Latent Tragedy and Anti-Allusion in *DRN* 3," in Papanghelis, Harrison and Frangoulidis: 2013, 113–133.

Croisille, J.-M. 1963. "Le sacrifice d'Iphigénie dans l'art romain et la littérature latine." *Latomus* 22: 209–225.

Crönert, W. 1907. "Die Epikureer in Syrien." *JÖAI* 10: 145–152.

Curran, L .C. 1969. "Catullus 64 and the Heroic Age." *YCS* 21: 169–192.

D'Anna, G. 1965. *Alcuni aspetti della polemica antiepicurea di Cicerone*. Rome.

Dale, F. R. 1958. "Caesar and Lucretius." *G&R* 5: 181–182.

Dalfen, J. (ed.) 1980. *Symmicta philologica Salisburgensia Georgio Pfligersdorffer sexagenario oblata*. Rome.

Damon, C. 1997. *The Mask of the Parasite: A Pathology of Roman Patronage*. Ann Arbor, MI.

Davis, G. 1991. *Polyhymnia: The Rhetoric of Horatian Lyric Discourse*. Berkeley and Los Angeles, CA.

(ed.) 2010. *A Companion to Horace*. Malden, MA.

De Lacy, P. 1941. "Cicero's Invective against Piso." *TAPA* 72: 49–58.

Delattre, D. 1984. "Philodème dans la 'Correspondance' de Cicéron." *BAGB*: 27–39.

Delattre, D. and J. Pigeaud (eds.) 2010. *Les Épicuriens*. Paris.

Dettmer, H. 1986. "*Meros amores*: A Note on Catullus 13.9." *QUCC* 23: 87–91.

1989. "Catullus 13: A Nose Is a Nose Is a Nose." *SyllClass* 1: 75–85.

DeWitt, N. W. 1954. *Epicurus and His Philosophy.* Minneapolis, MN.

Diano, C. 1940. "La Psicologia d'Epicuro e la teoria della passioni. Part I (section 2)." *Giornale critico della Filosofia Italiana,* 2nd ser. vol. 8: 151–165.

Dickey, E. and A. Chahoud (eds.) 2010. *Colloquial and Literary Latin.* Cambridge.

Diels, H. 1879. *Doxographi Graeci.* Berlin.

Dillon, J. and T. Long (eds.) 1988. *The Question of Eclecticism: Studies in Later Greek Philosophy.* Berkeley, CA.

Dobesch, G. 1985. "Politische Bemerkungen zu Ciceros Rede Pro Marcello," in Weber and Dobesch: 1985, 153–231.

Donini, P. 1988. "The History of the Concept of Eclecticism," in Dillon and Long: 1988, 15–33.

Donini, P. and B. Inwood 1999. "Stoic Ethics," in Algra et al: 1999, 675–738.

Dueck, D. 2009. "Poetic Quotations in Latin Prose Works of Philosophy." *Hermes* 137: 314–334.

Dyck, A. 2004. *A Commentary on Cicero, De Legibus.* Ann Arbor, MI.

Elliott, J. 2013. *Ennius and the Architecture of the Annales.* New York.

Englert, W. 1994. "Stoics and Epicureans on the Nature of Suicide," in Cleary and Wians: 1994, 67–96.

Erler, M. 1992a. "Orthodoxie und Anpassung. Philodem, ein Panaitios des Kepos?" *MH* 49: 171–200.

1992b. "Cicero und 'unorthodoxer' Epikureismus." *Anregung* 38: 307–322.

1994. "Die Schule Epikurs," in Flashar: 1994, 203–380.

2001. "Response to Voula Tsouna," in Auvray-Assayas and Delattre: 2001, 173–78.

2011. "Autodidact and Student: On the Relationship of Authority and Autonomy in Epicurus and the Epicurean Tradition," in Fish and Sanders: 2011, 9–28.

2016. "The Closing Columns of Philodemus' *On the Good King According to Homer, PHerc.* 1507 Cols. 95–98 (= Cols. 40–43 Dorandi)." *CronErcol* 46: 55–81.

2020. *Epicurus: An Introduction to His Practical Ethics and Politics.* Basel.

Erler, M. (ed.) 2000. *Epikureismus in der späten Republik und der Kaiserzeit. Akten der 2. Tagung der Karl-und-Gertrud-Abel-Stiftung vom 30. September–3. Oktober 1998 in Würzburg.* Stuttgart.

Essler, H. 2011. "Cicero's Use and Abuse of Epicurean Theology," in Fish and Sanders: 2011, 129–151.

Evans, M. 2004. "Can Epicureans Be Friends?" *AncPhil* 24: 407–424.

Fabrizi, V. 2012. *Mores veteresque novosque: rappresentazioni del passato e del presente di Roma negli Annales di Ennio.* Pisa.

Fantham, E. 2006. "'Dic si quid potes de Sexto Annali': The Literary Legacy of Ennius' Pyrrhic War." *Arethusa* 39: 549–568.

2009. "Caesar as an Intellectual," in M. T. Griffin (ed.), *A Companion to Julius Caesar.* Malden, MA, 141–156.

Farrell, J. 2008. "The Six Books of Lucretius' *De rerum natura*: Antecedents and Influence." *Dictynna* 5: 1–21.

Feeney, D. C. 1978. "Wild Beasts in the *De rerum natura*." *Prudentia* 10: 15–22.

Fish, J. 1998. "Is Death Nothing to Horace? A Brief Comparison with Philodemus and Lucretius." *CronErcol* 28: 99–104.

2011. "Not All Politicians Are Sisyphus: What Roman Epicureans Were Taught about Politics," in Fish and Sanders: 2011, 72–104.

2016. "The Closing Columns of Philodemus' *On the Good King According to Homer*, PHerc. 1507 Cols. 95–98 (= Cols. 40–43 Dorandi)." *CronErcol* 46: 55–81.

Fish, J. and K. Sanders (eds.) 2011. *Epicurus and the Epicurean Tradition*. Cambridge.

Fitzgerald, J. (ed.) 2008. *Passions and Moral Progress in Greco-Roman Thought*. London.

Fitzgerald, J. T., D. Obbink and G. S. Holland (eds.) 2004. *Philodemus and the New Testament World*. Leiden.

Fitzgerald, W. 1995. *Catullan Provocations: Lyric Poetry and the Drama of Position*. Berkeley, CA, Los Angeles, CA and London.

Flashar, H. (ed.) 1994. *Die Philosophie der Antike, Band 4: Die Hellenistische Philosophie I*. Basel.

Föllinger, S and G. M. Müller (eds.) 2013. *Der Dialog in der Antike: Formen und Funktionen einer literarischen Gattung zwischen Philosophie, Wissensvermittlung und dramatischer Inszenierung*. Berlin and Boston, MA.

Fordyce, C. J. 1961. *Catullus: A Commentary*. Oxford.

Fowler, D. 1989. "Lucretius and Politics," in Griffin and Barnes: 1989, 120–50. Reprinted in M. R. Gale (ed.), *Lucretius*. Oxford, 2007, 397–431.

2000. *Roman Constructions: Readings in Postmodern Latin*. Oxford.

2002. *Lucretius on Atomic Motion. A Commentary on De rerum natura 2.1, 332*. Oxford.

Frede, D. 2016. "Epicurus on the Importance of Friendship in the Good Life (*De Finibus* 1.65–70," in Annas and Betegh: 2016, 96–117.

Freudenburg, K. (ed.) 2005. *The Cambridge Companion to Roman Satire*. Cambridge.

2010. "*Horatius anceps*: Persona and Self-Revelation in Satire and Song," in Davis: 2010, 271–290.

Friedländer, P. 1941. "Pattern of Sound and Atomic Theory in Lucretius." *AJP* 62: 16–34.

Friedrich, G. 1908. *Catullus Veronensis liber*. Leipzig and Berlin.

Frischer, B. 1982. *The Sculpted Word: Epicureanism and Philosophical Recruitment in Ancient Greece*. Berkeley, CA.

Fuhrer, T. 2012. "Philosophische Schulen und ihre Kommunikationsräume im spätrepublikanischen und kaiserzeitlichen Rom," in Mundt: 2021, 241–252.

Furley, D. J. 1970. "Variations on Themes from Empedocles in Lucretius' Proem." *BICS* 17: 55–64.

1996. "The Earth in Epicureanism and Contemporary Astronomy," in Giannantoni and Gigante: 1996, 119–125.

1999. "Cosmology," in Algra et al.: 1999: 412–451.

Fussl, M. 1980. "Epikureismus im Umkreis Caesars," in Dalfern: 1980, 61–80.

Gaisser, J. H. 1995. "Threads in the Labyrinth: Competing Views and Voices in Catullus 64." *AJP* 11: 579–616.

Gale, M. R. 1994. *Myth and Poetry in Lucretius*. Cambridge.

2001. "Etymological Wordplay and Poetic Succession in Lucretius." *CP* 96: 168–172.

2007. "Lucretius and Previous Poetic Traditions," in Gillespie and Hardie: 2007, 59–75.

2009. *Lucretius: De rerum natura V*. Warminster.

Garani, M. 2007. *Empedocles Redivivus: Poetry and Analogy in Lucretius*. New York.

Garani, M. and D. Konstan (eds.) 2014. *The Philosophizing Muse*. Cambridge.

Garbarino, G. 2010. "Cesare e la cultura filosofica del suo tempo," in Urso: 2010, 207–221.

Garcea, A. 2012. *Caesar's De analogia*. Oxford.

Gatzemeier, S. 2013. *Ut ait Lucretius. Die Lukrezrezeption in der lateinischen Prosa bis Laktanz*. Göttingen.

Gellar-Goad, T. H. M. 2020. *Laughing Atoms, Laughing Matter: Lucretius' De Rerum Natura and Satire*. Ann Arbor, MI.

Giannantoni, G. and M. Gigante (eds.) 1996. *Epicureismo greco e romano. Atti del congresso internazionale, Napoli 19–26, maggio 1993, vol. 1*. Naples.

Gibson, R. and C. Whitton (eds.) Forthcoming. *Cambridge Critical Guide to Latin Studies*. Cambridge.

Giesecke, A. L. 2000. *Atoms, Ataraxy, and Allusion: Cross-Generic Imitation of the De Rerum Natura in Early Augustan Poetry*. Hildesheim, Zurich and New York.

Gigante, M. 1995. *Philodemus in Italy*. Trans. Dirk Obbink. Ann Arbor, MI.

Gigon, O. (ed.) 1978. *Lucrèce: Huit exposés suivis de discussions*. Geneva.

Gilbert, N. 2015. "Among Friends: Cicero and the Epicureans." Diss. Toronto.

2019. "Lucius Saufeius and His Lost Prehistory of Rome: Intellectual Culture in the Late Republic." *CP* 114.1: 25–46.

Gilbert, N., M. Graver and S. McConnell (eds.) Forthcoming. *Power and Persuasion in Cicero's Philosophy*. Cambridge.

Gildenhard, I. 2007. *Paideia Romana*. Cambridge.

2013. "Cicero's Dialogues: Historiography Manqué and the Evidence of Fiction," in Föllinger and Müller: 2013, 235–274.

Gillespie, S. and P. Hardie (eds.) 2007. *The Cambridge Companion to Lucretius*. Cambridge.

Giuffrida, P. 1950. *L'epicureismo nella letteratura latina nel I sec. av. Cristo II: Lucrezio e Catullo*. Turin.

Glucker, J. 1988. "Cicero's Philosophical Affiliations," in Dillon and Long: 1988, 34–69.

2012. "Cicero's Remarks on Translating Philosophical Terms – Some General Problems," in Glucker and Burnett: 2012, 37–96.

Glucker, J. and C. Burnett (eds.) 2012. *Greek into Latin from Antiquity until the Nineteenth Century.* London and Turin.

Goldberg, S. M. 1995. *Epic in Republican Rome.* New York.

2000. "Cicero and the Work of Tragedy," in Manuwald: 2000, 49–59.

Goldberg, S. M. and G. Manuwald. 2018. *Fragmentary Republican Latin: Ennius.* 2 vols. Cambridge, MA.

Goldhill, S. (ed.) 2008. *The End of Dialogue in Antiquity.* Cambridge and New York.

Goldschmidt, N. 2013. *Shaggy Crowns: Ennius' Annales and Vergil's Aeneid.* Oxford.

Goldschmidt, V. 1977. *La doctrine d'Épicure et le droit.* Paris.

Gordon, D. R. and D. B. Suits (eds.) 2003. *Epicurus: His Continuing Influence and Contemporary Relevance.* New York.

Gordon, P. 2004. "Remembering the Garden: The Trouble with Women in the School of Epicurus," in Fitzgerald, Obbink and Holland: 2004, 221–243.

2012. *The Invention and Gendering of Epicurus.* Ann Arbor, MI.

Görler, W. 1974. *Untersuchungen zu Ciceros Philosophie.* Heidelberg.

1995. "Silencing the Troublemaker: De Legibus I.39 and the Continuity of Cicero's Scepticism," in Powell: 1995b, 85–113.

Gorman, R. 2005. *The Socratic Method in the Dialogues of Cicero.* Stuttgart.

Gowers, E. 1993. *The Loaded Table: Representations of Food in Roman Literature.* Oxford.

Granarolo, J. 1967. *L'oeuvre de Catulle: Aspects religieux, éthiques et stylistiques.* Paris.

Griffin, M. 1986. "Philosophy, Cato, and Roman Suicide." *G&R* 33: 64–77; 192–202.

1989. "Philosophy, Politics, and Politicians at Rome," in Griffin and Barnes: 1989, 1–37.

1995. "Philosophical Badinage in Cicero's Letters to His Friends," in Powell: 1995b, 325–346.

1997. "The Composition of the Academica: Motives and versions," in Inwood and Mansfeld: 1997, 1–35.

2001. "Piso, Cicero and Their Audience," in Auvray-Assayas and Delattre: 2001, 85–99.

Griffin, M. and J. Barnes (eds.) 1989. *Philosophia Togata: Essays on Philosophy and Roman Society.* Oxford.

1997. *Philosophia Togata. II: Plato and Aristotle at Rome.* Oxford.

Griffin, M. T. (ed.) 2009. *A Companion to Julius Caesar.* Malden, MA.

Grimal, P. 1978. "La poème de Lucrèce en son temps," in Gigon: 1978, 233–270.

Gruen, E. 1992. *Culture and National Identify in Republican Rome.* Ithaca, NY.

Gurd, S. 2007. "Cicero and Revision, 61–46 BCE." *CA* 26: 49–80.

Hadot, P. 1995. *Philosophy as a Way of Life: Spiritual Exercises from Socrates to Foucault.* Trans. M. Chase. Malden, MA.

Hall, J. 1996. "Social Evasion and Aristocratic Manners in Cicero's *De Oratore.*" *AJP* 117: 96–118.

Hallett, J. P. 1978. "Divine Unction: Some Further Thoughts on Catullus 13." *Latomus* 37: 747–748.

Hammer, D. 2014. *Roman Political Thought from Cicero to Augustine*. Cambridge.

Hanchey, D. 2013a. "Rhetoric and the Immortal Soul in *Tusculan Disputation* 1." *SyllClass* 24: 77–103.

2013b. "Cicero, Exchange, and the Epicureans." *Phoenix* 67: 119–134.

2014. "Days of Future Passed: Fiction Forming Fact in Cicero's Dialogues." *CJ* 110: 61–77.

2015. "Conflicting Models of Exchange in Cicero's *Brutus.*" *Latomus* 74: 112–129.

Hankinson, R. J. 2013. "Lucretius, Epicurus, and the Logic of Multiple Explanations," in Lehoux, Morrison and Sharrock: 2013, 69–98.

Hanses, M. 2020. *The Life of Comedy after the Death of Plautus and Terence*. Ann Arbor, MI.

Hardie, P. 2007. "Lucretius and Later Latin Literature in Antiquity," in Gillespie and Hardie: 2007, 111–130.

Hanslik, R., A. Lesky and H. Schwabl (eds.) 1972. *Antidosis: Festschrift für W. Kraus zum 70. Geburtstag*. Vienna.

Hariman, R. 1995. *Political Style*. Chicago, IL.

Harrison, S. J. 2002. "Ennius and the Prologue to Lucretius *DRN* 1 (1.1–148)." *LICS* 1: 1–13.

Hatzimichali, M. 2011. *Potamo of Alexandria and the Emergence of Eclecticism*. Cambridge.

Heinze, R. (ed.) 1897. *T. Lucretius Carus: De Rerum Natura Buch III. With Commentary*. Leipzig.

Henry, W. B. (ed.) 2009. *Philodemus, On Death. With Translation and Notes*. Atlanta, GA.

Herrmann, L. 1956. "Catulle et Lucrèce." *Latomus* 15: 465–480.

Hessler, J. E. 2012. *Epikur. Brief an Menoikeus. Edition, Übersetzung, Einleitung, und Kommentar*. Basel.

Hiltbrünner, O. 1972. "Einladung zum epikureischen Freundesmal," in Hanslik, Lesky and Schwabl: 1972, 168–182.

Hinds, S. 1998. *Allusion and Intertext: Dynamics of Appropriation in Roman Poetry*. Cambridge.

Hine, H. 2016. "*Philosophi* and Philosophy: From Cicero to Apuleius," in Williams and Volk: 2016, 13–29.

Hirzel, R. 1882. *Untersuchungen zu Ciceros philosophischen Schriften II. De finibus. De officiis*. Leipzig.

Holmes, B. and W. H. Shearin (eds.) 2012. *Dynamic Reading*. Oxford.

Hope, V. M. 2009. *Roman Death: The Dying and the Dead in Ancient Rome*. London.

Horsfall, N. 1989. *Cornelius Nepos: A Selection*. Oxford.

Hourticq, L. 1946. *L'art et la littérature*. Paris.

Hutchinson, G. 2001. "The Date of *De Rerum Natura*." *CQ* 51: 150–162.

Inwood, B. 1990. "*Rhetorica Disputatio*: The Strategy of *de Finibus* II." *Apeiron* 23.4: 143–164.

International Occultation Timing Association 2017. "Observing the August 21, 2017 Total Solar Eclipse to Measure the Size of the Sun." 20 August 2017. http://occultations.org/eclipse2017/.

Inwood, B. and J. Mansfeld (eds.) 1997. *Assent and Argument: Studies in Cicero's Academic Books*. Leiden.

Irby, G. L. (ed.) 2016. *A Companion to Science, Technology, and Medicine in Ancient Greece and Rome*. Malden, MA.

Jocelyn, H. D. 1967. *The Tragedies of Ennius: The Fragments. With an Introduction and Commentary*. Cambridge.

Kajanto, I. 1969. "Balnea vina venus," in Bibauw: 1969, 357–367.

Kechagia, E. 2011. *Plutarch against Colotes; A Lesson in History of Philosophy*. Oxford.

Kenney, E. J. 1970. "Doctus Lucretius." *Mnemosyne* 23.4: 366–392. Reprinted in M. R. Gale (ed.), *Lucretius*. Oxford, 2007, 300–327.

(ed.) 1971. *Lucretius: De Rerum Natura Book III*. Cambridge.

(ed.) 2014. *Lucretius: De Rerum Natura Book III*. 2nd ed. Cambridge.

Knox, P. E. 2007. "Catullus and Callimachus," in Skinner: 2007, 151–171.

Knox, P. and C. Foss (eds.) 1998. *Style and Tradition: Studies in Honor of Wendell Clausen*. Stuttgart.

König, J. and G. Woolf (eds.) 2017. *Authority and Expertise in Ancient Scientific Culture*. Cambridge.

Konstan, D. 1977. *Catullus' Indictment of Rome: The Meaning of Catullus 64*. Amsterdam.

2007. "The Contemporary Political Context," in Skinner: 2007, 72–91.

2020. "Epicurean Phantasia." Πηγή/*Fons* 5: 1–18.

Konstan, D., D. Clay, C. E. Glad, J. C. Thom and J. Ware (eds.) 1998. *Philodemus: On Frank Criticism*. Atlanta, GA.

Krebs, C. B. 2013. "Caesar, Lucretius and the Dates of *De rerum natura* and the *Commentarii*." *CQ* 63: 772–779.

Kulka, T. 1996. *Kitsch and Art*. University Park, PA.

Kundera, M. 1984. *The Unbearable Lightness of Being*. Trans. Michael Heim. New York.

2006. *The Curtain: An Essay in Seven Parts*. Trans. Linda Asher. New York.

Laks, A. and M. Schofield (eds.) 1995. *Justice and Generosity. Studies in Hellenistic Social and Political Philosophy*. Cambridge.

Landolfi, L. 1982. "Tracce Filodemee di estetica e di epigrammatica simpotica in Catullo." *CronErcol* 12: 137–143.

Lattimore, R. 1942. *Themes in Greek and Latin Epitaphs*. Urbana, IL.

Lee, G. 2008. *Catullus: The Complete Poems*. Oxford.

Leeman, A. D., H. Pinkster and J. Wisse (eds.) 1996. *Marcus Tullius Cicero: De Oratore Libri III. Wissenschaftliche Kommentare zu griechischen und lateinischen Schriftstellern Band IV*. Heidelberg.

Lehoux, D., A. D. Morrison and A. Sharrock (eds.) 2013. *Lucretius: Poetry, Philosophy, Science.* Oxford.

Leslie, R. J. 1950. "The Epicureanism of Titus Pomponius Atticus." Diss. Columbia. Philadelphia.

Lévy, C. 1984. "La dialectique de Cicéron dans les livres II et IV du *De finibus*." *REL* 62: 111–127.

  1992. *Cicero Academicus. Recherches sur les Académiques et sur la philosophie cicéronienne.* Rome.

Lezra, J. and L. Blake (eds.) 2016. *Lucretius and Modernity: Epicurean Encounters Across Time and Disciplines.* New York.

Lieberg, G. 1962. *Puella divina: Die Gestalt der göttlichen Geliebten bei Catull im Zusammenhang der antiken Dichtung.* Amsterdam.

Lindsay, H. 1998. "The Biography of Atticus: Cornelius Nepos on the Philosophical and Ethical Background of Pomponius Atticus." *Latomus* 57: 324–336.

Littman, R. J. 1977. "The Unguent of Venus: Catullus 13." *Latomus* 36: 123–128.

Lloyd, G. E. R. 1987. *The Revolutions of Wisdom: Studies in the Claims and Practice of Ancient Greek Science.* Berkeley, CA.

Long, A. G. 2019. *Death and Immortality in Ancient Philosophy.* Cambridge.

Long, A. A. and D. Sedley (eds.) 1987. *The Hellenistic Philosophers.* 2 vols. Cambridge.

Lorca, A. M. 1996. "Lucrecio: una crítica ilustrada a la religión popular," in Giannantoni and Gigante: 1996, 851–864.

Luciani, S. 2005. "Amour sacré et amour profane chez Catulle et Lucrèce," in Poignault: 2005, 151–166.

Luper-Foy, S. 1987. "Annihilation." *PhilosQ* 37.148: 233–252.

McConnell, S. 2012. "Lucretius and Civil Strife." *Phoenix* 66: 97–121.

  2014. *Philosophical Life in Cicero's Letters.* Cambridge.

Mansfeld, J. 1993. "Aspects of Epicurean Theology." *Mnemosyne* 46: 172–210.

Manuwald, G. (ed.) 2000. *Identität und Alterität in der frührömischen Tragödie.* Würzburg.

Manuwald, G. 2011. *Roman Republican Theatre.* Cambridge.

  2012. *Tragicorum Romanorum Fragmenta, Vol. II: Ennius.* Göttingen.

Marcović, D. 2008. "Lucretius 1.471–7: Tragic Flames in *DRN*." *Mnemosyne* 61: 647–650.

Marcovich, M. 1982. "Catullus 13 and Philodemus 23." *QUCC* 11: 131–138.

Martha, C. 1896. *Le poème de Lucrèce.* Paris.

Masi, F. and S. Maso (eds.) 2013. *Fate, Chance and Fortune in Ancient Thought.* Amsterdam.

Maslowski, T. 1974. "The Chronology of Cicero's Anti-Epicureanism." *Eos* 62: 55–78.

Maso, S. 2008. *Capire e dissentire. Cicerone e la filosofia di Epicuro.* Naples.

Maurach, G. 1989. *Geschichte der römischen Philosophie.* Darmstadt.

Merlan, P. 1967. "Aristoteles' und Epikurs müssige Götter." *ZPhF* 4: 485–498.

Millar, F. 1988. "Cornelius Nepos, Atticus and the Roman Revolution." *G&R* 35: 40–55.

Minyard, J. D. 1985. *Lucretius and the Late Republic: An Essay in Roman Intellectual History*. Leiden.

Mitsis, P. 1988. *Epicurus' Ethical Theory. The Pleasures of Invulnerability*. Ithaca, NY and London.

    1989. "Epicurus on Death and the Duration of Life," in Cleary and Shartin: 1989, 303–322.

    2020. *The Oxford Handbook of Epicurus and Epicureanism*. Oxford.

Momigliano, A. 1941. Review of B. Farrington, *Science and Politics in the Ancient World*. *JRS* 31: 149–157.

Morel, P.-M. 2000. *Atome et Nécessité. Démocrite, Epicure, Lucrèce*. Paris.

    2013. "Epicuro e la desacralizzazione della necessità," in Masi and Maso: 2013, 159–175.

    2016. "Cicero and Epicurean Virtues (*De Finibus* 1–2)," in Annas and Betegh: 2016, 77–95.

Morford, M. 2002. *The Roman Philosophers from the Time of Cato the Censor to the Death of Marcus Aurelius*. London and New York.

Morisi, L. 2002. "Ifigenia e Polissena (Lucrezio in Catullo)." *MD* 49: 177–190.

Morisset, R. and G. Thévenot. 1950. *Les lettres latines*. Paris.

Mulgan, R. G. 1979. "Was Caesar an Epicurean?" *CW* 72: 337–339.

Mundt, F. (ed.) 2012. *Kommunikationsräume im kaiserzeitlichen Rom*. Berlin and Boston, MA.

Mynors, R. A. B. 1958. *C. Valerii Catulli Carmina*. Oxford.

Nagel, T. 1970. "Death." *Nous* 4.1: 73–80. Reprinted in Nagel: 1979, 1–10.

    1979. *Mortal Questions*. Cambridge.

    1986. *The View from Nowhere*. Oxford.

Nappa, C. 2001. *Aspects of Catullus' Social Fiction*. Frankfurt am Main.

Nethercut, J. S. 2012. "Provisional Poetics in Lucretius' *De rerum natura*." Diss. University of Pennsylvania.

    2014. "Ennius and the Revaluation of Traditional Historiography in Lucretius' *De Rerum Natura*," in Pieper and Ker: 2014, 435–461.

    2018. "The Alexandrian Footnote in Lucretius' *De Rerum Natura*." *Mnemosyne* 71: 75–99.

Nicgorski, W. 2002. "Cicero, Citizenship, and the Epicurean Temptation," in Allman and Beaty: 2002, 3–28.

Nightingale, A. 2015. "Sight and the Philosophy of Vision in Classical Greece: Democritus, Plato, and Aristotle," in Squire: 2015, 54–67.

Nisbet, R. G. M. 1961. *In L. Calpurnium Pisonem Oratio*. Oxford.

Nussbaum, M. 1994. *The Therapy of Desire: Theory and Practice in Hellenistic Ethics*. Princeton, NJ.

Obbink, D. (ed.) 1995. *Philodemus and Poetry: Poetic Theory and Practice in Lucretius, Philodemus, and Horace*. New York and Oxford.

O'Connor, D. K. 1989. "The Invulnerable Pleasures of Epicurean Friendship." *GRBS* 30: 165–186.

O'Keefe, T. 2001. "Is Epicurean Friendship Altruistic?" *Apeiron* 34: 269–305.

Panoussi, V. 2009. *Greek Tragedy in Vergil's "Aeneid": Ritual, Empire, and Intertext.* Cambridge.

Papanghelis, T. D., S. J. Harrison and S. Frangoulidis (eds.) 2013. *Generic Interfaces in Latin Literature: Encounters, Interactions and Transformations.* Berlin.

Paratore, E. 1973. "La problematica sull'epicureismo a Roma." *ANRW* 1.4: 116–204.

Perlwitz, O. 1992. *Titus Pomponius Atticus: Untersuchungen zur Person eines einflussreichen Ritters in der ausgehenden römischen Republik.* Stuttgart.

Perutelli, A. 1996. "Iphigenia in Lucrezio." *SCO* 46: 193–207.

Peters, W. T. 1963. *Landscape in Romano-Campanian Mural Paintings.* Assen.

Philippson, R. 1939. "M. Tullius Cicero: Die philosophischen Schriften." *RE* VIIA1: 1104–1192.

Pieper, C. and J. Ker (eds.) 2014. *Valuing the Past in the Greco-Roman World: Proceedings from the Penn-Leiden Colloquia on Ancient Values VII.* Leiden.

Pizzani, U. 1993. "La cultura filosofica di Cesare," in Poli: 1993, 163–189.

Poignault, R. (ed.) 2005. *Présence de Catulle et des élégiaques latins: actes du colloque tenu à Tours (28–30 novembre 2003).* Clermont-Ferrand.

Poli, D. (ed.) 1993. *La cultura in Cesare, Vol. 1.* Rome.

Pope, M. 2018a. "Ocular Penetration, Grammatical Objectivity, and an Indecent Proposal in *De Rerum Natura.*" *CP* 113.2: 206–212.

   2018b. "Seminal Verse: Atomic Orality and Aurality in *De Rerum Natura.*" *Eugesta* 8: 108–130.

Powell, J. G. F. (ed.) 1990. *Cicero: On Friendship and the Dream of Scipio.* Warminster.

   1995a. "Introduction: Cicero's Philosophical Works and their Background," in Powell: 1995b, 1–35.

   1995b. (ed.) *Cicero the Philosopher. Twelve Papers.* Oxford.

   1995c. "Cicero's Translations from Greek," in Powell: 1995b, 273–300.

Prinzen, H. 1998. *Ennius im Urteil der Antike.* Stuttgart.

Pucci, G. C. 1966. "Echi lucreziani in Cicerone." *SIFC* 38: 70–132.

Rambaud, M. 1969. "César et l'Épicurisme d'apres les Commentaires," in *Actes du VIIIe Congrès de l'Association Guillaume Budé.* Paris, 411–435.

   1984. "Le Pro Marcello et l'insinuation politique," in Chevallier: 1984, 43–56.

Raubitschek, A. E. 1949. "Phaidros and His Roman Pupils." *Hesperia* 18: 96–103.

Rawson, E. 1985. *Intellectual Life in the Late Roman Republic.* Baltimore, MD.

Reinhardt, T. 2002. "The Speech of Nature in Lucretius' *De Rerum Natura* 3.931–71." *CQ* 52: 291–304.

   2005. "The Language of Epicureanism in Cicero: The Case of Atomism," in Reinhardt, Lapidge and Adams: 2005, 151–177.

Reinhardt, T., M. Lapidge and J. N. Adams (eds.) 2005. *Aspects of the Language of Latin Prose.* Oxford and New York.

Richlin, A. 1988. "Systems of Food Imagery in Catullus." *CW* 81: 355–363.

Richter, G. 1965. *The Portraits of the Greeks*. London.

1971. *Engraved Gems of the Greeks, Etruscans, and Romans, Part II*. London.

Rigsby, K. 2008. "Hauranus the Epicurean." *CJ* 104: 19–22.

Rist, J. M. 1972. *Epicurus: An Introduction*. Cambridge.

Romeo, C. 1979. "Demetrio Lacone sulla grandezza del sole (PHerc 1013)." *CronErcol* 9: 11–35.

Rosenbaum, S. E. 1986. "How to Be Dead and Not Care: A Defense of Epicurus." *AphQ* 23: 217–225.

1989a. "Epicurus and Annihilation." *PhilosQ* 39: 81–90.

1989b. "The Symmetry Argument: Lucretius against the Fear of Death." *Philosophy and Phenomenological Research* 50: 353–373.

Roskam, G. 2007a. *Live Unnoticed (Λάθε βιώσας): On the Vicissitudes of an Epicurean Doctrine*. Leiden and Boston, MA.

2007b. *A Commentary on Plutarch's De latenter vivendo*. Leuven.

2012. "Will the Epicurean Sage Break the Law If He Is Perfectly Sure that He Will Escape Detection? A Difficult Problem Revisited." *TAPA* 142: 23–40.

2019. "Cicero against Cassius on Pleasure and Virtue. A Complicated Passage from *De finibus* (1,25)." *CQ* 69: 725–733.

Ross, D. O. 1969. *Style and Tradition in Catullus*. Cambridge, MA.

Rouse, W. H. D. 1975. *Lucretius*: On the Nature of Things. Revised by M. F. Smith. Cambridge, MA.

Rudolph, K. 2011. "Democritus' Perspectival Theory of Vision." *JHS* 131: 67–83.

2015. "Sight and the Presocratics: Approaches to Visual Perception in Early Greek Philosophy," in Squire: 2015, 36–53.

Sanders, K. R. 2011. "Philodemus and the Fear of Premature Death," in Fish and Sanders: 2011, 211–234.

Schefold, K. 1957. *Die Waende Pompejis: Topographisches Verzeichnis der Bildmotive*. Berlin.

Schiesaro, A. 1990. *Simulacrum et imago: gli argomenti analogici nel De rerum natura*. Pisa.

2007. "Lucretius and Roman Politics and History," in Gillespie and Hardie: 2007, 41–58.

Schilling, R. 1954. *La religion romaine de Vénus depuis les origines jusqu'au temps d'Auguste*. Paris.

Schmid, W. 1971. "Philodem als Dichter und als Philosoph: uber eine Athetese Kaibels in AP 9.570," in *Acta Conventus XI Eirene*, Warsaw, 201–207.

1984. *Ausgewählte philologische Schriften*. Berlin and New York.

Schofield, M. 2008. "Ciceronian Dialogue," in Goldhill: 2008, 63–84.

Schofield, M., M. Burnyeat and J. Barnes (eds.). 1980. *Doubt and Dogmatism: Studies in Hellenistic Epistemology*. Oxford and New York.

Scodel, R. 1980. *The Trojan Trilogy of Euripides*. Göttingen.

Seager, R. 2011. "Cicero and the 'False Dilemma,'" in Smith and Covino: 2011, 99–109.

Sedley, D. 1976. "Epicurus and the Mathematicians of Cyzicus." *CronErcol* 6: 23–54.

    1989. "Philosophical Allegiance in the Greco-Roman World," in Griffin and Barnes: 1989, 97–119.

    1996. "The Inferential Foundations of Epicurean Ethics," in Giannantoni and Gigante: 1996, 313–339.

    1997. "The Ethics of Brutus and Cassius." *JRS* 87: 41–53.

    1998. *Lucretius and the Transformation of Greek Wisdom.* Cambridge.

Seel, G. 1996. "Farà il saggio qualcosa che le leggi vietano, sapendo che non sarà scoperto?," in Giannantoni and Gigante: 1996, 341–360.

Seel, O. 1967. *Caesar-Studien.* Stuttgart.

Shackleton Bailey, D. R. 1965–70. *Cicero's Letters to Atticus.* 7 vols. Cambridge.

    1977. *Cicero's Epistulae ad familiares.* 2 vols. Cambridge.

    1980. *Cicero: Select Letters.* Cambridge.

Shapiro, S. O. 2014. "Socration or Philodemus? Catullus 47 and Prosopographical Excess." *CJ* 109: 385–405.

Shearin, W. 2012. "Haunting Nepos: Atticus and the Performance of Roman Epicurean Death," in Holmes and Shearin: 2012, 30–51.

Sider, D. 1987. "The Love Poetry of Philodemus." *AJP* 108: 310–324.

    1995. "The Epicurean Philosopher as Hellenistic Poet," in Obbink: 1995, 42–57.

    1997. *The Epigrams of Philodemos.* New York and Oxford.

Silverstein, H. S. 1980. "The Evil of Death." *JPh* 77.7: 401–424.

Skinner, M. B. 1976. "Iphigenia and Polyxena: A Lucretian Allusion in Catullus." *Pacific Coast Philology* 11: 52–61.

    1979. "Parasites and Strange Bedfellows: A Study in Catullus' Political Imagery." *Ramus* 8: 137–152.

    1989. "*Ut decuit cinaediorem*: Power, Gender and Urbanity in Catullus 10." *Helios* 16: 7–23.

    2001. "Among Those Present: Catullus 44 and 10." *Helios* 28: 57–73.

    2003. *Catullus in Verona: A Reading of the Elegiac Libellus, Poems 65–116.* Columbus, OH.

    (ed.) 2007. *A Companion to Catullus.* Malden, MA and Oxford.

Skutsch, O. 1985. *The Annals of Q. Ennius: Edited with Introduction and Commentary.* Oxford.

Smith, C. and R. Covino (eds.) 2011. *Praise and Blame in Roman Republican Rhetoric.* Swansea.

Snyder, J. M. 1980. *Puns and Poetry in Lucretius' De Rerum Natura.* Amsterdam.

Squire, M. (ed.) 2015. *Sight and the Ancient Senses.* London.

Steel, C. E. W. 2005. *Reading Cicero. Genre and Performance in Late Republican Rome.* London.

    2013. "Structure, Meaning and Authority in Cicero's Dialogues," in Föllinger and Müller: 2013, 221–234.

Stem, R. 2012. *The Political Biographies of Cornelius Nepos.* Ann Arbor, MI.

Stokes, M. 1995. "Cicero on Epicurean Pleasures," in Powell: 1995b, 145–170.

Striker, G. 1977. "Epicurus on the Truth of Sense Impressions." *AGPh* 59.2: 125–142.

  1989. "Commentary on Mitsis: Epicurus on Death and the Duration of Life," in Cleary and Sharkin: 1989, 323–328.

  1995. "Cicero and Greek Philosophy." *HSCPh* 97: 53–61.

  1996. "Epicurean Hedonism," in Striker: 1996, 196–208.

Striker, G. (ed.) 1996. *Essays on Hellenistic Epistemology and Ethics.* Cambridge and New York.

Stroup, S. C. 2010. *Catullus, Cicero, and a Society of Patrons: The Generation of the Text.* Cambridge.

Suerbaum, W. 1995. "Der Pyrrhos-Krieg in Ennius' Annales VI im Lichte der ersten Ennius-Papyri aus Herculaneum." *ZPE* 106: 31–52.

  2002. *Die archaische Literatur: Von den Anfängen bis Sullas Tod.* Munich.

Syme, R. 1956. "Piso and Veranius in Catullus." *C&M* 17: 129–134.

Tait, J. I. M. 1941. "Philodemus' Influence on the Latin Poets." Dissertation: Bryn Mawr College.

Tamás, A. 2016. "Erroneous Gazes: Lucretian Poetics in Catullus 64." *JRS* 106: 1–20.

Taormina, D. 2016. "'What Is Known through Sense Perception Is an Image.' Plotinus' tr. 32 (Enn. V 5) 1.12–19: An Anti-Epicurean Argument?," in Taormina and Longo: 2016, 113–310.

Taormina, D. P. and A. Longo (eds.) 2016. *Plotinus and Epicurus: Matter, Perception, Pleasure.* Cambridge.

Taylor, B. 2016. "Rationalism and the Theatre in Lucretius." *CQ* 66: 140–154.

Taylor, C. C. W. 1980. "All Perceptions Are True," in Schofield, Burnyeat and Barnes: 1980, 105–124.

Thibodeau, P. 2016. "Ancient Optics: Theories and Problems of Vision," in Irby: 2016, 130–144.

Thomas, C. 2017. "Putting a Ring on It: 2017 Total Solar Eclipse," NASA AFRC2017–0233-009. www.nasa.gov/centers/armstrong/multimedia/image gallery/2017_total_solar_eclipse/AFRC2017-0233-009.html.

Thomas, R. F. 1994. "This Little Piggy Had Roast Beef (Catullus 47)." *Prudentia* 26: 147–152.

Titchener, F. 2003. "Cornelius Nepos and the Biographical Tradition." *G&R* 35: 40–55.

Torres, M. 2018. *Epicuro, epicúreos y el epicureísmo en Roma.* Madrid.

Trapp, M. B. 2007. *Philosophy in the Roman Empire: Ethics, Politics and Society.* Aldershot.

  2017. "Philosophical Authority in the Imperial Period," in König and Woolf:2017, 27–57.

Trappes-Lomax, J. M. 2007. *Catullus: A Textual Reappraisal.* Swansea.

Tsouna, V. 2001. "Cicéron et Philodème: quelques considérations sur l'éthique," in Auvray-Assayas and Delattre: 2001, 159–172.

2007. *The Ethics of Philodemus.* Oxford.

2012. *Philodemus: On Household Management.* Atlanta, GA.

Tutrone, F. 2017. "Granting Epicurean Wisdom at Rome: Exchange and Reciprocity in Lucretius' Didactic (*DRN* 1.921–950)." *HSCPh* 109: 275–337.

Urso, G (ed.) 2010. *Cesare: precursore o visionario?* Pisa.

Valachova, C. 2018. "The Garden and the Forum: Epicurean Adherence and Political Affiliation in the Late Republic," in van der Blom, Gray and Steel: 2018, 147–164.

van der Blom, H., C. Gray and C. Steel (eds.) 2018. *Institutions and Ideology in Republican Rome: Speech, Audience, and Decision.* Cambridge.

van den Steen, T. 2009. "Injustice: An Epicurean Guarantee for Justice." *QUCC NS* 93: 137–150.

Vander Waerdt, P. A. 1987. "The Justice of the Epicurean Wise Man." *CQNS* 37: 402–422.

Verde, F. 2013. "ΤΥΧΗ e ΛΟΓΙΣΜΟΣ nell'epicureismo," in Masi and Maso: 2013, 177–197.

2016. "Epicuro e la grandezza del sole: sul testo di *Pyth.* 91." *Méthexis* 28: 104–110.

2017. Review of F. A. Bakker, *Epicurean Meteorology: Sources, Method, Scope and Organization. BMCR* 2017.06.38.

Vessey, D. W. T. C. 1971. "Thoughts on Two Poems of Catullus: 13 and 30." *Latomus* 30: 45–55.

Vogt, K. M. 2016. "All Sense-Perceptions Are True: Epicurean Responses to Skepticism and Relativism," in Lerza and Blake: 2016, 145–159.

Volk, K. 2010. "Lucretius' Prayer for Peace and the Date of *De Rerum Natura.*" *CQ* 60: 127–131.

2021. *The Roman Republic of Letters: Scholarship, Philosophy, and Politics in the Age of Cicero and Caesar.* Princeton, NJ.

Forthcoming a. "Philosophy," in Gibson and Whitton.

Forthcoming b. "Towards a Definition of sapientia: Philosophy in Cicero's Pro Marcello," in Gilbert, Graver and McConnell.

Wallach, B. P. 1976. *Lucretius and the Diatribe against the Fear of Death: De Rerum Natura III, 830–1094.* Leiden.

Wardle, D. 2009. "Caesar and Religion," in Griffin: 2009, 100–111.

Warren, J. 2002. *Epicurus and Democritean Ethics: An Archaeology of Ataraxia.* Cambridge.

2004. *Facing Death: Epicurus and His Critics.* Oxford.

2007. "Lucretius and Greek Philosophy," in Gillespie and Hardie: 2007, 19–32.

(ed.) 2009. *The Cambridge Companion to Epicureanism.* Cambridge.

2014. "The Symmetry Problem," in S. Luper (ed.), *The Cambridge Companion to Life and Death.* Cambridge, 165–180.

2016. "Epicurean Pleasure in Cicero's *De Finibus,*" in Annas and Betegh: 2016, 41–76.

Weber, E. and G. Dobesch (eds.) 1985. *Römische Geschichte, Altertumskunde und Epigraphik: Festschrift für Artur Betz zur Vollendung seines 80. Lebensjahres.* Vienna.

Welch, K. E. 1996. "T. Pomponius Atticus: A Banker in Politics?" *Historia* 45: 450–471.

West, D. A. 1969. *The Imagery and Poetry of Lucretius.* Edinburgh.

Westman, R. 1955. *Plutarch gegen Kolotes. Seine Schrift "Adversus Colotem" als philosophiegeschichtliche Quelle.* Helsingfors.

White, P. 2010. *Cicero in Letters: Epistolary Relations of the Late Republic.* New York.

Whitlatch, L. 2014. "Empiricist Dogs and the Superiority of Philosophy in Lucretius' *De Rerum Natura*." *CW* 108.1: 45–66.

Willi, A. 2010. "Campaigning for Utilitas: Style, Grammar, and Philosophy in C. Iulius Caesar," in Dickey and Chahoud: 2010, 229–242.

Williams, B. 1973. "The Makropulos Case: Reflections on the Tedium of Immortality," in *Problems of the Self: Philosophical Papers 1956–1972.* Cambridge, 82–100.

Williams D. G. and Volk, K. (eds.) 2016. *Roman Reflections: Studies in Latin Philosophy.* New York.

Wirth, J. M. 2015. *Commiserating with Devastated Things: Milan Kundera and the Entitlements of Thinking.* Oxford.

Wiseman, T. P. 1969. *Catullan Questions.* Leicester.

       2015. *The Roman Audience: Classical Literature as Social History.* Oxford.

Wolfsdorf, D. 2013. *Pleasure in Ancient Greek Philosophy.* Cambridge.

Woltjer, J. 1877. *Lucretii philosophia cum fontibus comparata: specimen litterarium, quo inquiritur quatenus Epicuri philosophiam tradiderit Lucretius.* Groningen.

Woolf, R. 2015. *Cicero. The Philosophy of a Roman Sceptic.* London and New York.

Wray, D. 2001. *Catullus and the Poetics of Roman Manhood.* Cambridge.

Yona, S. 2018. *Epicurean Ethics in Horace: The Psychology of Satire.* Oxford.

Zanker, P. 1995. *The Mask of Socrates: the Image of the Intellectual in Antiquity.* Berkeley, CA.

Zetzel, J. 1998. "*De Republica* and *De Rerum Natura*," in Knox and Foss: 1998, 230–247.

General Index

Aeschylus, 152–153, 159
Algra, Kiempe, 170, 172, 175–176, 179, 184
Amafinius, 14
ancestors
    achievements of, 15, 26–30
    representations of, 141
Anderson, W. S., 5, 142–143
animals
    and transmigration of souls, 164–166
    resemblance of Epicureans to, 45–46
Antiochus of Ascalon, 64
Aristippus, 15–16
Aristotle, 16, 18, 67, 140
Asmis, Elizabeth, viii, 1, 5, 50, 71, 75, 79, 91,
    93, 99, 114, 121, 137, 174, 180–181, 183
Atticus
    Epicureanism of, 18, 36, 58–60, 98, 140
Aulus Gellius, 148, 151
Auvray-Assayas, Clara, 3

Bailey, Shackleton, 59
Bakker, Frederik, 174–176
Barnes, Jonathan, 2, 169–170, 173–174, 180,
    183–184
Benferhat, Yasmina, 33, 35, 39, 57, 59, 61, 64,
    67, 72–73, 75, 77–78, 97, 99–100
Beretta, Marco, 175
Boissier, Gaston, 59
Boyle, Rebecca, 168

Caesar
    and ambition, 72
    and death, 75–81
    and familiarity with Lucretius, 73–74
    as threat to the Republic, 38–39, 52
    education of, 73–74
calculus, See measurement
Callimachus
    as model for Catullus, 92
    as model for Philodemus, 92

Carneades, 16, 26, 55, 60, 62–63
Cassandra, 160–161
Cassius, 23, 31, 33, 36, 41, 56–57, 61, 69, 71,
    86, 98, 144
Castner, C. J., 35, 57, 59, 65–68, 73–74, 77, 83,
    99
Catiline, 75
Cato, 55, 70–71, 76–77, 82
Catullus
    and criticism of patrons, 95
    and friendship compared to Lucretius, 97–100
    as crazed, 101–107
    as hostile to Epicureanism, 88–89
    as rival of Philodemus, 90–94
    pessimism of, 100–101
Chrysippus, 15–16, 82
Cicero
    and anti-Epicurean rhetoric, 39–44
    and conversion tactics, 60–68
    and criticism of Caesar, 76–80
    and criticism of Piso, 33–34, 72–73, 94
    and criticism of Torquatus, 30–32, 34–35
    and Greek intellectual framework, 14–22
    and his sources, 22–23
    and Roman achievements, 26–28
    and Roman virtue, 24–26
    and the Garden, 28–29
    as opposed to measurement, 48–53
    as translator, 24
circumlocution
    as rhetorical strategy, 39–42, 44, 46, 54
coniunctum
    vs. eventum, 158
convivium, 94
Crassus, 26, 37, 40–42, 64
criteria
    and philosophical allegiance, 54
criticism
    of Epicurus, 4–8, 14, 23, 34–36, 38–42,
        49–54, 67, 69–70

204